Teaching in Post-Compulsory Education

Policy, practice and values

EDITED BY ANTHONY COLES

🦌 **David Fulton** Publishers

David Fulton Publishers Ltd
The Chiswick Centre, 414 Chiswick High Road, London W4 5TF

www.fultonpublishers.co.uk

First published in Great Britain in 2004 by David Fulton Publishers
10 9 8 7 6 5 4 3 2 1

Note: The right of Anthony Coles to be identified as the editor of this work has been
asserted by him in accordance with the Copyright, Designs and Patents Act 1988.

David Fulton Publishers is a division of Granada Learning Limited, part of ITV plc.

British Library Cataloguing in Publication Data
A catalogue record for this book is available from the British Library.

ISBN 1 84312 233 2

Typeset by RefineCatch Ltd
Printed and bound in Great Britain

Contents

Acknowledgements

The publishers are grateful to the following persons and organisations for permission to reproduce the following figures in this book:

Figures 5.1, 5.2 – Organisation for Economic Co-operation and Development (1997) *Literacy Skills for the Knowledge Society*, Paris: OECD Publishing.

Figures 7.1, 7.2, 7.3 – Learning Skills Council, *International Adult Literacy Survey, 1994–1998*.

Figure 10.2 – Healey, M. and Jenkins, A. (2000) 'Kolb's Experiential Learning Theory and its application in geography in higher education,' *Journal of Geography*, 99: 185–95.

Preface

Teaching in Post-compulsory Education: Policy, practice and values is designed as a reader for anyone interested in issues affecting the adult education and training sector today. The book can be used to support work towards teacher training courses, such as the Cert Ed or PGCE and masters modules targeted towards the Further Education (FE) sector. Equally, the issues discussed are highly relevant to those engaged in Continuing Professional Development (CPD) in any post-compulsory teaching or training environment.

Such is the state of flux in post-compulsory education that it is even difficult to arrive at a suitable definition. 'Post-compulsory' implies 'post-16', yet one of the most significant issues affecting the sector is the participation of learners aged 14–16. Equally, 'FE' tends to imply college-based provision, yet a large amount of learning takes place in work, private and community settings. The term 'FE' as used in this book includes the widest possible definition of learning outside the formal school system. Similarly, 'FE teacher' encompasses the lecturer, trainer and classroom support role.

Chapters can be read in their entirety to get an overview of the topic, or sections used selectively according to need. Throughout the text, **Reflective questions** are provided to stimulate thinking on the personal relevance of issues and **Discussion points** present questions relating to the development of key issues in a wider context. **Indicative tasks** provide examples of activities that could contribute to assignment work, though it's strongly advisable to check with tutors whether a particular task is relevant. Each chapter includes a mind-map indicating which Further Education National Training Organisation (FENTO) Teaching and Learning Standards could be relevant to the topics covered and key points are summarised at the end as an aid to selecting relevant material. Comprehensive references to the most useful sources are included to aid further research, together with a list of useful websites. A glossary of acronyms and terminology relating to the sector is also provided.

Chapter 4, 'Learning to learn', and Chapter 9, 'Reflection and critical reasoning in educational contexts', contain guidance on developing skills relevant to completing assignments. These chapters can be used to assist with the reader's assignments, or the development of appropriate skills with learners.

About the contributors

Anthony Coles

Tony is a Senior Lecturer in Education at the University of Central England. He is Course Director for the Cert HE (FE) programme and has research interests in the pedagogy of ICT use in the classroom and work-based learning. He is also involved in several projects on the impact of including the 14–16 age range in FE. He has been involved in the ICT component of the Raising Expectations and Achievements in Literacy for Children from African-Caribbean Backgrounds (REAL) project and is working on a project evaluating the role of the FENTO Standards in colleges. Tony sits on the Universities Council for the Education of Teachers (UCET) 14–19 Working Group and is an 'Expert Advisor' for Theme 2 of *Success for All* for the Standards Unit.

Peter Hipkiss

Peter is an Assistant Principal at Walsall College of Arts and Technology. He has recently completed his PhD thesis entitled 'Growth and change in post-incorporated further education: a case study of three colleges with special reference to franchising'.

Janet Hoskyns

Janet is Professor and Head of the School of Post-compulsory Education at the University of Central England. She has research interests in music and arts education and training, with a particular focus at present on community and higher education; mentoring and supporting professional development through mentoring; the 14–19 curriculum and relationships between colleges and secondary schools. Janet is currently undertaking research in community liaison for the Guildhall School of Music and Drama funded by the Youth Music Foundation. She is Director of an evaluation team researching and evaluating the Cornwall Youth Music Action Zone 2 and Bristol and Gloucester Youth Music Action Zone 'REMIX' and part of a faculty team evaluating Creative Partnerships in Birmingham.

Tricia Le Gallais

Tricia is a Senior Lecturer in Education at the University of Central England. Formerly a researcher at Stourbridge College, she has interests in the role of the researcher in FE and current developments in the 14–19 sector.

Catherine Matheson

Catherine's interests lie mainly in widening participation and socio-cultural representations of learners and teachers.

David Matheson

David is Course Director for the MA in Education at the University of Central England. He has research interests in lifelong learning and how cultural identity and education are related. David is also interested in the history of education and the development of identity through and in education.

Jim McGrath

Jim is a Senior Lecturer in Education at the University of Central England. He is also the Deputy MA Programme Director. He has recently been awarded an EdD on management strategies in educational institutions.

Debra Wilson

Debra is Business and Community Outreach Manager at Newman College of Higher Education. She is working towards a PhD on disaffected learners.

Glynis Worrow

Glynis is a Senior Lecturer in Education at the University of Central England. Formerly the Cert HE (FE) Course Director, she currently has responsibility for partnerships.

SECTION

1

Background to teaching in post-compulsory education

1

Post-compulsory education and training: an historical perspective

Anthony Coles

Technical education and the growth of the post-compulsory sector

THE 'POST-COMPULSORY' sector is distinguished from other education sectors in its diversity. Herein lies one of the most significant problems for government strategists, curriculum planners and senior managers when planning and implementing structural change. The extent of the diversity is such that even the name of the sector can be controversial. 'Post-compulsory', 'FE' (further education) and 'adult education' are all labels that are used. The pace of change means that even these terms soon become inappropriate. For example, 'post-compulsory' implies a sector comprising learners who are over 16 years of age. In fact, much younger learners have been attending colleges for years and current '14–19' initiatives such as the Increased Flexibility Programme (IFP) are at the forefront of strategic planning in the sector. It's even debatable whether the age of 16 can be regarded as the transition between compulsory and post-compulsory education given expectations that the majority of young people will stay in full-time education or training until the age of 18.

Working in FE is demanding, but highly rewarding because of the diversity of learners, including their age, cultural background and experience, for example. Diversity can also be found in the subjects on offer, of which over 2,000 have been identified. These subjects differ substantially in terms of the pedagogic models used in teaching and learning. From the academic to the vocational and the craft to the recreational, full time and part time, they're all distinguished by a curriculum folklore perpetuated by the academic/vocational divide recognised by Helena Kennedy in *Learning Works*:

> Further education suffers because of prevailing British attitudes. Not only does there remain a very carefully calibrated hierarchy of worthwhile achievement, which has clearly established routes and which privileges academic success well above any other accomplishment, but there

is also an appalling ignorance amongst decision-makers and opinion-formers about what goes on in further education. It is so alien to their experience.

(FEFC 1997: 1)

The problem is that it's impossible to precisely define standards for criteria such as teaching and learning, assessment and quality assurance that can be equally applied across all subject areas. The approach by the Further Education National Training Organisation (FENTO), which is the organisation responsible for workforce development across the FE sector, has been to devise a set of standards relating to operational aspects of FE such as teaching and learning, management and governance. If describing the sector in its current form is problematic, describing its roots is a challenge. This section will address the derivation of the institutions that form our current FE colleges and related organisations.

Until recently, pupils leaving school at 16 have had limited experience of vocational subjects. The demands of the National Curriculum have tended to restrict technical subjects to information and communication technology (ICT), design and technology, art and design, and science. These subjects are closely related to some of the main vocational curriculum areas. For example, the subjects available as six unit (single award) Advanced Vocational Certificate in Education (Advanced VCE) are:

- Art and design
- Business
- Construction and built environment
- Engineering
- Health and social care
- Information and communication technology
- Land and environment
- Leisure and recreation
- Manufacturing
- Media: communication and production
- Performing arts
- Retail and distributive services
- Science
- Travel and tourism

A minority of these curriculum areas involve subjects taken at school. More recently, schools have offered vocational subjects such as the GCSE (Vocational Subjects) double award and Advanced VCE, which are available in many of the areas listed above. However, recruitment of suitably qualified staff to some areas has been problematic.

Specialist School status has provided a partial solution and vocational subjects are more popular and feasible in these institutions, which have more staff in the specialist curriculum area. The Specialist Schools Trust website (see 'Useful websites' at the end of the chapter) has further information on this topic.

The role of the FE college has traditionally been to provide vocational experience beyond the dominantly academic curriculum provided in schools. However, with the market economy in education initiated in the 1980s, it is common for FE colleges to offer academic subjects at GCSE and 'A' Level. Consequently there is often competition between providers such as schools, sixth form colleges and FE colleges for students; hence the trend towards schools and sixth form colleges offering vocational subjects. Although it's possible to take a cynical view on the role of competition, the value of providing choice cannot be overstated as a mechanism for widening participation and influencing quality.

It would be expected that applied disciplines (the 'practical arts' as described by Lewis 1999, including technological, vocational and professional education) should be able to achieve the status of traditional academic subjects (such as English, history and mathematics) as a result of their intrinsic value to society. Although the Church and landed elite are often cited as being prejudiced against the practical arts, possibly in order to dominate the working classes, the academic/vocational divide has its roots in the Greek culture of Plato. The debate concerns the purity of knowledge; essentially that the purest form of knowledge is the most valuable and valid and that practical subjects represent a 'second class' of knowledge, lacking the credentials of pure knowledge.

The purpose of the above discussion has been to emphasise the complexity of FE, the rapid change in the sector during recent years and the trichotomy between academic, vocational and 'trade' curriculum areas. These debates are not new, indeed it's remarkable that the literature relating to the development of formalised technical education in the nineteenth century describes many similar issues.

Discussion points

1 What is the evidence for the academic/vocational divide from your institution?
2 What are the barriers to participation resulting from the academic/vocational divide in your curriculum area?
3 Research three initiatives designed to enhance the status of vocational subjects.
4 What are the differences in assessment methodology for academic and vocational aspects of your curriculum area?

Reflective questions

1 How do you distinguish between academic and vocational content in your subject? To what extent is this distinction valid?

2 What changes could be made to your schemes of work to enhance the value of skills in relation to knowledge?

3 Read the annual report for your curriculum area. What are the action points proposed that could influence the academic/vocational divide? How could you change your practice to ensure that these influences have a positive effect on your learners' experience?

The political climate of the early to mid-nineteenth century was such that the power residing with the landowner class resulted in caution over allowing too much technical knowledge to be in the possession of others; there was a lack of incentive to promote vocational training in case this led to a transfer of power to the proletariat. The dominant method of technical education was the apprenticeship with the focus on the development of skills, rather than knowledge. Green (1999) commented that the rapid industrialisation of the period appeared to owe little to state support for technical training. This is important when considering the derivation of the current system as we tend to consider it a given that improving vocational education is a good thing for individuals and the state; this has not always been the case.

The roots of modern FE colleges are often considered to reside in the first 'Mechanics' Institutes' founded by George Birkbeck in Edinburgh and London between 1821 and 1823. Birkbeck was a physician and Professor of Natural Philosophy in Glasgow. He delivered lectures on the 'mechanical arts' that became so popular that he found a home for them in the new Mechanics' Institute. The institutes provided a library and a focus for the self-improvement of the working classes and an opportunity for social activities. Many women attended, having the opportunity to engage in philosophical discussions for the first time. There were often conflicts over the purpose of the movement, with some advocating them as vehicles for social change, including the emancipation of women and the working classes. The movement spread rapidly across the country and there were around 300 institutes by the mid-nineteenth century. The London Mechanics' Institute became Birkbeck College in 1907.

Given the importance of vocational education to economic development, it would seem reasonable that the state would provide financial support for the developing movement. However scepticism and concerns over transfer of power to the working classes resulted in voluntary subscription being a major source of funds. The new wealth of the industrialists brought political power and an incentive to invest in vocational education with a vision that this would lead to greater competitiveness; this was particularly important given the substantial investment in training made by European competitors. Science also entered the school curriculum at this time, reinforcing the greater importance attached to technical education.

The role of local authorities in vocational education began as a result of the Samuelson *Commission on Technical Instruction* (1884) and the resulting Technical Instruction Act (1889). The legislation enabled the public rates to be used to fund vocational education, though popularity forced additional funding to be sought from a local alcohol tax ('whiskey money'). North East Wales Institute of Higher Education was one of the first institutions formed as a result of the Act. The 1902 Education Act established Local Education Authorities (LEAs), grammar schools and junior technical schools, providing a choice of academic or technical education at age 13. There are interesting parallels with current 14–19 initiatives here. Other organisations, particularly Day Continuation Schools, Trade Schools and Evening Institutes were involved in providing technical education. There was also a major role for the City and Guilds of London Institute in directing the technical education curriculum and sourcing the necessary funding. German Technical High Schools were seen as important models for post-school technical education in the UK.

The terms 'further education' and 'technical colleges' came into use following the *Regulations for Technical Schools, Schools of Art and other forms of provision for Further Education* (HMSO) in 1914. 'Technical Colleges' were established to provide extended periods of technical education and these were termed 'Colleges of Further Education' in the 1926 and 1934 *Regulations for Further Education* (HMSO 1926, 1934). These organisations became responsible for awarding National Certificates and National Diplomas after the First World War; qualifications which survive to the present day.

The 1944 Education Act raised the school leaving age to 15 and incorporated some of the organisations described above (Junior Technical Schools, for example) into the secondary component of the current three-tier system of Primary, Secondary and Higher education. The latter resulted in national colleges organised on a regional, area and local basis. Many of these are the direct predecessors of today's FE colleges.

This discussion of the origins of FE explains the diversity of the current system, particularly as other components of FE, namely adult education and the apprenticeship system are still to be described.

Discussion points

1 How does the history of your own institution relate to the general history of FE described above?

2 Which of the influences on the development of FE resonate with current issues in the sector (the developments in the 14–16 sector, for example)? Are proposed solutions to current issues likely to result in similar or different outcomes to those in the past?

Reflective question

Consider the factors likely to influence participation among your learners. Given the tensions between the state, industry, institutions and individuals, what steps could you take to reduce barriers to participation?

Adult recreational learning

The motivation behind adult learning is often self-improvement, possibly with the objective of gaining qualifications or experience in order to improve employment prospects or as an enrichment activity. Although much adult education takes place in FE colleges, many of the alternative providers have roots in nineteenth-century movements, many of which had a mission to promote social change among the working classes through a form of liberal education. The distinction between adults learning for pleasure and those learning for personal development is difficult to make. Much tacit learning results from recreation and engagement in recreational programmes may encourage people from under-represented groups to pursue learning for other reasons. This has resulted in greater significance being attached to recreational learning by government and the inclusion of the sector in arrangements for inspection – one of the roles of the Adult Learning Inspectorate (ALI).

The importance of a flourishing adult education programme has been recognised in reports such as *The Learning Age* (DfEE 1998) and *Learning to Succeed* (DfEE 1999), and the Learning and Skills Act 2000, which established the Learning and Skills Council with a remit to meet local learning needs and champion the cause of lifelong learning and the achievement of a 'learning society' (see Raggett *et al.* 1995 for further reading). These were valuable steps towards halting a decline in the provision of adult liberal education (NIACE 1998), including the decision that the Further Education Funding Council should fund programmes, which do not lead to qualifications (called 'non-Schedule 2 activity'). Other initiatives include the Adult and Community Learning Fund (supports community learning projects) and the Adult and Community Learning Quality Support Programme (provides support materials for those delivering adult and community learning – see 'Useful websites').

The Adult School Movement arose at the end of the nineteenth century from a desire to improve the literacy skills of the working classes to enable them to engage with the Bible more effectively. Although run on non-sectarian principles, the Methodist William Singleton and Quaker Samuel Fox were involved in the establishment of the movement, which had 80,000 members by 1914. Indeed the Religious Society of Friends (Quakers) had a significant influence on the development of adult education through the Adult School Movement and the Educational Settlements. The First World War resulted in a serious decline in numbers, although much of the ethos survives in the remaining Educational Settlements and the Workers' Educational Association.

The first Educational Settlement was formed in Leeds in 1909. The settlement movement was established by Samuel and Henrietta Bennett in 1884 in Toynbee House, Tower Hamlets. Key influences include the Adult School Movement, the polymath John Ruskin and social reformer Thomas Carlyle. The movement aimed to establish residential communities to alleviate poverty and develop community leadership skills through education. The movement gained momentum and led to the formation of the Educational Settlements Association in 1920. Educational Settlements run non-residential part-time courses designed to allow people to share educational experiences in a friendly atmosphere (Drews and Fieldhouse 1996). Existing institutions with links to the educational settlement movement include Toynbee House, Letchworth Adult Education Settlement, the Percival Guildhouse in Rugby, Bristol Folk House and Fircroft College in Birmingham. These institutions are linked with the community education programmes of universities and offer courses such as languages, arts and crafts and personal development. Some courses carry accreditation for Credit Accumulation and Transfer Scheme (CATS) points, which can be used towards diplomas or degrees including music, science, archaeology and literature.

The Workers' Educational Association (WEA) was founded to provide continuing education for working people, based on the philosophy of liberal education; essentially having the purpose of enabling people to realise their full potential and become active participants in their community. The WEA celebrated its centenary in 2003 and currently offers 13,000 courses to 110,000 adults on a wide range of subjects. Courses are run as evening classes or offered to community groups (often funded by the European Union or the Lottery) with a view to reducing social exclusion through community learning and the development of basic skills. The public and private sector are involved in the WEA Workplace Learning Programme which offers courses on basic skills, study skills and work-related topics including health and safety, equal opportunities and union representation. Albert Mansbridge founded the WEA (Marsh 2002). Mansbridge was a teacher within the Co-operative Movement (the original co-operative societies extended their philosophy to providing educational opportunities for the working classes) and was involved in the University Extension Movement. He felt that the latter organisation supported the middle classes and that co-operation between these organisations to provide education for the working classes would be beneficial. The first courses were offered in Rochdale (also the home of the Co-operative Movement) in 1908.

The University Extension Movement is still very active. Cambridge University offered the first extramural courses in 1873. Lecturers would travel all over the country to deliver courses on a wide range of subjects. The Institute of Continuing Education offers a wide range of courses at a number of outreach centres, as weekend courses and summer schools.

Although strictly outside the remit of this book as it is a higher education institution, the contribution of the Open University (OU, established by Royal Charter in 1969) to adult education should not be overlooked. Although primarily offering routes to a degree, certificate- or diploma-level courses are also available. The OU has around 200,000 students and is a world leader in distance learning, particularly through the use of ICT to provide learning opportunities in the students' home or workplace and facilitate communication between students and tutors. The OU has always been highly proactive at ensuring that those with disabilities have equal opportunities to study.

For those no longer in gainful employment, the Third Age Trust (U3A, or University of the Third Age) was formed in 1982 and has over 500 groups with 130,000 learners organised on a regional basis. Each group makes use of the expertise of members to provide courses in subjects of interest. This is recreational learning in the true sense as qualifications are not awarded.

Opportunities for adult education using e-learning methods have increased significantly over the last few years. In addition to the OU, Learndirect is a major provider. The University for Industry (UfI) founded Learndirect in 1998 with the objective of providing a wide range of courses for adults to promote workforce development and lifelong learning. The organisation operates via a regional network of centres. The courses tend to be orientated towards the development of work-related skills such as basic skills, business and management and IT for those in work, seeking work or excluded from other education opportunities. BBC Learning for Adults also provide a range of online courses.

There are many issues surrounding the use of ICT to deliver courses to excluded groups. Although the use of ICT has the potential to reach millions of learners, those most in need are likely to lack the skills and resources to access learning – an example of the 'digital divide'. Only those with the necessary skills and resources are able to develop their skills and knowledge.

Apprenticeship

The traditional notion of the apprentice is one in which a keen novice is nurtured by a supportive mentor to a point where he or she becomes fully competent at a complex task. These notions tend to be based on our experience of post-Industrial Revolution craft professions. While this may have been the case for a period spanning 100 years or so from the late nineteenth century, it was preceded and followed by something quite different.

Although the process of learning a trade from someone more knowledgeable has been practised for thousands of years, the traditional apprenticeship has its roots in the indenture system of the Middle Ages. Indentures were contracts between the 'master' and the parent or guardian of the novice apprentice. The term 'master' gives a flavour of the relationship. The apprentice would work for years, gradually becoming a competent tradesperson, but for 'compensation' in the form of food, clothing and small amounts of money. The relationship was far from altruistic on the part of the master, indeed the subversion of youth in this way has been considered a form of social control. The culmination was the production by the apprentice of a 'masterpiece' for presentation to the guild (a craft association) in order to become a 'freeman'. The process was often accompanied by a completion ritual or 'rite of passage' to mark the transition to adulthood (Lane 1996).

The Industrial Revolution brought changes in working practices and labour shortages. With the prospect of economic prosperity from manufacturing industry, apprentices became more valued in their own right and were employees paid a salary. There was social status associated with the role, which was thought to provide a lifetime of employment. Industrialisation changed the nature of some apprenticeships in that mechanisation achieved some of the more repetitive work, with skilled tradespeople being responsible for the more skilled tasks.

The decline in manufacturing industry in the second half of the twentieth century resulted in poorer prospects for apprentices. Together with the growth of service industries, often perceived as providing an easier life than a craft profession, the number of apprentices fell to an extent that they represented less than 1 per cent of the workforce in 1990 (Fuller and Unwin 2003). The result was a serious skills shortage and wage inflation. The increase in participation in full-time education among 16-year-olds was also a contributory factor as the result was dominantly academic qualifications, rather than training (Steedman *et al.* 1998).

There has been a history of non-intervention in the apprenticeship system by government, rather it was left to employer to recruit and train according to demand. The formation of the Industrial Training Boards (ITBs) in 1964 marked the beginning of a closer relationship between government and employers. ITBs formulated the apprenticeship curriculum. Trade unions were also heavily involved in managing apprenticeships. ITBs were the forerunners of a series of employer-led organisations designed to improve standards in work-based training, including the Manpower Services Commission, the Training Agency, Training and Enterprise Councils (TECs) and National Training Organisations (NTOs). Each sector (engineering, for example) has an NTO that is responsible for workforce development and setting national standards.

The need for improvements in the structure of work-based training has been apparent for many years, particularly when comparisons are made with other countries (Keep 1996). For example, half the number of UK workers have vocational qualifications when compared with Germany (OECD 2001) and only one in four economically active people have a qualification, or have qualifications below the equivalent of National Vocational Qualification (NVQ) Level 4 (Campbell 2001).

Our current model of work-based training (the 'new vocationalism') has its roots in the Holland Report (HMSO 1977) and schemes such as the Youth Opportunities Programme (YOP) and New Training Initiative, which were designed to modernise the traditional craft apprenticeship, but met with limited success as trainees felt that thy were exploited. The YOP scheme was replaced by the Youth Training Scheme (YTS) in 1983 and later by the two-year YTS2. These schemes were supported pre-vocational courses under the

Technical Vocational Education Initiative (TVEI) leading to the award of a Certificate in Pre-vocational Education (CPVE). These schemes carried rather low status, however, and were often seen as devices to place school leavers in non-existent jobs. For the first time the availability of work-based training places was supply-, rather than demand-led.

The Modern Apprenticeship (MA) was introduced in 1994 in an attempt to reduce the decline in the number of traditional apprenticeships and it represented the first significant peacetime involvement of government in apprenticeships. The intention was that recruits to the MA scheme had employed status and were expected to work towards an NVQ Level 3 (unlike previous schemes such as YTS which involved Level 2 qualifications) and take Key Skills units at Level 2. FE colleges or private training providers were usually involved to provide support and assessment for the qualification. In 2001, MAs were designated as 'Foundation MA' (FMA) at Level 2 and 'Advanced MA' (AMA) at Level 3 and recruits did not have to have employed status. National Diplomas were considered suitable alternatives to the NVQ.

The introduction of MAs involved some fundamental changes to the established apprenticeship system, with the involvement of private training providers and more off-the-job training – factors that may have marginalised the effectiveness of a well-established system: 'the shift from employer-led, to an agency-led training provision has fractured the relationship between communities and apprenticeship' (Fuller and Unwin 1998: 156). These authors also criticised the role of off-the-job training as decontextualising the learning experience. MAs also differed from their predecessors in that many trainees tended to be older (the scheme is available to those up to the age of 24), some already having a Level 3 qualification, or even a degree. A major difference was also the inclusion within the MA scheme of sectors not traditionally associated with apprenticeships, such as business administration and customer care, for example. Business administration was the largest MA sector in 2001, having 35 per cent more recruits than engineering (Fuller and Unwin 2003).

Many significant points in relation to the apprenticeship as a method of learning emerge from the distinction between the traditional apprenticeship and the MA. The apprenticeship traditionally had a greater bearing on the life of a young person than the provision of a career. Family connections were important in many traditional apprenticeships and with this the notion of being part of a community. Interaction within the community, including the apprentice, master and other workers, for example, has been considered crucial to the learning process. Lave and Wenger (1991) emphasised the importance of learning being 'situated' with a 'community of practice' in their influential book *Situated Learning: legitimate peripheral participation*. 'Legitimate peripheral participation' refers to the process of transition on the part of the apprentice from at first being a novice (on the periphery of the community) to a fully fledged expert. The multi-agency MA model may have a detrimental influence on the mentor-protégé relationship. In another influential publication Engestrom *et al.* (1995) emphasised the role of the apprenticeship in the transition between adaptive learning (the development of imitation skills) and expansive learning (skills of critical analysis, for example). The 'authenticity' of the activity was considered crucial, hence the questionable validity of simulation experiences provided by off-the-job training.

Development of vocational education in Europe

The purpose of this section is to draw some comparisons between vocational training in the UK and other countries. This is a significant topic that cannot be covered in detail here, but key issues will be identified from some major authors in the field and references to useful sources of information will be provided.

International comparisons are often useful to establish the standing of UK education and training against partners and economic competitors. The Organisation for Economic Co-operation and Development (OECD) produce an annual Education Policy Analysis, for example, see OECD 2001 and 2002. These documents provide a detailed qualitative and quantitative analysis of various aspects of education policy in OECD countries. Although all education sectors are covered, some reports are particularly relevant to post-compulsory education. For example, 'Rethinking Human Capital' (OECD 2002) takes an international perspective on the knowledge and skills required to promote personal, social and economic well-being. Some particularly useful quantitative information on the learning and skills sector in the UK has been provided by Campbell (2001) for comparative purposes.

The 1980s represented a period of significant growth in adult education (in this context 'adult education' refers to recreational, vocational, work-based and basic skills education) in Europe (Tuijnman 1996). Growth occurred in terms of participation and investment by public and private sectors in education and training. The only educational sector to show a significant decline during this period was liberal adult education, possibly as priorities shifted towards work-related qualifications. Growth in the Nordic countries such as Norway and Sweden was less marked, mainly due to existing high participation rates, though vocational education increased significantly.

The need for increased participation in adult education stemmed from a re-training of the existing workforce due to the ageing population and consequent shortage in young trainees. New technologies were also introduced at a significant rate during this period, together with a shift from manufacturing industry towards service industries.

Urbanisation and workforce mobility also contributed to the need for education and training. Furthermore, just as potential students are becoming more mobile, educational institutions recognise the cultural and commercial benefits of offering their services directly to overseas students, or delivering their courses via distance learning, including e-learning. The market for training and education has been particularly strong from emerging economies (OECD 2001). Although the General Agreement on Trade Services (GATS) includes clauses designed to remove barriers to educational trade, it has been recognised that there is much work to do on harmonising qualification structures and improving communication. Inherent in this process are risks associated with the commercialisation of education: 'The major change is that adult education is increasingly becoming part and parcel of the commodity market, to be developed, bought and sold under conditions of competitiveness and profitability' (Tuijnman 1996: 40).

The European Union (EU) 'Lisbon Strategy' had the goal of making Europe: 'The most competitive and dynamic knowledge-based economy in the world, capable of sustainable economic growth with more and better jobs and greater social cohesion' (Council of the European Union 2001: 4). The objectives of the Lisbon Strategy were to:

- increase the quality and effectiveness of education and training systems in the EU
- facilitate access for all to education and training systems
- open-up education and training systems to the wider world.

These were bold objectives, but the report lacked detail on how they could be achieved. Later, in 2002, the Copenhagen declaration emphasised the need for co-operation with vocational education and training programmes and the need for a 'common currency' of qualifications and competencies, particularly given the proposed expansion of the EU. The declaration provided specific proposals on how EU countries could develop collaborative arrangements in vocational education and training with regard to:

- a single framework for competences and qualifications
- a common system of credit transfer
- common criteria and principles for quality assurance
- common principles for the validation of non-formal and informal learning
- lifelong guidance.

Indicative task

The motivation behind adult learning is varied. The desire for personal development or enrichment, career progression or employment can encourage adults to seek opportunities to learn. The nature of the motivation can have an impact on the individual's ability to engage in learning and achieve their desired goals. Teachers need to respond to their learners' motivation and ambition in order to provide an appropriate programme.

Devise a questionnaire based on the motivational factors discussed in this chapter to determine what motivates your learners. Analyse the questionnaire to determine the most significant factors and evaluate the strengths and weaknesses of your programme in terms of its ability to meet their requirements. What changes are needed in order to more fully meet their needs? Maslow's hierarchy of needs and Roger's and Knowles' theories of andragogy would be relevant theory to introduce. Textbooks such as Petty (2004) cover these issues.

Summary

- FE is a diverse sector encompassing craft, vocational and academic curriculum areas.

- The roots of FE are found in the Mechanics' Institutes of the nineteenth century and a range of other initiatives during that period such as Junior Technical Schools.

- There have been many political, social, economic and cultural influences over the development of the sector.

- The diversity of the current FE sector results from the varied roots and influences described above.

- Adult recreational learning has an important contribution to make to personal enrichment and tacit learning.

- The Adult School Movement, Educational Settlements, the WEA and the University Extension Movement have had a significant influence on the development of modern adult education.

- Apprenticeship is a long-established method of learning a trade. Economic circumstances dictate the popularity of apprenticeships, though government intervention with schemes such as the Modern Apprenticeship have become common.

- Demographic and political change have contributed to a globalisation of education, with trends towards internationally transferable qualifications.

- This historical background has led to the current FENTO Teaching and Learning Standards (see Figure 1.1). Full details of these standards are available at the FENTO website (see 'Useful websites').

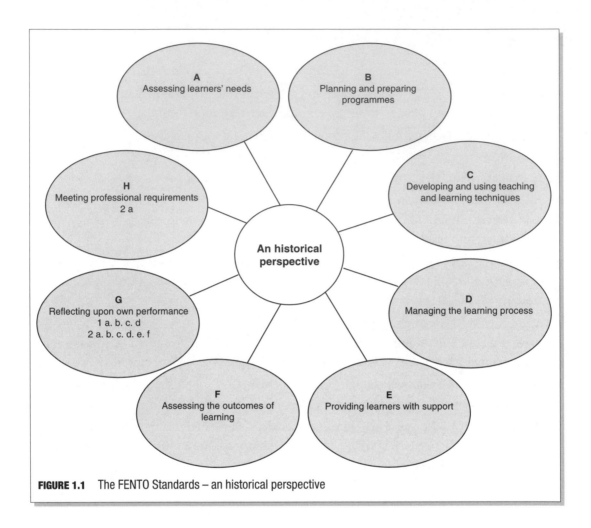

FIGURE 1.1 The FENTO Standards – an historical perspective

Useful websites

www.ali.ac.uk

Adult Learning Inspectorate (ALI): online news, updates, reports and statistics about the inspection process in FE colleges.

Last accessed 7 May 2004

www.bopcris.ac.uk

The British Official Publications Collaborative Reader Information Service (BOPCRIS): an online archive of government publications.

Last accessed 7 May 2004

www.cont-ed.cam.ac.uk
The Institute of Continuing Education at Cambridge University: provides news and information about the Institute.
Last accessed 7 May 2004

www.elwa.org.uk
Details of MA in Wales: provides information relating to post-16 education and training in Wales.
Last accessed 7 May 2004

www.fento.ac.uk
The Further Education National Training Organisation (FENTO) website
Last accessed 7 May 2004

www.ifsnetwork.org
The International Federation of Settlements and Neighbourhood Centres: online site that provides a background to the origin of the centres and their history.
Last accessed 7 May 2004

www.infed.org/lifelonglearning
Information on informal and adult learning
Last accessed 7 May 2004

www.learndirect.co.uk
Learndirect: provides online courses and learning information.
Last accessed 7 May 2004

www.lifelonglearning.co.uk
Department for Education and Skills (DfES) site to encourage and promote lifelong learning.
Last accessed 7 May 2004

www.ni-assembly.gov.uk
Official website of the Northern Ireland Assembly: details of MA in Northern Ireland.
Last accessed 7 May 2004

www.pro.gov.uk
The National Archives Online Catalogue: a summary of the developments in technical education and links to archived documents.
Last accessed 7 May 2004

www.qualityacl.org.uk
Joint Learning and Skills Council (LSC)/DfES/National Institute for Adult Continuing Education (NIACE) site to support those delivering adult and community learning.
Last accessed 7 May 2004

www.schoolsnetwork.org.uk
The Specialist Schools Trust: useful information on GCSEs in vocational subjects.
Last accessed 7 May 2004

www.scotland.gov.uk
Scottish Executive website: provides details of MA in Scotland.
Last accessed 7 May 2004

www.support4learning.com/education/adult.htm
Information about adult learning opportunities
Last accessed 7 May 2004

www.u3a.org.uk
The Third Age Trust: promotes lifelong learning for older people who are no longer in gainful employment.
Last accessed 7 May 2004

www.waytolearn.co.uk
Government website to promote adult learning
Last accessed 7 May 2004

www.wea.org.uk
The Workers' Educational Association (WEA): news, courses and information about learning in the workplace.
Last accessed 7 May 2004

References

Campbell, M. (2001) *Skills in England 2001: the research report*. Leeds: Policy Research Institute.

Council of the European Union (2001) *The concrete future objectives of education and training systems*, Report from the Education Council to the European Council. Brussels: EU.

DfEE (1998) *The Learning Age: a renaissance for a new Britain*. London: DfEE.

DfEE (1999) *Learning to Succeed: a new framework for post-16 learning*. London: DfEE.

Drews, W. and Fieldhouse, R. (1996) 'Residential colleges and non-residential settlements and centres', in Fieldhouse, R. and associates (eds) *A History of Modern British Adult Education*. Leicester: NIACE.

Education Act (1902) London: HMSO.

Education Act (1944) London: HMSO.

Engestrom, Y., Engestrom, R. and Karkkainen, M. (1995) 'Polycontextuality and boundary crossing in expert cognition: learning and problem solving in complex work activities', *Learning and Cognition* **5**, 319–36.

FEFC (1997) *Learning Works: widening participation in further education*. Coventry: FEFC.

Fuller, A. and Unwin, L. (1998) 'Reconceptualising Apprenticeship: exploring the relationship between work and learning', *Journal of Vocational Education and Training* **50**, 153–73.

Fuller, A. and Unwin, L. (2003) 'Creating a "Modern Apprenticeship": a critique of the UK's multi-sector, social inclusion approach', *Journal of Education and Work* **16**, 5–25.

Green, A. (1999) 'Technical education and state formation in nineteenth-century England and France', in Moon, B. and Murphy, P. (eds) *Curriculum in Context*. London: Paul Chapman Publishing.

HMSO (1914) *Regulations for Technical Schools, Schools of Art and other forms of provision for Further Education*. London: HMSO.

HMSO (1926) *Regulations for Further Education*. London: HMSO.

HMSO (1934) *Regulations for Further Education*. London: HMSO.

HMSO (1977) *Young People and Work*. London: HMSO.

Keep, E. (1996) 'Missing presumed skilled: training policy in the UK', in Edwards, R., Sieminski, S. and Zeldin, D. (eds) *Adult Learners, Education and Training*. London: Routledge.

Lane, J. (1996) *Apprenticeship in England, 1600–1914*. London: UCL Press.

Lave, J. and Wenger, E. (1991) *Situated Learning: legitimate peripheral participation*. Cambridge: Cambridge University Press.

Learning and Skills Act (2000). London: HMSO.

Lewis, T. (1999) 'Valid knowledge and the problem of practical arts curricula', in Moon, B. and Murphy, P. (eds) *Curriculum in Context*. London: The Open University/Paul Chapman.

Marsh, G. (2002) *Mansbridge: A life*. London: WEA.

NIACE (1997) *Learning for the Twenty-first Century: first report of the National Advisory Group for Continuing Education and Lifelong Learning*. Leicester: NIACE.

NIACE (1998) *Creating Learning Cultures: next steps in achieving the learning age*. Leicester: NIACE.

OECD (2001) *Education Policy Analysis 2001*. Paris: OECD.

OECD (2002) *Education Policy Analysis 2002*. Paris: OECD.

Petty, G. (2004) *Teaching Today: a practical guide*. London: Nelson Thornes.

Raggett, P., Edwards, R. and Small, N. (eds) (1995) *The Learning Society: challenges and trends*. London: Routledge.

Samuelson, H. C. (1884) *Commission on Technical Instruction*. London: HMSO.

Steedman, H., Gospel, H. and Ryan, P. (1998) *Apprenticeship: a strategy for growth*. London: LSE.

Technical Instruction Act (1889) London: HMSO.

Tuijnman, A. C. (1996) 'The expansion of adult education and training in Europe: trends and issues', in Raggett, P., Edwards, R. and Small, N. (eds) *The Learning Society: challeges and trends*. London: The Open University/Routledge.

2

Policy and practice in post-compulsory education

Anthony Coles

The response to social and economic change

COMPARISONS BETWEEN THE standard and extent of work-related education and training in the UK and other countries (by OECD – Organisation for Economic Co-operation and Development, for example) indicate fewer people entering training or higher education in the UK. Despite a 50 per cent target for participation in higher education, this is lower than many other countries. The immediate reaction to adverse comparisons is, quite reasonably, to examine ways to increase participation and to improve the quality of provision. The problem is that this response doesn't take into account the underpinning reasons for apparently low participation rates.

Interesting parallels can be drawn between the changes in market conditions and the response of the education system. The term 'Fordism' has been used to describe the notion of a standardised product for a mass-market using production-line assembly methods (Murray 1989). Traditionally, organisations using this approach had bureau-cratic 'pyramidal' management structures. Technological advances have resulted in what has been described as 'post-Fordist' methods in which industry can respond more immediately to customer requirements with a bespoke product. These organisations have a more devolved management structure with staff taking more responsibility for their own decisions (see also Chapter 11). The problem is that these individuals need a wider range of skills to be able to respond to the more diverse technological, manage-ment and production requirements. There have also been changes to the structure of organisations with various functions being devolved to satellite companies that can be used or discarded according to market conditions (Edwards 1996).

Ritzer (1993) discussed the concept of 'McDonaldisation' of education. In contrast with the notion of Fordism, in which industry has become more focused on customer requirements, Ritzer considered that the commercialisation of education had resulted in students becoming consumers of a product based on the 'product' being *predictable* (based on set outcomes), *calculable* (target driven), *efficient* (e-learning materials used for mass education, for example) and *controlled* in the sense that the curriculum and delivery are centrally determined. With the focus on individual learners, particularly in the 14–19 sector with individual learning plans and blended approaches involving various providers, a post-Fordist description may appear more apt. The danger is trying to apply a single label to a complex situation.

Discussion points

Consider the descriptions of 'Fordism', 'post-Fordism' and 'McDonaldisation' above.

1 Which model best describes the current education system from your perspective?
2 Is the system moving towards a particular model?
3 Are such metaphors useful in describing trends in education?

The decline of manufacturing industry since the 1960s has resulted in a shift in demand for manufacturing skills to those relevant to service industries. Similarly, changes in employment patterns with an increase in those engaged in part-time and short-contract work has resulted in a change in the purpose of education and training from 'up-skilling' to 're-skilling'. Haughton (1996: 132) commented that 'there is a need to shift fundamentally from the old attitude of training for life to one of training for change'. He drew attention to the need for the 'polyvalent worker'; one able to operate within a variety of spheres. The example of a kitchen fitter was provided, who needs the skills of an electrician, plumber and carpenter. Haughton considered that a 'skills mismatch' exists, rather than a skills shortage. The mismatch arises from the existence of a supply of skilled workers, but a lack of access to employment for them as a result of various barriers. Barriers could include: discrimination on grounds of age or gender; recruitment practices, as employers expect applicants to conform to social norms; pay, shift patterns and holidays; and local infrastructure, such as transport and childcare. He considered that entry to employment and return to work initiatives can also result in discrimination against those with qualifications, as financial incentives can make the unqualified a more attractive proposition.

Keep (1996: 96) criticised the organisation of provision, suggesting that 'the fact that the design and development of an effective [vocational education and training] system has for so long eluded the UK indicates that the problem's causes are deep-rooted and structural'. He identified problems arising from the UK employers (unlike those in most other countries) such as being prepared to recruit staff at age 16 without a commitment to provide further training. Other issues considered to be significant were poor technical training among managers resulting in resistance to innovation; voluntarist, short-term policies with little legislative backing; and the poor image of schemes such as Modern Apprenticeships, when compared with established training models.

Local and national policy

A bewildering array of White Papers, Green Papers and discussion documents appear relating to FE and work-based training. Some are heavy on rhetoric, but offer little in terms of policy changes that are likely to make a real difference. There are exceptions, however. The Kennedy Report *Learning Works* (FEFC 1997) remains a significant document and has influenced the widening participation agenda (see also Chapter 7). *Skills for Life* (DfEE 2001) and the Moser Report *A Fresh Start* (DfEE 1999a) have brought considerable developments to the area of adult literacy and numeracy (see also Chapter 5). The reforming agenda of *Success for All: reforming further education and training* (DfES 2002a) has permeated much of the sector.

Success for All seemed to encompass the characteristics of the FE sector; a recognition of its diversity and role in social and economic development. The effects of funding mechanisms, lack of investment and the education marketplace leading to increased provision for the advantaged at the expense of the disadvantaged were recognised as leading to poor quality provision in many areas. Strengths were recognised too, particularly those relating to promoting social inclusion, widening participation and responding to local and employer needs. The innovative teaching practices of some staff were also praised. The report highlighted the need for reform in the 14–19 sector with regard to improving opportunities for access to vocational education and the importance of building on established initiatives to improve basic skills provision. The reform was planned under four themes.

Theme 1 – Meeting needs, improving choice

The need to be more responsive to local needs was identified and the Learning and Skills Council (LSC) was charged with producing strategic area reviews (SARs) in order to identify 'learner, community and employers' needs'. These have taken place in 47 LSCs (DfES 2003a). Once complete the reviews would enable local LSCs to target resources appropriately taking providers' strengths into account. Proposals were made to increase the number of Centres of Vocational Excellence (CoVEs) and currently half of all colleges have such a centre and improved partnerships between providers in order to meet the development of 14–19 provision. Developments in the 14–19 sector include the establishment of 39 'pathfinder' areas and 280 Increased Flexibility Programmes (see also Chapter 8). The Entry to Employment (E2E) scheme established under this theme provides for progression to an improved Modern Apprenticeship (MA) programme. A significant development for the planning activity of FE colleges is that LSC funding has been made available to the private and voluntary sector and work-based learning providers can compete for basic skills funding.

Theme 2 – Putting teaching, training and learning at the heart of what we do

The Standards Unit was formed in January 2003 within the DfES with a remit to identify the most effective teaching and learning strategies in specific curriculum areas and produce support materials and training programmes for teachers and other staff. The Unit is also responsible for developing e-learning strategies. Expert groups have been established to advise on the most effective ways of developing teaching and learning in a range of curriculum areas such as science, business, construction and E2E. A network of teaching and learning practitioners supports each curriculum area.

Theme 3 – Developing the leaders, teachers, lecturers, trainers and support staff of the future

Targets were set to have 90 per cent of full-time and 60 per cent of part-time FE teachers qualified by 2005/06. These targets are being extended to include community, private and work-based provision where LSC funding is claimed. Various incentives such as training bursaries, 'golden hellos' and the repayment of student loans have been included to address the considerable shortages of teachers in some areas, including construction and some aspects of ICT. The formation of the Lifelong Learning Sector Skills Council (LLLSSC) for post-16 learning will identify and formulate plans to address skills needs in this area. A Centre for Excellence and Leadership was established to improve the skills of managers in the FE sector.

Theme 4 – Developing a framework for quality and success

Three-year funding plans linked to floor (minimum acceptable) targets for factors such as achievement and staff development have been agreed between providers and Local Learning and Skills Councils (LLSCs). Increased funding was promised for the achievement of targets.

A new funding regime

The LSC have developed a new funding strategy in response to *Success for All* (DfES 2002a). 'Plan-led' funding is based on the LSC's current funding formula involving:

- **Programme funding** determined by the number of starters, finishers and continuing students
- **Learner-related factors** including achievement, disadvantage and fee-remission
- **Institution factors** including area costs and specialist status.

Problems with the current system have related to inflexibility, the extensive bureaucracy and retrospective clawback if targets were not met. The plan-led approach (LSC 2003a), implemented in 2004, is based on three-year development plans negotiated between providers and their local LSC resulting in a three-year funding arrangement.

The plans take national, regional, local and sectorial factors into account as well as the LSC Strategic Area Review. The advantage is that funding for the subsequent year is guaranteed, providing that certain Headline Improvement Targets are met. These should be achievable, but demanding and take account of local needs and past performance. The Headline Targets are:

- Target 1 Learner numbers
  Targets for learner numbers will be set relating to the 16 to 18 and 19+ age groups. Targets for work-based learners will be based on average numbers in learning (AiL) and for E2E on the number of starts.

- Target 2 Employer engagement
  Targets will be based on extending work with employers and enhancing the employability of learners. How these factors will be measured is not clear as there is no baseline data.

- Target 3 Success rates
  Floor targets will be set based on national data for achievement. Typically, these vary from 35 to 55 per cent depending on the subject and sector. Floor targets and previous success rates are used to determine targets for improvement. The 'success rate' will include components of retention and achievement.

- Target 4 Professional qualifications
  Providers will need to set improvement targets for part-time and full-time staff achieving qualified status. Where all staff are qualified, Continuing Professional Development (CPD) targets must be set. Adult and community and work-based providers will also need to set targets.

Further advantages relate to the abolition of retrospective clawback (although targets are subject to a 3 per cent tolerance), a simpler 'regularity' audit in which the funding audit is discontinued, but the spending audit is maintained. Block funding is available for Additional Learning Support and some short courses so that providers can use funds flexibly to meet community needs. Finally, the February and May census dates will be abolished, leaving one in October, thereby reducing bureaucracy.

Premium-rate funding is available to providers to recognise and reward excellence (LSC 2003b). Real terms increases of up to 9 per cent are available over three years (2 per cent more than Standard Additional Funding). Methods used to measure success are an issue, but the DfES, the Office for Standards in Education (Ofsted) and the Adult Learning Inspectorate (ALI) are working on a range of measures, including a value-added approach to obtain a representative 'scorecard'. In order to qualify for premium-rate funding, a provider must meet the following criterion 1 plus either 2 or 3:

- Criterion 1 Progress against the three-year development plan
  Meeting or exceeding milestones towards the Headline Target, with a distinctive contribution to LSC strategic priorities.

- Criterion 2 Excellent performance evidenced through inspection
  At least 2/3 learners in areas graded 1 or 2 in inspection, with others graded at least 3; management graded 1 or 2.

- Criterion 3 Reaching the threshold premium funding indicator through the measure of a curriculum-adjusted success rate
  Success rates take account of a 'curriculum profile' in relation to the levels of qualifications offered and the mix between long and short courses.

Inevitably the new regime results in discord as provision offered traditionally by one institution may not meet LLSC strategic plans, consequently courses have to be closed. The LSC has been described as a 'monopsony': a situation in which there is a single purchaser (Ainley 2003). This gives LSCs the power to fund provision from private training providers if they so choose. In practice, this could create a much larger and more competitive marketplace in FE than took place post-incorporation in which several providers, including colleges, private training providers and work-based trainers could bid for contracts. Clearly, 'widening participation' has been interpreted liberally here, with providers being included in the equation. Ainley questioned the potential role of the LSC in funding HE institutions as part of their workforce development strategy. 'Regional universities', probably drawn from the 'new' universities, could form part of the LSC's remit for meeting local and regional needs. Parallels were also drawn with the old polytechnics in this respect.

Competition is on the horizon here too as private companies gain the opportunity to award degrees. Ainley described the developments in 14–19 (or as he suggested '14–30') provision envisaged by *Success for All* (DfES 2002a). *Learning to Succeed* (DfEE 1999b) and the Green Paper *14–19: extending opportunities, raising standards* (DfES 2002b) as 'a seamless web' in which further and higher education are part of a single strategy.

Indicative task

Research the performance of your organisation over the past three years. Annual reports and inspection reports would be useful resources.

As far as possible, evaluate the progress of your organisation towards meeting previous targets in the four Headline Improvement Targets described above.

Given the criteria for premium-rate funding identified here in this chapter, in general terms (given that Headline Targets and success measures are not available) is your institution well placed to qualify? If not, what changes are necessary to make improvements?

The FENTO Standards and the development of FE teacher education

The Further Education National Training Organisation (FENTO) is responsible for setting and implementing the national standards required of a teacher in further education. FENTO is one of many sector-specific ('sectors' including construction, engineering and care, for example) National Training Organisations (NTOs) having responsibility for developing occupational standards for their particular sector (FENTO 1999). FENTO is not the only NTO with an education-related remit; PAULO is responsible for the Adult and Community Education and Youth Work sector and the Higher Education Staff Development Agency (HESDA) for the HE sector. However, FENTO has had a more significant influence on its designated sector than these latter organisations. The role of FENTO and its relation to other organisations involved in FE teacher training has been discussed by Lucas (2004) in his article 'The "FENTO Fandango" '.

There has been much criticism among FE teachers and their trainers about the role and strategies adopted by FENTO. However, the organisation has made a positive contribution to the sector by managing to produce, in consultation with stakeholders such as employers, unions and government departments, a set of standards (the Teaching and Learning Standards) encompassing the diverse roles of FE teachers. Most would regard the Standards as imperfect, but nonetheless they represent a significant step forward.

The limitations of the Teaching and Learning Standards were to some extent ameliorated by the development of standards relating to other facets of working in FE. The standards can be found on the FENTO website (see 'Useful websites' at the end of the chapter). Currently FENTO supports standards in:

- Teaching and learning
  The standards specify the skills and knowledge required of an FE practitioner. They have been used to devise FE teacher training programmes, for staff development and appraisal purposes and internal observation of teaching.

- Management
  These standards specify the 'management roles and functions needed to deliver the core business' of FE and are based on a 'generic' model, which assumes that the 'function remains the same in all roles and at all levels . . . but that the context and scope differ according to the remit of particular jobs in varying organisational structures'. They were developed from National Vocational Qualifications (NVQs) and Head Teachers' standards, among others. They are designed to inform the development of appropriate qualifications.

- ILT
  The ILT (Information and Learning Technology) Standards 'provide a framework within which to identify the competences and knowledge necessary to perform effectively with the help of new technology'. They are designed to support the implementation of both the Teaching and Learning and the Management Standards.

- Support roles
  The diversity of support roles in FE is recognised and the function of support staff is defined as: '(supporting) learners and facilitate teaching in the FE environment'. The

document is a report in which gaps have been identified between existing relevant standards (such as those from the Employment NTO) relating to the functions of nearly 160,000 full- and part-time support staff in England and Wales. These are draft standards and FENTO has published a tender for the development of full standards.

- Governors and clerks
  These standards support the 'recruitment, training and appraisal' of college governors and are designed to assist their professional development with a view to improving the quality of college governance.

- English for Speakers of Other Languages (ESOL), literacy and numeracy
  Standards are published at Level 3 and Level 4 for teachers of adult literacy, numeracy and ESOL. These are designed to specify the skills, knowledge and understanding needed by specialist teachers in these areas (FENTO 2003).

Reflective questions

The Teaching and Learning Standards are used to map skills and knowledge in FE teacher training programmes. Choose one of the other standards above and assess your skills against the requirements. Have you identified any particular deficits? What action could you take to gain the necessary skills and knowledge?

The most common application of the Teaching and Learning Standards is to inform the development of FE teacher training programmes. However, following the introduction of the Standards, the Department for Education and Employment (DfEE) commissioned a series of case study projects based on piloting a variety of applications in FE and HE (Peeke 2000). A total of 19 projects were published covering the development of teacher training programmes, recruitment, observation of teaching and learning, appraisal, continuing professional development and reflective practice. The publication provides a rich resource of exemplar material. Peeke concluded that the Standards are useful for identifying gaps in provision and challenging current practice, though there were problems with staff time and motivation for implementing the Standards in different contexts and some of the language used to define the knowledge and skills required was rather impenetrable. The Standards lacked clarity on appropriate levels for the development of qualifications and some Standards were considered appropriate to CPD, rather than trainee teachers. The relevance to work-based trainers was also questioned. The Standards were found useful for CPD and recruitment, but they were difficult to apply to the observation of teaching. Appraisal was an effective use, though the Standards were not relevant to all job roles (support staff, for example).

Standards are not new to educationalists. In common with FE teachers, trainee schoolteachers need to meet specific occupational standards set by the Teacher Training Agency (TTA). Most would agree that a minimum set of core standards is important for any profession, but there is a debate about how standards are used for training professionals. For example, is it satisfactory to regard training as complete once the minimum standards have been met? Most would argue that the definition of a 'profession' should include reference to the need to engage in continuing development. Herein lies one of the most significant issues relating to the training and development of FE teachers.

Many of the chapters in this book refer to the academic/vocational divide and the long history of tensions between government and employers resulting from opaque responsibilities for vocational training. Similar tensions have determined the course of teacher training in the FE sector. At the heart of the issue is the distinction between FE teachers as subject specialists who happen to teach and FE teachers as teachers who happen to have vocational experience. Perhaps one answer can be obtained by asking the teachers themselves. For example, when asked to define their role, many plumbing lecturers would call themselves 'plumbers', rather than 'teachers'; indeed, pre-incorporation and changes to FE teachers' contracts, it was common for college staff to engage in a considerable amount of specialism-related work during the (much longer) holidays. In the public sector, 'nurse educators' would call themselves 'nurses' primarily. Conversely, teachers of academic subjects such as sociology would be more likely to call themselves 'teachers', rather than 'sociologists'. These distinctions are deep-rooted since they emanate from historical models of workforce development in which the apprenticeship was the dominant method to acquire work-related skills. The increasing amounts of training transferred to simulated environments in colleges institutionalised the process and the expectation was that trainers (or 'masters' in the apprenticeship vernacular) would comply with the conventions of the new training environment. They also emanate from notions of self-image and aspirations.

Unfortunately, there doesn't seem to be a resolution in sight to the identity of FE or FE teachers. The vast majority of NTOs produce standards that are used to develop competence-based NVQs. Although FENTO is currently the exception, the FENTO Standards evolved from a competence-based model devised by the Further Education Development Agency (FEDA) and the DfEE (DfEE/FEDA 1995). There was a precedent for the use of a competence approach with the D32 and related assessor and verifier awards developed by the Training and Development Lead Body (TDLB) in the early 1990s. However, this has not been an approach used widely in the education profession and it was rejected, probably because it would have reduced the status of FE teachers compared with their school-based colleagues. FENTO retains a role in endorsing FE teacher training awards and appears to be taking a proactive role in overseeing the delivery of these programmes.

Professional representation is another issue. The status of schoolteachers has been raised by the formation of the General Teaching Council (GTC), which is responsible for upholding professional standards; the British Medical Association being a similar model. Similarly, the award of 'QTS' (Qualified Teacher Status) and a DfES registration number confers further status. Several years after these arrangements were implemented, it is still unclear what the future holds for FE teachers. The formation of Sector Skills Councils (alliances of NTOs covering wider segments of employment) incorporating FENTO doesn't augur well for the professionalisation of FE if the sector maintains an alliance with these organisations. In order to attain parity of status with schoolteachers, a professional body independent of employers is needed and the award of 'QTS' (not a divisive variant specifying 'FE') is essential (see also Chapter 3). The political hurdles are considerable though; employers would be reluctant to lose control of their teaching and training, while school-orientated organisations would feel their professionalism diluted by association with FE.

The *Success for All* strategy and the Ofsted survey report on the initial training of further education teachers (Ofsted 2003; see also Chapter 8) emphasised the importance of improving the quality of teacher education in the FE sector. The Ofsted report identified 'good practice within fundamental structural weaknesses' (Ofsted 2003). Qualifications for FE teachers have only been compulsory since 2001 following a DfEE consultation paper in 2000 (DfEE 2000) in response to which there was a lively debate over such issues as qualifications for part-time and experienced staff. In response to the Ofsted report, the DfES produced a consultation document (DfES 2003b) entitled *The Future of Initial Teacher Education for the Learning and Skills Sector*. The document expressed the need for FE teachers 'to be experts in their own field, well grounded in generic pedagogy alongside the specific skills of teaching their subject' (p. 4). The need for FE teachers to be able to respond to the needs of diverse learners in terms of age, disability and level was stressed, together with the development of their learners' literacy, numeracy and IT skills.

The need to be able to develop learners' basic and Key skills has been an emerging requirement for FE teachers in response to *Success for All* and the national strategy for improving adult literacy and numeracy, *Skills for Life* (DfEE 2001); indeed one for which many new entrants to the profession are poorly prepared. It's not uncommon for potential trainees to question why they should need skills not traditionally associated with their discipline, sometimes with consternation as graduates find themselves unqualified for training because they lack a Level 2 numeracy qualification, for example. The response to this issue has been for FENTO and the DfES to develop a minimum core of language, literacy, numeracy and ESOL at Level 3 for inclusion in all FE teacher training programmes (DfES/FENTO 2002a, b) and Level 4 to inform the development of specialist qualifications for teachers of literacy, numeracy and ESOL.

The qualification structure for FE teachers in Scotland consists of a much more coherent model than that in England and Wales. Recommendations made by the Anderson Committee resulted in occupational standards for FE teachers in Scotland being written by a working group of practitioners. The Standards represent statements of competence that the Scottish Qualifications Authority (SQA) and the Further Education Professional Development Forum (FEPDF) have used to produce specifications for the award of Teaching Qualification (Further Education) or TQ(FE). The qualification consists of units that can be credited to an award at Introductory, Certificate, Diploma and finally TQ(FE) level. Courses are approved by FEPDF and are delivered in higher and further education institutions. Credit transfer and Accreditation of Prior Learning are possible and progression to a BA degree is available (see 'Useful websites' for further details).

Summary

- The standards and extent of post-16 education and training in the UK compares poorly with that in most of our economic competitors.

- Technology has enabled industry to move from standardised products for a mass market using production-line assembly methods (Fordism) to bespoke products to meet individual requirements (post-Fordism).

- The 'McDonaldisation' of education refers to a *predictable*, *calculable*, *efficient* and *controlled* product. There is a tension between applying post-Fordism and McDonaldisation to recent changes in post-16 education.

- Superficially, poor comparisons may be the result of inadequate and poor quality training, though the focus may be on 'up-skilling', rather than 're-skilling' to produce a multi-skilled workforce.

- Poor comparisons may be the result of a 'skills mismatch'; a situation in which skilled individuals exist, but are prevented from entering employment.

- *Success for All* (DfES 2002a) resulted in: LSCs conducting Strategic Area Reviews; the establishment of the Standards Unit to improve the quality of teaching and learning in the sector; targets for FE teacher qualifications; the formation of the Lifelong Learning Sector Skills Council and three-year funding plans linked to Strategic Area Reviews.

- The three-year funding regime under the LSC involves a provider development plan. Funding is linked to meeting four Headline Targets for: learner numbers; employer engagement; success rates and professional qualifications.

- Premium-rate funding is available for providers meeting or exceeding Headline Target milestones; excellent performance evidenced through inspection and/or reaching a defined minimum success rate.

- The FENTO Teaching and Learning Standards can be used for recruitment, observation of teaching, appraisal, qualification development, and continuing professional development

- The FENTO Teaching and Learning Standards are accompanied by standards for: management; information and learning technology; support roles; governors and clerks; teachers of English as a Second or Other Language; teachers of literacy and teachers of numeracy.

- There are issues over the parity of esteem of FE teachers in relation to those in schools and professional recognition in terms of qualifications and professional bodies.

- The FENTO Teaching and Learning Standards relating to policy and practice are shown in Figure 2.1. Full details of these standards are available at the FENTO website (see 'Useful websites').

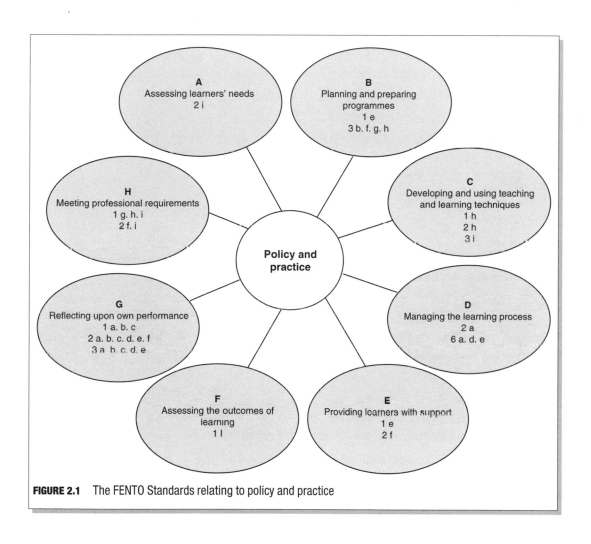

FIGURE 2.1   The FENTO Standards relating to policy and practice

Useful websites

www.ali.ac.uk

The Adult Learning Inspectorate (ALI): a government-funded body responsible for raising the standards of education and training for young people and adults in England, by inspecting and reporting on the quality of learning provision they receive.

Last accessed 7 May 2004

www.aoc.co.uk

The Association of Colleges (AOC): promotes the interests of further education colleges in England and Wales.

Last accessed 7 May 2004

www.collegemanager.co.uk

The *Times Educational Supplement* FE Focus

Last accessed 7 May 2004

www.dfes.gov.uk

The Department for Education and Skills (DfES) website

Last accessed 7 May 2004

www.fento.ac.uk

The Further Education National Training Organisation (FENTO): responsible for workforce development across the UK in the further education sector.

Last accessed 7 May 2004

www.fepdfscotland.co.uk/standards.htm

The Further Education Professional Development Forum (FEPDF) site with details of Scottish FE teaching qualifications.

Last accessed 7 May 2004

www.lsc.gov.uk

The Learning and Skills Council (LSC): responsible for funding and planning education and training for over-16-year-olds in England.

Last accessed 7 May 2004

www.lsda.org.uk

The Learning and Skills Development Agency (LSDA): a strategic national resource for the development of policy and practice in post-16 education and training.

Last accessed 7 May 2004

www.ofsted.gov.uk

The Office for Standards in Education (Ofsted): the non-ministerial government department which helps to improve the quality and standards of education and childcare through independent inspection and regulation.

Last accessed 7 May 2004

www.teach-tta.gov.uk
The Teacher Training Agency
Last accessed 7 May

www.tes.co.uk
The *Times Educational Supplement*
Last accessed 7 May 2004

www.thes.co.uk
The *Times Higher Educational Supplement*
Last accessed 7 May 2004

References

Ainley, P. (2003) 'Towards a seamless web or a new tertiary tripartism? The emerging shape of post-14 education and training in England', *British Journal of Educational Studies* **51**(4), 390–407.

DfEE (1999a) *Improving Literacy and Numeracy: a fresh start*. The report of the working group chaired by Sir Claus Moser. London: DfEE.

DfEE (1999b) *Learning to Succeed: a new framework for post-16 learning*. London: DfEE.

DfEE (2000) *Consultation Paper on the Introduction of Compulsory Teaching Qualifications for FE College Teachers*. London: DfEE.

DfEE (2001) *Skills for Life: the national strategy for improving adult literacy and numeracy skills*. London: DfEE.

DfEE/FEDA (1995) *Mapping the FE Sector*. Peterborough: FEDA.

DfES (2002a) *Success for All: reforming further education and training*. London: DfES.

DfES (2002b) *14–19: extending opportunities, raising standards*. London: DfES.

DfES (2003a) *Success for All: the first year*. London: DfES.

DfES (2003b) *The Future of Initial Teacher Education for the Learning and Skills Sector: an agenda for reform*. London: DfES.

DfES/FENTO (2002a) *Subject Specifications for Teachers of Adult Literacy and Numeracy*. London: DfES/FENTO.

DfES/FENTO (2002b) *Subject Specifications for Teachers of English as a Second or Other Language (ESOL)*. London: DfES/FENTO.

Edwards, R. (1996) 'The inevitable future? Post-Fordism in work and learning', in Edwards, R., Sieminski, S. and Zeldin, D. (eds) *Adult Learners, Education and Training*. London: Routledge.

FEFC (1997) *Learning Works: widening participation in further education*. Coventry: FEFC.

FENTO (1999) *Standards for Teaching and Learning in Further Education in England and Wales*. London: FENTO.

FENTO (2003) *Subject Specifications for Teachers of Adult Literacy and Numeracy*. London: FENTO.

Haughton, G. (1996) 'Skills mismatch and policy response', in Edwards, R., Sieminski, S. and Zeldin, D. (eds) *Adult Learners, Education and Training*. London: Routledge.

Keep, E. (1996) 'Missing presumed skilled: training policy in the UK', in Edwards, R., Sieminski, S. and Zeldin, D. (eds) *Adult Learners, Education and Training*. London: Routledge.

LSC (2003a) *Success for All: implementation of the framework for quality and success*. Circular 03/09. London: LSC.

LSC (2003b) *Success for All: recognizing and rewarding excellence in colleges and other providers of further education – arrangements for premium rate funding.* Circular 03/16. London: LSC.

Lucas, N. (2004) 'The "FENTO Fandango": national standards, compulsory teaching qualifications and the growing regulation of FE college teachers', *Journal of Further and Higher Education* **28**, 35–51.

Murray, R. (1989) 'Fordism and post-Fordism', in Hall, S. and Jacques, M. (eds) *New Times: the changing face of politics in the 1990s.* London: Lawrence and Wishart.

Ofsted (2003) *The Initial Training of Further Education Teachers.* London: Ofsted.

Peeke, G. (2000) *Standards in Action.* London: FENTO.

Ritzer, G. (1993) *The McDonaldization of Society: an investigation into the changing character of contemporary social life.* California: Pine Forge Press.

3

The role of the post-compulsory teacher

Janet Hoskyns

Introduction

THE PURPOSE OF this chapter is to consider the variety of roles an FE teacher can be required to undertake and some of the ways in which those roles may effectively be discharged. Although the term 'FE teacher' is used in this book, 'lecturer' is commonly used, but several other terms relate to teaching roles in FE.

The Common Inspection Framework for inspecting post-16 education and training (Ofsted/ALI 2001) uses the following definition of an FE teacher as:

> Someone responsible for teaching or training. As well as those specifically referred to as teachers or trainers, the term includes lecturers, tutors, instructors, supervisors, technicians and assessors when they have a teaching or training function and others involved in providing learning support.

> (Ofsted/ALI 2001: Inside cover)

There is a significant debate about the distinction between these roles, with considerable differences in job descriptions and salaries. For example, the 'instructor' grade does not normally involve planning lessons and marking. 'Assessors' may not be engaged in classroom-based teaching, but in visiting employers to assess NVQs, for example. The wider role of the FE teacher could also encompass that of, for example a:

- mentor
- counsellor
- tutor
- facilitator
- manager
- team leader
- administrator

- adjudicator

- mediator.

The role of the FE teacher is more difficult to define than that of the schoolteacher as the sector is much more diverse than the school sector in terms of the learners, models of curriculum delivery and subject areas, for example.

We recognise that many who work in post-compulsory education fulfil some aspects of the FE teacher's role as indicated above. Government statements and statutes since 2001 require FE teachers to be trained for their role, whether while they work (in-service) or before they take on a post (pre-service), and they need to gain accreditation to ensure that the status is securely maintained. By 2010 the Government expectation is that all serving FE teachers will be trained for their role and will have met the appropriate Further Education National Training Organisation (FENTO) Standards relating to their employment. Accountability has become more and more important in all sections of public service employment over the past 20 years. Teaching is no exception and further and adult education teachers are accountable for their work and achievements in the same way as any other public servant.

Most FE teachers will have a full- or part-time contract that stipulates how they're employed and their conditions of service. When compared with other professions, there is a considerable amount of part-time and temporary employment in post-compulsory teaching. Part-time working is part of the ethos of the sector and can be seen as a strength in terms of the added diversity, but it brings problems with complexity, continuity and communication.

At the time of writing, further developments are proposed, including amendments to the standards that FE teachers should achieve and qualification ladders, which would allow them to follow an acknowledged pathway for continuing professional development. The role of the post-compulsory teacher is under much scrutiny from Ofsted (Office for Standards in Education) and the DfES (Department for Education and Skills). The area of basic skills is viewed as critical for development in FE, particularly in terms of the competence of FE teachers. Consequently there are opportunities for specialist pre-entry, literacy, numeracy and English for Speakers of Other Languages (ESOL) routes to a teaching qualification and from 2004, FE teacher training courses will have to meet certain core basic skills requirements.

The level of interest in the role of the FE teachers indicates that it is recognised as being important, but also that it is likely to be subject to further adaptation and development over the next few years.

Discussion points

1 What factors might affect or change the FE teacher's role in the next few years?

2 List the differences between the role of an FE teacher and that of a schoolteacher. How do these differences impact upon the nature of the skills required?

Reflective questions

1 Evaluate your skills and expertise in the various roles described above. Which are your strongest areas and which are your weakest? What strategies could you adopt to build on your strengths and remedy your weaknesses?

2 Consider occasions when teamwork and co-operation have been difficult because of the balance between full- and part-time teachers. How is this managed in your own workplace? How do you ensure that the balance does not adversely affect the learners' experience?

Inspection, observation of teaching and appraisal

Since 1997, when the Blair government's slogan 'education, education, education' was coined, a number of reports have been published and legislation enacted that recognise that the learning and skills sector had been underfunded and under-recognised. At a time when schoolteachers' pay and conditions had been improved, very little had been done to ensure that FE teachers enjoyed the same status or that they were entitled to training in the same way as schoolteachers. The Kennedy (FEFC 1997) and Moser (DfEE 1999) reports also revealed that many young people and adults in the sector were not always being taught by appropriately experienced and qualified practitioners. Consequently, steps were taken to improve the training and practice of FE teachers by surveying their teaching and inspecting it against national criteria in order to improve the quality of classroom practice.

Since incorporation of FE colleges, a number of systems have been adopted in an attempt to standardise practice, thus allowing comparisons to be made. In recent years Ofsted and the Adult Learning Inspectorate (ALI) have taken responsibility for ensuring that teaching takes place in appropriate surroundings, and that it achieves the intended and expected outcomes. In addition, DfES papers including *Success for All* (DfES 2002) and others have led to target setting by management and other measures designed to ensure that value for money and high standards are achieved in the sector.

Increasingly government wishes to control these aspects of the education system and to be able to report statistically on the progress of institutions towards agreed standards and outcomes. As a result of lengthy consultations with the then Further Education

Funding Council (FEFC) and the Association of Colleges (AoC), Ofsted set up a section devoted to the inspection of post-16 education and ALI was established as a result of the Learning and Skills Act (2000). ALI was to inspect adult learning, for example work-based learning, learning by those over 19 in FE colleges, Jobcentre and Learndirect programmes, community-based learning and prison education (in conjunction with Ofsted). ALI and OFSTED share inspection of FE colleges and 14–19 provision. The Common Inspection Framework (common to Ofsted and ALI) is the result of much debate and deliberation, and all FE colleges (including school sixth forms and sixth form colleges) come within their inspection brief. The first inspections under the new framework began in April 2001 (see also Ofsted 2002). Ofsted are responsible for inspecting FE teacher training in higher education establishments.

Much of the practice of inspection is built upon the Section 10 inspection of schools, in particular in the inspection of teaching and the ways in which this is graded. Colleges now take considerable responsibility for assuring the quality of teaching and learning in institutions as a result of regular Ofsted inspections and in response to many of the criticisms made. This self-assessment exercise includes the observation of teaching, which focuses almost exclusively on the learners' perceptions. The seven main questions in the Common Inspection Framework are:

- How well do learners achieve?

- How effective are teaching, training and learning?

- How are achievement and learning affected by resources?

- How effective are the assessment and monitoring of learning?

- How well do the programmes and courses meet the needs and interests of learners?

- How well are learners guided and supported?

- How effective are leadership and management in raising achievement and supporting all learners?

(Ofsted/ALI 2001: 6)

In view of these aims, and the regular cycle of inspection, colleges now have systems for observing teaching and monitoring support, resources and management in all programmes.

Discussion points

How is monitoring of teaching carried out in your own institution? Is it linked to other forms of individual review and performance management? If so how?

Indicative task

1 Obtain a copy of a recent inspection report for your institution, or a similar institution.

2 List the strengths and weakness relating to your curriculum area.

3 Compare the strengths and weaknesses of your curriculum area with those of the institution.

4 Prepare a response to the inspection report recommending strategies to address areas in need of improvement.

Reporting attendance and achievement

As noted earlier, with regard to inspection, all colleges and other institutions receiving LSC (Learning and Skills Council) funding for the training they offer are required to report twice a year on their enrolments and achievements. If many students enrol but few achieve then funding is likely to be withdrawn from that particular course, which is why college teachers are endlessly required to monitor attendance and achievement in very concrete ways. In addition, the Government has set targets for involvement in higher education of 50 per cent for the 18–30 age group by 2010. In order to meet these targets recruitment and achievement in the post-16 sector will have to rise: in 2000 only three out of four young people between the ages of 16 and 18 remained in education and only 50 per cent of 16-year-olds were achieving five GCSEs at grades A–C. Targets and performance tables are used extensively as levers to improve standards. The effect of these upon the FE teacher is that they must produce documentary evidence of student attendance and achievement to support rising standards and improvements in the sector. The reporting of achievement is also required when an inspection takes place. For example, inspectors are required to evaluate the adequacy and suitability of staff and specialist equipment, in order to complete their inspection of how achievement and learning are affected by resources (Ofsted/ALI 2001: 9).

Relationship with QTS

The status of the teacher in further education has long been contentious. Changes to government policy during the 1990s contrived to erode this still further. Since the 1970s schoolteachers in the maintained or compulsory sector, have been required to be graduates and to undertake professional training or education that allows them to be registered as qualified teachers: this is known as Qualified Teacher Status (QTS) and confers the rights, duties and responsibilities of state registration for teaching in state schools. Registration with the General Teaching Council (GTC) is also required. The GTC is the professional body for teaching, which is responsible for professional standards and development. Such a system has never existed in post-compulsory education because much of the workforce is already involved in a professional activity as well as teaching.

The qualification levels and expectations among FE teachers are enormously variable, depending on what is taught to whom and in what circumstances. For example, a teacher of bricklaying may have undertaken an apprenticeship in the past and have gained qualifications to show what level of bricklaying has been achieved, but never have considered gaining a degree in bricklaying, since employment in the sector depends upon professional qualification not academic levels. It would be unreasonable to require the bricklayer to become a graduate merely to allow him or her to teach their subject specialism in college on three days each week. Equally, some professional courses rely on, for example, solicitors teaching for a few sessions each year, so some flexibility is needed if the system is to continue in its present form. FENTO, which published its *Standards for Teaching and Supporting Learning in Further Education in England and Wales* in 1999 (FENTO 1999), has created the basis for an equivalent status to be developed. In 2004 consultation is continuing to establish whether a form of Qualified Teacher of FE (QTFE) status might be appropriate and achievable. Similarly, the relevance of a professional body equivalent to the GTC is being debated. With it would come a number of requirements but also some benefits. The advantages might be that FE teachers would have a recognised status that could be transferred between institutions. Disadvantages might include registration and the difficulty of defining what constitutes a teacher, particularly in work-based situations.

Discussion points

1 What other benefits would there be if qualified status for FE teachers were instituted?

2 What would be the effects of a professional body being responsible for standards in FE?

3 How may a professional body such as the GTC differ from an organisation such as FENTO?

Engaging in Continuing Professional Development (CPD)

As is clearly indicated in the FENTO Standards, there is an expectation of all teachers that they will engage in continuing updating and furthering their professional development throughout their careers. Having completed an initial qualification in teaching, many FE teachers wish to pursue their career further, to achieve a higher level qualification, which may lead to more responsibility or to gain further understanding and experience in their subject specialist area. All teachers are learners too, and the continuation of professional development is an expectation in most professions, allowing for teachers to continue learning whatever their age and experience. Common sources of professional development are:

- use of Cert Ed credits towards a degree
- in-service programmes providing accreditation in skills such as mentoring and counselling
- courses run by private training providers such as Matrix and Network Training on topics such as accelerated learning, differentiation and updates on current initiatives
- masters programmes targeted towards the FE sector including modules on topics such as research methods, widening participation, education management and lifelong learning
- management qualifications such as the Certificate in Management Studies
- subject-specific courses
- courses designed to develop skills in new subjects such as ESOL.

Staff development funds are usually available from employers, though priorities are usually set in strategic plans, so these are worth reading before choices are made. The development programme may be administered by a staff development officer. Sometimes a financial contribution may be made to training that only indirectly benefits the employer. Masters programmes sometimes fall into this category.

Reflective question

Consider what further professional development might be useful and relevant to you in the next couple of years.

Assessment

Section F of the FENTO Standards covers every possible kind of assessment which a lecturer will normally need to employ. Assessment begins with assessing learners' needs (diagnostic assessment) and continues through the teaching programme (involving formative assessment) at regular intervals until the course objectives have been achieved, at which point summative assessment takes place. This is a traditional model but there are many variations on this theme, for example an NVQ may involve regular summative assessment.

Teaching, learning and assessment are the three pillars of the teaching triangle and assessment permeates all of them. It is not and should not be thought of as an optional extra occurring right at the end of a programme, rather it involves teachers and students making judgements about progress and motivation from the moment a course begins until it is concluded. Assessment is an integral part of teaching and learning, but the principles governing a responsibility for assessment lie with each individual teacher and the learners for whom they are responsible.

When devising assessment instruments, or evaluating them for assignment purposes, always consider the following points:

- *Validity* – Does the assessment test the learning outcomes intended?
- *Reliability* – Does the assessment give a representative indication of the skills of the learner?
- *Functionality* – Does the assessment methodology work effectively?

Remember that it's important that different teachers arrive at the same results if marking an assessment, so always include a marking scheme. It's also important to moderate results, so cross-marking is always needed if the assessment is summative.

Effective record keeping is vital as inspectors and external verifiers or moderators will want to see your results. If you intend to assess NVQs, then you will almost certainly need to take additional qualifications such as the 'A' (assessor) and 'V' (verifier) awards.

Discussion point

Why is assessment such a crucial part of an FE teacher's role?

Reflective questions

1 Evaluate one of your assessment instruments in terms of validity, reliability and functionality.
2 How could it be improved against these criteria?

Providing tutorial support

Section E of the FENTO Standards relates to the kinds of support that learners are likely to need. Tutorial support is normally related to learning and academic issues although tutorial support and pastoral care may often be linked and in some cases are provided by the same person. For purposes of clarity and in order to distinguish between the different roles, these two will be discussed separately, while acknowledging that overlap may inevitably occur.

Most FE teachers will have a tutorial group of students for whom they are responsible. Such responsibility will include ensuring students are fully enrolled for appropriate courses, take part in induction programmes and are able to access the learning support they require and to which they are entitled. Students will normally have regular meetings with their tutor and will complete learning action plans. Learning plans will commonly involve a negotiated response to issues such as:

- progress towards learning targets
- attendance
- effort
- Key Skills
- coursework
- assessments
- enrichment activities
- university applications
- discussion of references
- part-time work
- personal issues relating to learning
- career aspirations.

The personal tutor is usually the first person to be consulted when there are concerns over attendance or achievement, for example. This is often in response to referral systems in which teachers comment on performance issues. Some FE colleges operate a 'supertutor' system, which involves specified teachers taking responsibility for a relatively large number of learners. The philosophy here is that these individuals should become more skilled at the tutor role and have more time for individual support.

Indicative task

Identify the kind of tutorial support which might be needed in the following different cases:

1 an adult learner who has difficulty gaining access to computer technology despite attending a beginners' course for using IT;

2 an 18-year-old 'A' Level student who cannot or will not (it is not clear which) use the college library to find recommended texts that are needed to complete coursework assignments;

3 a student in construction who is intimidated by the other students, thinking they are all competent and he/she is not, so can't get started on the practical project work required.

Tutorial support is also provided as part of teaching sessions for individuals and groups, according to need. This will be related to specific academic needs perceived by the lecturer and that may already have been highlighted on entry to the course as part of the analysis of learning needs and the individual learning plan.

Interaction with parents and guardians is also an important aspect of the role of the tutor. Considerable tact and diplomacy are needed, particularly when there may be a false impression of the progress being made.

Pastoral care and counselling

There will be occasions when students approach their tutor or subject teacher for advice and guidance about pastoral issues. In most colleges this service is the responsibility of a range of different providers, some internal to the college and others by visiting staff offering particular support. It is important that teachers are aware of what is available and know how to refer individuals where this is necessary. In addition, all students have an entitlement to support for their learning and it is important for personal tutors to be aware of referral procedures and sources of support. These could include advice on:

- contraception or pregnancy
- rehabilitation from drug or alcohol habits
- financial matters
- accommodation
- learning disabilities
- general health matters
- relationships
- sexuality
- careers.

Individual teachers should be aware of issues they can deal with personally and those which should normally be referred on to the other services. There are usually opportunities for students in need of particular advice, be it medical, social or financial, to seek guidance from a trained counsellor. Nevertheless, if there is trust between a teacher and a student then it may well be to their regular tutor, someone they know and can rely upon, that the student will turn first.

Reflective question

Consider the examples of circumstances listed above in which referral may take place. With regard to your own expertise, which particular problems would you feel comfortable dealing with yourself and which would you find it necessary to make a referral within or outside the organisation?

Management

Management is a critical aspect of the role of the FE teacher. This topic is covered in more detail in Chapter 11. Although 'management' implies 'course management', the management of learners in the classroom involves many similar skills. These skills are addressed in FE teacher training programmes, but it is rare to find explicit course- and people-management skills addressed. The FENTO Standards emphasise the importance of developing interpersonal skills in order to collaborate effectively within and outside the institution. Examples of functions relating to the management role are:

- maintaining attendance records
- recording assessment results
- interacting with awarding bodies for external verification, coursework and moderation purposes
- taking part in and chairing course team meetings
- reporting to and chairing exam boards
- managing colleagues (often as course leader in the absence of seniority)
- liaising with managers within the institution
- engaging in marketing activities.

Skills relating to these roles can be gained as part of continuing professional development, though some are critical at an early stage in a career, such as effective organisation as many records are vital to the progress of learners.

Reflective question

List the management roles in your current work and evaluate your development needs in order to become more effective in these areas.

Using ICT in teaching

Information and communications technology is widely used in the workplace and increasingly at home. It has long been noted that although students are normally conversant with the tools of their trade, many teachers are less likely to use IT to communicate and disseminate knowledge. There are areas where using IT would be difficult if not impossible, but increasingly digital technology has applications in all subject areas and can be used to support and enhance learning. For students with a preference for visual learning, then a display on an interactive whiteboard or an image that links to the particular topic may be of great importance. Why, in the digital era, would trainee accountants use a paper and pencil, when the software available on hand-held, laptop and desktop computers can automate many of the calculations they would normally use? Until recently both schools and colleges were often underresourced in appropriate technology for use in the classroom, but this situation is slowly beginning to change. We would not advocate using technology for its own sake, but to improve and enhance learning and learning opportunities.

There are major government initiatives to increase access to ICT among all walks of life. For example, UK Online has the objective of enabling everyone in the UK to have access to the Internet and e-mail if they wish and there are many other ways in which ICT can increase access to learning.

Such is the significance of the ability of ICT to enhancing learning that FENTO have devised separate *Standards for Information and Learning Technology* (FENTO 2001). The 'learning technology' in the title implies more than 'IT'; indeed technology in the classroom includes using computers, but also devices such as data loggers in science, satellite navigation systems in geography, digital sound and light systems and such widely available equipment as videos and cameras.

Indicative task

Search the DfES, lifelong learning and FENTO websites (see 'Useful websites') to find evidence of different ways in which ICT can be used in teaching.

Summary

- The role of the FE teacher is very diverse. It requires a range of skills which may be gained through experience of another trade or profession, or may need to be developed through training.

- Statutory qualifications for FE teachers are in place and new programmes will be required to incorporate a core of basic skills. Specialist routes are available in pre-entry, numeracy, literacy and ESOL.

- Ofsted and ALI are responsible for inspecting teaching and learning in FE against the Common Inspection Framework.

- Self-assessment takes place in institutions as an evaluation tool and in preparation for inspection. This includes observation of classroom practice.

- Reporting attendance and achievement is a duty of the FE teacher and is necessary for monitoring progress and reporting to funding and inspection bodies.

- Professional recognition is a current agenda for the FE teaching profession, with parity of esteem and salary in relation to schoolteachers an objective. The attainment of QTS status and membership of a professional body may be involved.

- Continuing professional development is part of the role of the teacher.

- Assessments must be valid, reliable and functional. Diagnostic, formative and summative assessment are critical to the learning process.

- The role of the tutor is complex and requires significant interpersonal skills.

- Guidance and counselling involves difficult judgements on the need for referral.

- Management and administration are skills not normally incorporated within FE teacher education programmes, nonetheless they are essential to the role.
- The FENTO Teaching and Learning Standards relating to the wider role of the FE teacher are shown in Figure 3.1. Full details of these standards are available at the FENTO website (see 'Useful websites').

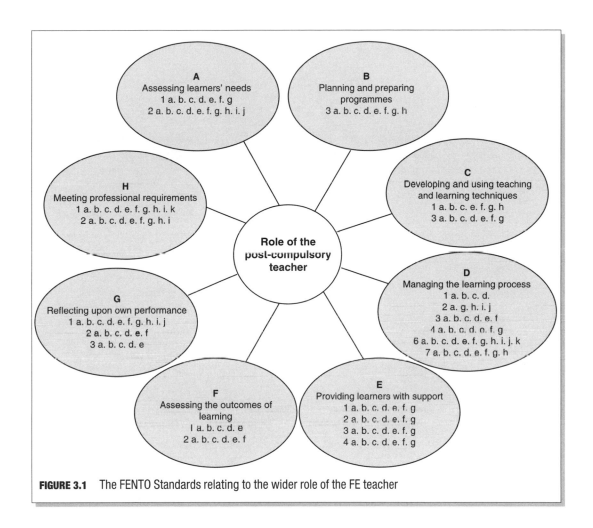

FIGURE 3.1 The FENTO Standards relating to the wider role of the FE teacher

Useful websites

www.dfes.gov.uk
Department for Education and Skills website
Last accessed 7 May 2004

www.fento.ac.uk
Further Education National Training Organisation (FENTO) website: training organisation responsible for workforce development across the UK in the further education sector.
Last accessed 7 May 2004

www.lifelonglearning.co.uk
DfES site to encourage and promote lifelong learning.
Last accessed 7 May 2004

www.ofsted.gov.uk
The Office for Standards in Education (Ofsted) website
Last accessed 7 May 2004

References

DfEE (1999) *Improving Literacy and Numeracy: a fresh start*. The report of the working group chaired by Sir Claus Moser. London: DfEE.

DfES (2002) *Success for All: reforming further education and training*. London: HMSO.

FEFC (1997) *Learning Works: widening participation in further education*. Report of the Further Education Funding Council's committee on widening participation in further education. Coventry: FEFC.

FENTO (1999) *Standards for Teaching and Supporting Learning in Further Education in England and Wales*. London: FENTO.

FENTO (2001) *Standards for Information and Learning Technology*. London: FENTO.

Learning and Skills Act (2000). London: HMSO.

Ofsted (2002) *A Handbook for Inspecting Colleges HMI 464*. London: Ofsted.

Ofsted/ALI (2001) *The Common Inspection Framework HMI 263*. London: Ofsted and ALI.
http://www.OfSTED.gov.uk/publications/index.cfm OfSTED

Practice and values in post-compulsory education

Learning to learn

Glynis Worrow

Introduction

THE PRESSURES OF 'delivering' a curriculum in order to meet objectives, targets and assessments often result in a lack of time to explore learners' individual needs and develop teaching and learning strategies in response to these needs. This chapter emphasises the importance of individual experience as a resource for learning. A range of learning style models is addressed and suggestions are made for linking these to experiential learning. The roles of socialisation and collaboration are discussed and practical suggestions are made for the utilisation of concepts that have a particular relevance to building on learners' experience, such as collaborative learning, discovery learning and deep and surface learning. A technique for active reading is included in order to develop a selective approach to using learning resources and finally, a guide to writing for academic and assignment purposes is provided.

What is learning?

Smith (1993: 34) stated that 'Psychologists and educators don't agree on, or even claim to be able to say . . . what learning is.'

The diversity of learning theories from the Behavourist, Neo-behaviourist, Cognitivist, Humanist and Gestaltist schools (cited in Curzon 2004), to the more recent theoretical concepts of adult learning described by Freire, Gagne, Knowles, Mezirow and Rogers (cited in Jarvis 1995), emphasise the challenges faced by trainee teachers in applying theory to practice. A tension emerges between what the tutor wants the student to learn and what they want to learn.

Although learning theories are diverse, many emphasise the importance of recognising the individuality of the learner and ensuring that new learning is set in the context of a learner's previous experience; essentially creating new experiences by modifying those already in existence. This is particularly well exemplified by the constructivist approach described by Bruner (1966) and can be regarded as 'spiral learning' where learning a new concept requires a learner to recall what they already know in order to add new learning. Learning is 'situated' in the learners' own experience (Lave and Wenger 1991). As teachers we are involved in providing learners with access to new knowledge and experiences in order to produce a change in behaviour. Behaviour in this context relates to the new learning. A major aspect of changing behaviour is to enable learners to become independent of the teacher such that they're able to respond to new situations with confidence.

The teacher requires the ability to make judgements on how, when and where new knowledge and experience is introduced. Knowledge of the learners' previous experience and ensuring that learners are aware of the relevance of their own experience is therefore vital. Smith (1993: 78) commented that 'The more one understands the self as learner; the better-equipped one is to learn.' For the new trainee teacher this introduces a new dimension to the role of the teacher, namely that of enabling their learners to understand the relevance of their own experiences to their learning and how to use information on their learning styles to become more proficient learners; essentially to learn how to learn. This is by no means an easy task given the pressures of targets and inspections, indeed, 'this learning theory is all very well, but I don't have time to teach my students how to learn' was a recent comment by a trainee teacher. The key message here is that providing information to learners is just a part of teaching and learning. However sophisticated the presentation, a critical aspect of the learning process is marginalised if learning skills are neglected.

The range of settings in which learning takes place and the diversity of learners in terms of age, social background and culture in the post-compulsory sector provide a challenge for the teacher to integrate learning to learn within an often crowded curriculum. Labelling a series of lessons as 'study skills' or 'learning how to learn' is likely to disengage and demotivate many learners as they may fail to see the relevance of what they're doing. Learning skills must be integrated within the curriculum using exercises based on the learners' experience and expectations.

Despite the reluctance on the part of learners to engage in tasks perceived as unrelated to their curriculum, there is usually a positive response to exercises designed to encourage self-evaluation and reflection. This is particularly the case when the outcome categorises learners according to specified criteria; these exercises can lead to very productive group work involving a comparison between perceived and measured learning styles.

Learning styles

There is a range of learning style approaches

Learning style questionnaires can provide a useful induction exercise, providing that the questions are at an appropriate level for the learners and that the results are discussed and explained. Honey and Mumford (1982) designed a learning style questionnaire that is commonly used in this situation. Many learners remember their learning style and this can provide the motivation to reflect further on their learning characteristics. Many students on teacher training courses have completed a variety of these questionnaires themselves but when asked have never used them with their students, again often citing lack of time as an issue.

Honey and Mumford's questionnaire categorises learners under four headings:

■ **Activists** enjoy the here and now, are open-minded and enthusiastic about anything new, are easily bored and have a tendency to want to become the centre of all activities.

■ **Reflectors** like to stand back and think and look at things from different angles before making conclusions. They are generally cautious, usually taking a back seat in discussions and tend to postpone decision making.

■ **Theorists** think in a logical way, can be perfectionists, like to analyse and synthesise, can be detached and can reject anything that doesn't fit their approach.

■ **Pragmatists** are usually down to earth, keen to try new things, have lots of new ideas, are impatient with others who don't share their enthusiasm and can be impressionable.

Although Honey and Mumford's questionnaire is the most commonly used tool to identify learning preferences, other approaches include those by:

■ Kolb (Kolb 1984)

■ Myers-Briggs

■ 4-MAT system

■ Gregorc

■ Bandler and Grinder (Bandler *et al.* 1981)

■ Dunn and Dunn (Dunn 2000)

■ Gardner (Gardner and Hatch 1989).

Each of these learning style approaches has strengths and weaknesses and some are more useful with particular learners than others. Most are copyright and some are only available commercially. The critical point is to encourage learners to reflect on how they learn and that they understand the implication of the result of whichever questionnaire is used. In practice, most groups contain individuals with different learning styles; the implication is that the teacher needs to devise teaching strategies to appeal to this range.

As teachers, learning styles should be used to enable students to:

■ try new things in different ways – for **pragmatists** and **activists**

■ start classes with different types of literature – for **theorists**

- prepare tasks that require analysis and decision-making skills for **pragmatists** but to enable **reflectors** to use their preferred learning styles.

Encouraging learners to use their own learning style

The planning of learning in the form of a case study or a problem-solving exercise can be useful to encourage learners to use their own learning style. One approach is to use the content of the lesson in the form of a problem in search of a solution. For example, ask your students:

- *How* do *you* think *you* can solve this problem?

- *How* are *you* going to make a start?

- *What* skills do *you* need?

- *How* have *you* solved problems like this in the past?

This approach is invoking the principles of problem-based learning (Boud and Feletti 1997) to encourage learners to individualise their approach to a particular topic.

When learners are asked about significant learning experiences, the response usually relates to something that has gone wrong or a situation involving failure or embarrassment. These memories bring back feelings of fear and inadequacy but discussion can enable students to share with others how they overcame their problems and yield strategies useful to everyone in the group. This is an example of the value of shared experience; the curriculum is the one common experience shared by learners, even if their backgrounds differ in many other ways. If, therefore, we learn more from mistakes, errors or embarrassment, why are we reluctant and panic when presented with a situation that may result in failure? If the teacher creates a supportive environment in which learners feel comfortable and able to fail without embarrassment, the process of failure can be extremely constructive. In addition to the learning that can result, the ability of individuals to adopt strategies to enable them to cope with failure is an important life skill.

When planning for future lessons, a variety of methods that utilise students' preferred styles should be included. In a whole-class environment this may mean presenting the content of the lesson using pictures, music and or rhythmic approaches. Ask students how they have learned best in the past. Examples provided may include listening to music to study, total silence, having some background noise or working with others. When students on initial teacher training (ITT) courses are asked this question, the answer usually includes listening to colleagues in class and at break times, small-group work and exercises to apply their learning for the benefit of their practice. Consider the opportunities available for your learners to engage in informal learning (learning that takes place away from traditional learning contexts: see Coffield (2000) for a review of related concepts such as non-formal and tacit learning). This is one of many examples of situations in which your knowledge of learners' backgrounds can be useful. What are their opportunities for informal learning? How can you embrace these opportunities to help them to make links with their formal learning? This adds a whole new resource to your teaching toolkit.

Reflective questions

1 How could you use learning style questionnaires with your learners and how would you ensure that the results are shared and understood by them?

2 What common experiences are likely to be shared by your learners and what exercises could you prepare to enable them to share experiences?

3 How might you encourage less confident learners to engage in sharing their experiences?

Multiple intelligences

Gardner defined 'intelligences' as 'the ability to solve problems that are of consequence in a particular cultural setting or community' (Gardner and Hatch 1989). Their research into the nature and realisation of human potential focused on how humans solve problems. The role of cultural setting and community is particularly relevant to the discussion here.

From this research it is suggested that there are at least seven basic 'intelligences' (or facets of human cognition) that teachers should address when planning lessons. These are:

1 **Linguistic** – the ability to structure rules, sounds and the meaning of language

2 **Logical/mathematical** – the ability to perceive logical patterns and relationships, cause and effect, functions and complex processes

3 **Musical** – sensitivity to rhythm, pitch, melody and tone

4 **Visual/spatial** – the ability to perceive colours, lines, shapes and the relationship between them

5 **Bodily-kinaesthetic** – the ability to co-ordinate muscles, balance etc. in physical movement

6 **Interpersonal** – sensitivity to body language and voice tone together with discrimination and response to personal cues

7 **Intrapersonal** – honesty and accuracy in terms of one's strengths and weaknesses, an awareness of one's own mood and motivation, self-discipline and self-esteem.

Individuals have strengths and weaknesses in each area, therefore a knowledge of learners' aptitudes should inform the planning of teaching and learning, with a focus on the particular intelligences of each person.

Discussion points

1 If this is the case, how might tutors utilise these learning capabilities within the learning environment?

2 What are the possible implications for learners with learning and/or other disabilities and how could you ameliorate these difficulties?

Reflective questions

Consider a situation in which you have recently engaged in learning.

1 Which of these 'intelligences' were addressed during your course?

2 Were they applicable to your preferred learning characteristics?

3 What changes could have been made to relate to your preferred characteristics?

Experiential learning

The Lewin/Kolb Experiential Learning Cycle (Kolb 1984) provides a most useful description of the adult learning process. The model can be linked to Honey and Mumford's four descriptors to provide a tangible sequence for planning a lesson in order to appeal to a range of learning styles (Table 4.1).

An example of a basic skills lesson to develop the skill of listening and responding to spoken language in which the Lewin/Kolb cycle is used could be:

■ **Reflection on experience**
Learners list situations in which they have had to listen to spoken language and then respond. They share these experiences within a small group. The teacher summarises the circumstances to the whole class.

■ **Abstract conceptualisation**
An audio tape of situations involving spoken language, such as buying a train ticket or ordering a meal is played to the class. Individually learners consider their response.

TABLE 4. 1 Relationship between the Lewin/Kolb cycle and Honey and Mumford's descriptors

Lewin/Kolb stage	Honey and Mumford descriptor
Concrete experience	Activists prefer doing and experiencing
Reflection on experience	Reflectors observe and reflect
Abstract conceptualisation	Theorists want to understand underlying reasons, concepts and relationships
Active experimentation	Pragmatists like to have a go and to try things to see if they work

- **Active experimentation**

  In pairs, learners take it in turn to ask the question and respond verbally.

- **Concrete experience**

  Problems arising from the exercise are discussed in a whole-class situation and another scenario is provided to pairs in order to practise their learning.

In principle, the cycle can be joined at any stage, indeed this can be used to vary the learning experience.

Carl Rogers (Rogers and Freiberg 1994) considered that experiential learning is equivalent to personal change and growth. His view was that teachers should be facilitators and set a positive climate for learning, clarify the purpose of the learning, organise and make learning resources available, balance intellectual and emotional components of learning and share feelings and thoughts with learners. Hammond and Collins (1991) also suggested that teachers build a co-operative learning environment and intellectual climate. This involves including learners in decision making, scheduling individual, small-group and whole-group tasks and using practical exercises in order to obtain feedback on the learners' experience.

Therefore Rogers, Hammond and Collins suggest that learning is facilitated when the learning environment:

- encourages complete participation by the learner who has control over the direction and nature of the learning

- is based on direct confrontation with practical, social or personal problems

- includes a method of assessing progress and/or success

- includes peer teaching, self-assessment and learning through group projects.

Carl Rogers' guiding principle was that:

> All individuals have within themselves the ability to guide their own lives in a manner that is both personally satisfying and socially constructive. In a particular type of helping relationship we free the individual to find their inner wisdom and confidence, and they will make increasingly healthier and more constructive choices.
>
> (Rogers and Freiberg 1994: xiv)

Discussion points

1 Consider Rogers' guiding principle and discuss its strengths and weaknesses when applied to your own learning/teaching environment.

2 Compare the differences between descriptions of your role as a 'teacher', 'facilitator' and 'learning manager'.

Reflective questions

1 What part does the Lewin/Kolb cycle play in your teaching at present?

2 How and when do you enable students to reflect on their learning?

3 How might you use the Experiential Learning Cycle in your teaching?

4 Can you identify lessons in which you will be a facilitator?

Social development theory

Vygotsky (1978: 57) stated that:

> Every function in the child's cultural development appears twice: first, on the social level, and later on the individual level, first between people (interpsychological) and then inside the child (intrapsychological). This applies equally to voluntary attention, logical memory and the formation of concepts. All the higher functions originate as actual relationships between individuals.

His theory is the notion that any potential for cognitive development is limited to 'the distance between the actual developmental level as determined by independent problem solving and the level of potential development as determined through problem solving under the guidance or in collaboration with more capable peers'. He calls this distance the 'Zone of Proximal Development' (ZPD).

This zone is created in the course of working collaboratively where students socially interact. This interaction creates links between individuals and their cultural and historical settings. An individual's culture creates distinct behaviours; social interaction with others of differing cultures can transform natural inclinations and develop new forms of behaviour. Therefore, full cognitive development requires social interaction. Lave and Wenger (1991) studied the interaction between apprentices and their 'masters' (tailors and midwives, for example). Their work reinforces the importance of situated learning and emphasises the value of social interaction and the need for learning to take place in an authentic context. Students should therefore, be provided with opportunities to problem solve and to learn together in a realistic learning environment, with tutor/expert guidance.

Vygotsky observed that when children work together on complex tasks, they assist each other in much the same way as adults assist children. He concluded that this social interaction is pivotal in enabling learners to solve difficult problems they cannot solve independently.

Bandura's (1986) social learning theory describes and explains human behaviour in terms of 'continuous reciprocal interaction between cognitive, behavioural and environmental influences'. The implication is that social interaction is prerequisite for learning and that behaviourist methodologies based on stimulus response alone would not be effective to enable human beings to engage in higher-order learning. Bandura's theory encompasses attention, retention, reproduction and motivation and suggests that the highest level of learning is achieved by organising, rehearsing and then enacting. Individuals are more likely to adopt this behaviour if it results in outcomes they value or if the model has admired status.

The collaborative learning environment

Vygotsky's research suggested that human beings are products of culture and biology and that any intellectual functioning is a product of our language, history and sociological background. Language was considered to be the key mediator of learning; the vehicle by which we assimilate our culture and organise our thinking. The relevance of this to the teacher, particularly in the diverse post-compulsory sector, is that learning needs to be presented in the language of the learner in order to be accessible. In this context 'language' refers to the vernacular used by learners, rather than necessarily their first language, though clearly this is also a highly significant issue.

Vygotsky also suggests that children use an 'inner speech', that is they learn when they engage in activities and dialogue with others. 'Inner speech' in this context means the things we say to ourselves as we are learning. Children first learn to watch others going through this process, but gradually this inner dialogue internalises, so becoming a way of regulating their own behaviour (learning) in a variety of contexts. Adults also do this by listening and socialising with peers, colleagues and family, for example.

To use these theories in practice you will need to:

- plan meaningful group work and enable students to sit with learners of varying ability
- continuously move from group to group to ensure each group is focused, on track and to check progress
- ensure that 'expert' assistance is on hand at all times
- suggest students talk 'out loud' if it helps clarify the situation, i.e. talk about what they are thinking.

Discovery learning

Discovery learning releases unexplored levels of knowledge, skills and attitudes. Bruner, influenced by the work of Piaget, suggested that the process of discovery learning is the most authentic (consider the importance attached to 'authenticity' by Lave and Wenger already described) method of understanding the principles of a subject. This process can be used in conjunction with a problem-solving approach to enable learners to explore various solutions using previous learning in conjunction with a research task.

Discovery learning theorists suggest that learners come into contact with a fact, object or process and experience **apprehension**, followed by a cognitive process in which learners make sense of the new learning (construct new 'meaning', or the process of **meaning making**) and put it into a form that the brain will accept: the **acquisition** phase. Finally, the new learning is internalised into the memory such that it can be recovered and used to demonstrate learning to an external observer. The key point here is the role of apprehension (or bewilderment) in the learning process.

Discussion point

Learners in post-compulsory education are often from diverse social and cultural backgrounds. If your groups consist of diverse learners, what are the implications for learning given the importance of cultural interaction?

Reflective questions

1 These ideas often seem quite theoretical and difficult to contextualise. Use the discussion above to summarise the meaning of terms such as 'situated learning', 'constructivism' and 'authenticity'. How are these concepts manifested in your current teaching?

2 Given their prevalence in current discourses on teaching and learning, how could you adapt your methodology to incorporate them more regularly?

Deep and surface learning

Learning to learn is a skill that needs to be consciously developed in order for a learner to understand their capabilities for learning. Reading, repetition and recall usually lead to relatively superficial, or 'surface learning'. This type of learning may meet the immediate needs of an examination, for example, but it has a limited duration and cannot be applied in new situations.

Approaches to 'deep learning' concentrate on meaning and understanding. Encouraging learners to address the following questions can develop deep learning:

■ What is the learning that needs to take place?

■ What are the concepts?

■ What previous knowledge is available to build on?

Encourage your learners to be sensitive to words and develop strategies for under-standing and unlocking their meaning. Suggest that they write down the concepts that they already know and consider ways for them to build on previous knowledge. Dictionaries, glossaries and many other resource materials can be useful. Learners can read key documents and highlight words and phrases that they don't understand. A useful exercise for them is to research the meaning of these words and phrases and then to devise a mind-map to link their ideas and build understanding.

- Why is the learning in question important?

Ask your learners to give reasons and explanations for engaging in the learning. Ask them to summarise the process that they believe would be most effective in order for the learning to take place and draw a diagram or flow chart as a summary.

- How does the concept work?
- What is its structure?
- How could it be explained to others?

Remember the importance of language. Use questions to encourage learners to verbalise their ideas. Ask them to suggest questions that they could ask each other in order to foster collaboration and the sharing of ideas in their own cultural context. Drawings and diagrams can be useful to visualise most concepts (how to make a com-pression joint between two pipes, the structure of the National Health Service, the process for booking a flight), including those in the affective domain. The technique of 'imaginisation' is useful for exploring attitudes and opinions in which learners draw metaphorical representations of envy, hate, love and trust, for example. Maintain a focus on the task by asking them to produce regular précis and summaries of their learning. This will develop the skill of 'active listening' so that they can focus on the most significant issues.

Peer-teaching activities can be particularly useful for sharing experiences and developing understanding. Try the 'jigsaw' approach in which small groups research aspects of a concept and produce an aid to assist them to teach their part of the concept to others. This is achieved by learners swapping groups and 'teaching' their part of the concept to their new group. Ensure that everyone has a lesson on each component and include a plenary activity to draw the concept together.

Discussion point

Discuss the possible consequences for learners of presenting information solely using handouts in the absence of using group discussions and research tasks.

Reflective questions

1 How and when are you going to use these strategies for learning with your groups of students?

2 What opportunities are you going to give your students to share their learning to learn strategies with others?

3 How do you enable students to work as individuals?

Dealing with ideas

Ideas often appear at the most inconvenient times: while driving, in the middle of the night, or in the supermarket, for example. These are times when the mind can wander and use 'spare capacity' to reflect upon and process problems that often seem intractable. Most teacher training courses encourage the use of reflective diaries. These provide a record of thoughts related to learning and how they impact upon personal and professional development. Consider asking learners to keep a small spiral bound notebook with them so that they can record thoughts when they occur at these inconvenient times. Mobile phones can also be used to keep a record of ideas and some have a voice-recording feature to keep a verbal record.

Periodically provide an opportunity for learners to share thoughts in the classroom. It may be necessary to negotiate at the beginning whether their notes should be made available to the class, or whether they should be confidential. Learners can select which point to share and a useful exercise can be to pool resources and produce a poster on how the ideas relate to their previous learning. These thoughts will be the result of highly contextualised learning as they will have resulted from culturally related stimuli.

Learning to read for academic study

The topic of 'reading for academic purposes' is sometimes greeted with scepticism by learners, particularly those with extensive previous experience. However, the skills involved, including 'active reading' can be very useful in order to focus reading on the task in hand and save considerable amounts of time.

Learning to read for a specific purpose, for example for academic work, is different from the reading for pleasure. This doesn't imply that academic reading is not pleasurable, but the style of writing that needs to be read may contain words or phrases that the reader has not experienced before. Education theory is a complex subject drawing from a range of different disciplines. It isn't reasonable to expect trainee teachers to be knowledgeable in all these fields. This is the case with most learning. Therefore techniques need to be adopted to come to an understanding of the new material; this can be particularly challenging in the case of distance learning courses for which tutor support may not always be available.

There are several different approaches to active reading. Most involve reading at least part of the text several times. These techniques will be useful for your own learning, but they can be developed with your learners too. When faced with a piece of text, for example an article:

- Establish the provenance of the writing by looking at the authors and source. This is essential when using material from the Internet as it may not be peer-reviewed. This will help you to make judgements on the validity of the opinions provided. You can usually have confidence in the provenance if the material is provided by your tutor. Make a note of the publication details for citation purposes.

- Use sections such as the contents, introduction, conclusion and summary to work out whether the source is useful and if so, where the relevant information is likely to be. Each section has a very specific function. For example, the introduction should identify the range of relevant topics covered and the conclusion should emphasise the key issues in relation to the theme of the writing. Note that long government reports often have an 'Executive Summary', sometimes as a separate document.

- Either read the whole document or a section as appropriate. Make a list of new words and use a dictionary or textbook to find their meaning. Write the meaning against the word to start your own glossary. Remember that it often helps to define new terms when writing an assignment to clarify that you understand them.

- Re-read the relevant section(s), but at the end of each sub-section, summarise your learning in your own words using a notebook or 'post-it' notes (useful to stick on relevant pages if you're using a library book). It can be helpful to have a list of the relevant topics to hand to maintain a focus on the task.

- Review your notes once the task has been completed. This is usually sufficient to give you an idea of what the text is about and you should start to understand the meaning of what you have read. Re-visit the text another day, reading your notes first. Then paragraph by paragraph read the actual text again. Make a note of anything that you don't understand so that it can be discussed with colleagues or a tutor.

This may seem time consuming, but with practice it takes less time and is more effective that trying to read the whole text several times with extensive non-targeted note-taking.

Reflective questions

1 How do you develop your learners' study skills?

2 Make a list of the skills they use most and identify which need to be supported further.

3 Plan activities to develop the skills identified above.

Indicative task

1 Research the different learning style diagnostic tools and choose the most appropriate for your learners. Use the tool with your learners (see also 'reflective questions' above).

2 Plan a session in which you use information on your learners from induction (remember confidentiality) to devise opportunities for them to make use of informal learning situations.

3 Evaluate the effectiveness of you new strategy when compared with your previous methods. Which aspects would you use again and why? Which wouldn't you use and why?

Academic essay writing

Writing for any purpose is always a challenge, but the way in which you write must be tailored to the context of the writing. A letter to a friend would be written in a different way to a memo to your line manager. Each type of writing has its particular characteristics and conventions. These are particularly evident in the difference between writing letters and e-mails, the latter being more of a conversational style. This is also the case when writing for academic purposes. The most likely form of academic writing that you will need to do is for an assignment. Although the detail of assignments varies according to where you're studying, the conventions are similar.

Planning and organising

The key point is to make sure that you demonstrate that you have fulfilled the assessment criteria. These are written for you as well as for those marking the work. Planning is an essential tool to organise your ideas. Here is a general strategy that can be applied to most assignments:

- Begin by identifying the essential elements of the task. These will be found in the assignment brief. Make separate notes of them. Look at the assessment criteria and make a note of what exactly is required from the task. It may help to look for *process* words such as describe, compare, explain, contrast and discuss. These tell you what to do, so ensure that you understand their meaning.

- Identify the information needed to complete the task. This may relate to educational theories, your own experiences (reflections), your learners' views, institutional strategies or national policy, for example. What do you know already? What do you need to find out? Where will you be able to find the information? A mind-map can be a useful planning tool to help you to structure your work.

- Gather the information from a range of resources. These may include the Internet, the library, institutional documents, government reports, newspaper articles, journals, course handouts or your reflective diary, for example. Read the resources and summarise the necessary information. Guidance on this is provided above. Keep re-visiting the assignment brief to make sure that you're on-task. Remember to record the references for all your sources, including the page numbers for quotations as it can be very time consuming to re-visit sources.

- Plan how you will organise the information in your account. Use the assessment strategy, the assessment criteria and other information from your tutors to inform this process. Be prepared to revise your plan in the light of new information or your initial writing.

Structuring your account

There may be specific guidance on this, but in general assignments are divided into three sections, introduction, main body and conclusion. It's advisable to complete the main body before the introduction and conclusion.

- Use the introduction to describe your setting and your role. Remember that those marking the assignment may not know you, so this needs to be explained for each assignment. State the key themes to be addressed in the main body and any particular approach taken (for example, have you included any original field research, or has the research been desk-based?). The introduction is rarely more than a couple of paragraphs.

- The main body of the essay should contain paragraphs that begin with a sentence describing the theme of the paragraph. Subsequent sentences normally describe relevant theory and present conflicting debates. Include your own (substantiated) views and relate theory to your own practice. The last point is usually very important and will often have a significant effect on the grade achieved. Try to give concrete examples from your practice that confirm or refute ideas from the literature. These examples could be backed-up with quotations, data from your own research, institutional reports or other sources related to your practice, for example. Only use quotations if the form of words is critical to the meaning, otherwise use your own words and reference the source.

- The conclusion should summarise the main points in the assignment, state the key issues arising and identify any developments for future practice that would be beneficial in the light of your arguments.

Technical points

It is important that attention is paid to the following technical points:

- Ensure that your work is fully referenced according to the method required by your institution. You must comply exactly with the referencing style (Harvard, for example) as it's critical that someone is able to follow up your work if necessary and full referencing avoids accusations of plagiarism. Remember to include page numbers for quotations. Long quotations tend to be provided indented in a separate paragraph, shorter quotations can be included in the text, though try to avoid long quotations.

- Generally, numbers or bullet-pointed lists are not favoured. Try to use continuous prose.

- If you use tables or figures (diagrams, pictures, graphs and charts) ensure that you include a legend (a description) and a number. Always ensure that you refer to the table or figure in the text. Similarly, material in appendices (questionnaires, documents, observation forms or assessment materials, for example) should always be referenced and discussed in the text.

Editing and proofreading

Finally, check your work as follows:

- Leave at least two days for proofreading and be prepared to change your first draft if necessary. Is the account coherent? Does it flow? Check spelling and punctuation. Have you included your references? Include the word count at the end and remember to check that you're within the maximum number of words. Use the assessment criteria to produce a list of essential components to confirm that you have completed all the tasks. For example, if the assessment criterion requires you to *show evidence of personal learning arising from the study of this module*, check your work for this evidence and tick the list.

- Swap with a critical friend. 'Critical' in this context means someone who can provide constructive comments and supportive feedback. Peer support is welcomed by most institutions, but take care not to copy sections from each other.

Above all, plan your time carefully, set realistic goals, use a diary or wall planner, have a break at regular intervals, reward yourself with something for comfort and do the most difficult parts first as this will give you the confidence and motivation to continue. Before handing in your work, ensure you have an additional copy.

Summary

- Learners engage in new learning most effectively by building on prior experience.
- Teachers must know their learners in order to provide opportunities for situated learning.
- Learning style approaches are useful for learners to understand how they learn and for teachers to plan their teaching.
- A variety of learning style diagnostic tools are available, but they need to be used with caution to ensure that teachers can act upon the results and that learners understand their significance.

- Gardner's multiple intelligences (Gardner and Hatch 1989) can provide a framework for evaluating the extent to which teaching methods relate to a range of preferred learning styles.

- Teachers can employ learners' informal learning, providing that they're aware of opportunities for this form of learning to take place.

- The Experiential Learning Cycle can be used to plan lessons and encourage learners to become independent.

- Bafflement is an important aspect of discovery learning.

- The use of language, shared experience in a cultural context and questioning can promote deep learning.

- Reflective diaries can be useful tools for all learners to manage ideas.

- Reading for academic purposes involves distinct stages differing from those used for other purposes that help to focus and reinforce learning.

- Writing for academic and assignment purposes involves task-focused phases including research, drafting and editing.

- The FENTO Teaching and Learning Standards relating to aspects of learning to learn are shown in Figure 4.1. Full details of these standards are available at the FENTO website (see 'Useful websites').

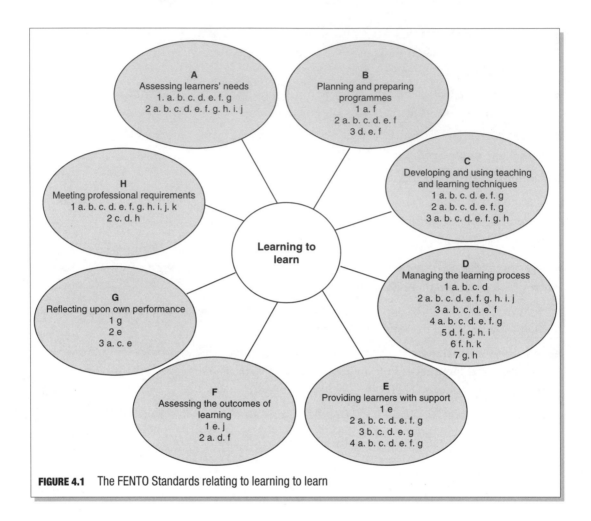

FIGURE 4.1 The FENTO Standards relating to learning to learn

Useful websites

www.aboutlearning.com
The 4-MAT System
Last accessed 7 May 2004

www.fento.ac.uk
The Further Education National Training Organisation (FENTO) website
Last accessed 7 May 2004

www.gregorc.com
Gregorc Style Delineator: includes links and services to promote self-learning.
Last accessed 7 May 2004

www.learningstyles.net
Information on different approaches to learning styles
Last accessed 7 May 2004

www.myersbriggs.org
Myers-Briggs learning style tests
Last accessed 7 May 2004

www.peterhoney.com
Honey and Mumford learning style questionnaire
Last accessed 7 May 2004

www.studygs.net
Study guides and strategies
Last accessed 7 May 2004

References

Bandler, R., Grinder, J. and O'Stevens, J. (1981) *Frogs into Princes: neuro linguistic programming*. Moab, Utah: Real People Press.

Bandura, A. (1986) *Social Foundations of Thought and Action: a social cognitive theory*. Englewood Cliffs, NJ: Prentice-Hall.

Boud, D. and Feletti, G. (1997) *The Challenge of Problem-based Learning*. London: Kogan Page.

Bruner, J. (1966) *Toward a Theory of Instruction*. Cambridge, MA: Harvard University Press.

Child, D. (2004) *Psychology and the Teacher*, 7th edn. London: Continuum.

Claxton, G., Atkinson, T., Osborne, M. and Wallace, M. (eds) (1996) *Liberating the Learner*. London: Routledge.

Coffield, F. (2000) *The Necessity of Informal Learning*. Bristol: The Policy Press.

Curzon, L. B. (2004) *Teaching in Further Education*, 6th edn. London: Continuum.

Dunn, R. (2000) 'Learning styles: theory, research, and practice', *National Forum of Applied Educational Research Journal* **13**(1), 3–22.

Eastcott, D. and Farmer, R. (1993) *Planning Teaching for Active Learning*. Effective Learning and Teaching in Higher Education Module 3. CVCP Universities Staff Development and Training Unit. London: CVCP.

Gardner, H. and Hatch, T. (1989) 'Multiple intelligences go to school: educational implications of the theory of multiple intelligences', *Educational Researcher* **18**(8), 4–9.

Hammond, M. and Collins, R. (1991) *Self Directed Learning*. East Brunswick, NJ: Nichols/GP Publishing.

Honey, P. and Mumford, A. (1982) *Manual of Learning Styles*. London: P. Honey.

Jarvis, P. (1995) *Adult and Continuing Education*, 2nd edn. London: Routledge.

Kolb, D. A. (1984) *Experiential Learning. Experience as the source of learning and development*. Englewood Cliffs, NJ: Prentice-Hall.

Lave, J. and Wenger, E. (1991) *Situated Learning: legitimate peripheral participation*. Cambridge: Cambridge University Press.

Rogers, C. and Freiberg, H. J. (1994) *Freedom to Learn*, 3rd edn. New York: Merrill.

Smith, R. M. (1993) *Learning How to Learn*. Buckingham: OUP.

Vygotsky, L. S. (1978) *Mind in Society*. Cambridge, MA: Harvard University Press.

5

Supporting skills for life with adult learners

Anthony Coles

Introduction

IT HAS LONG been recognised that a sound standard of literacy and numeracy provides the key to individual and national prosperity. While these are priority areas within the compulsory or pre-16 education sector supported by the National Literacy and Numeracy Strategies, there is a considerable need to develop these skills among adults. The term 'basic skills', or more particularly 'adult basic skills' (ABS), is used to describe literacy and numeracy skills pertinent to post-compulsory education. ABS also includes the provision of language skills to those for whom English is their second language; this is usually called English for Speakers of Other Languages, or ESOL. From 2004, information and communication technology, or ICT will also become a basic skill.

There are a considerable number of issues relating to ABS relevant to the FE teacher. ABS support is provided by most FE colleges and specialist staff are employed to teach these groups. From 2004 newly qualified teachers of ABS will be required to have a specialist ABS qualification at National Qualifications Framework (NQF) Level 4 in addition to a Cert Ed or PGCE. Teachers of all other subjects in an FE environment are expected to have the ability to support basic skills with their learners. To this end, Cert Ed and PGCE courses will be required to develop trainees' literacy and numeracy skills to NQF Level 3. This chapter will address the current issues relevant to ABS in the FE context.

The background to ABS in the United Kingdom

Serious deficiencies in adult literacy and numeracy in the UK were identified in the report of the working group chaired by Sir Claus Moser in 1999 (DfEE 1999). The report suggested that approximately one in five adults in the UK are illiterate and a similar figure was quoted as having very poor numeracy skills. The situation with regard to numeracy was considered to be much worse, however, as there were conflicting reports on the extent of the problem an estimate of 40 per cent having 'numeracy problems' was considered realistic. One of the problems with quoting figures such as these is that data appear to conflict according to the source and research methodology used. It is clear that there are considerable variations in the levels of literacy and numeracy in the UK population, from acute functional illiteracy and innumeracy to minor deficiencies in particular skills. Even these minor deficiencies can often present serious difficulties to the individuals concerned. The UK compared unfavourably with other countries as illustrated by Figures 5.1 and 5.2 quoted in the report.

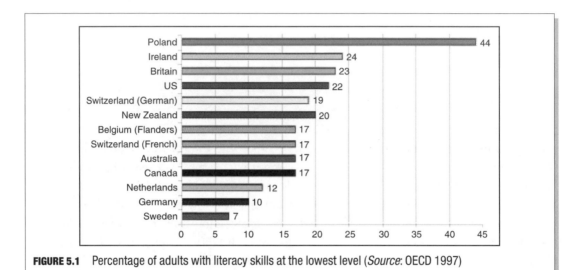

FIGURE 5.1   Percentage of adults with literacy skills at the lowest level (*Source*: OECD 1997)

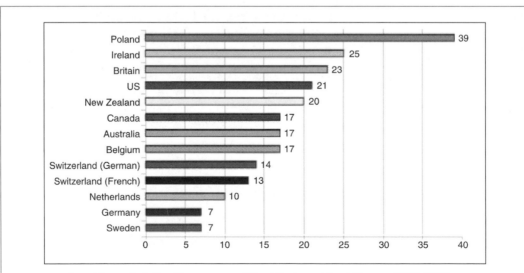

FIGURE 5.2   Percentage of adults with numeracy skills at the lowest level (*Source*: OECD 1997)

Particular problems were found in ethnic minority groups for whom English was not their first language, with one in four being unable to write their name or address or use a calendar.

The costs to the individual and society of poor literacy and numeracy skills are significant. Unsurprisingly, individuals with poor skills are less likely to be in employment and if employed, earn significantly less than their literate and numerate colleagues. Increased social exclusion, crime and poverty are endemic in areas in which the population has poor literacy and numeracy skills. In addition to the cost to individuals, UK business and hence the economy also suffer with estimates varying from £5 to £10 billion each year. Without intervention this problem is likely to grow given the increased skill levels required to use new technologies in the workplace.

The most significant reasons for the poor skill levels were considered to result from poor quality schooling, poor ABS provision and lack of motivation among potential learners: 'The teaching of basic skills to adults is often marginalised, remaining something of a Cinderella service. In fact it needs to become a key part in the strategy for lifelong learning and for national renewal generally' (DfEE 1999: 1).

The report recognised that progress had been made in improving the levels of ABS with initiatives designed to widen participation and foster lifelong learning as well as more targeted campaigns involving New Deal, community learning and family literacy programmes. However, significant weaknesses were identified, including a lack of a national strategy, poor co-ordination of provision including that in FE, a lack of staff training and qualification framework, an inconsistent inspection system and a lack of employer involvement.

The response to the weaknesses identified above was to propose a national strategy to 'virtually eliminate' functional illiteracy and innumeracy. The strategy would include a qualification structure, core curriculum, a set of standards to be met by teachers of ABS and targets for improvement. The targets are summarised in Table 5.1.

TABLE 5.1 Possible literacy and numeracy targets for 2005 and 2010 (percentage with adequate levels of literacy or numeracy) (*Source*: DfEE 1999: 5)

	Now	2005	2010
Literacy			
All adults	80	84	90
People aged 19	83	90	95
Numeracy			
All adults	60	64	70
People aged 19	60	85	90

The response to the Moser Report was published in *Skills for Life: the national strategy for improving adult literacy and numeracy skills* (DfEE 2001). The objectives of the strategy were to focus resources on those in the greatest need with a target of improving the literacy and numeracy skills of 750,000 adults by 2004, supported with additional funding of £1.5 billion.

The concentration of need within specific groups such as the unemployed, public sector employees and the low-skilled workforce was recognised. The priority groups are summarised in Table 5.2.

With such diversity, a wide range of agencies were identified as crucial to the success of the programme, including:

- Employment Service programmes
- Benefits Agency
- Local Authorities
- Learning partnerships
- Health services
- Information, Advice and Guidance

TABLE 5.2 Priority groups for improvement of literacy and numeracy skills (*Source*: adapted from DfEE 2001: 14)

Those with literacy and numeracy needs in regular contact with government and its agencies, comprising:	Around 200,000 public sector employees with literacy and numeracy needs in:	Approximately 1.5 million low-skilled people in employment with literacy and numeracy needs, particularly:	Other groups at high risk of exclusion due to poor literacy and numeracy skills, including:
■ 280,000 unemployed people ■ 1.5 million other benefit claimants ■ Around 250,000 prisoners and people supervised in the community	■ Central government ■ Local government ■ Armed Forces ■ National Health Service	■ Those in occupations and sectors with low average literacy and numeracy rates ■ Young people in employment	■ Around 60,000 homeless people with literacy and numeracy needs ■ Up to 1 million refugees, successful asylum seekers and other speakers of English as an additional language ■ Parents with poor basic skills, including the 250,000 lone parents with no qualifications ■ Around 1.7 million adults with literacy and numeracy needs who live in disadvantaged communities

- Religious bodies
- Community and voluntary organisations
- Health services
- Refugee Council and similar bodies
- Prison Service
- Age Concern and similar charities
- Probation Service
- Football clubs
- Public sector employers
- Trade unions

- Partnerships
- Libraries
- National training organisations
- Voluntary and community organisations
- Small Business Service
- Local Learning and Skills Councils
- Connexions Service
- Residents' associations
- Social Services
- Private sector employers

The Learning and Skills Council (LSC) was designated to plan, fund and monitor progress towards targets, with Ofsted and the Adult Learning Inspectorate (ALI) charged with devising and implementing an inspection framework. The Basic Skills Agency (BSA) would extend its experience in schools by providing support and advice, producing materials and disseminating best practice. In order to enable diverse groups to access learning, a range of delivery methods were proposed such as full-time and part-time courses, self-study, including mentored learning and Learndirect and dedicated provision such as that for families and specific minority groups.

Central to the proposal was recognition that standards needed to be raised by developing paper-based and electronic diagnostic tests to adequately assess prior knowledge and skills. The Qualifications and Curriculum Authority (QCA) was asked to devise a new set of National Standards which would inform the Basic Skills Agency in the production of a National Core Curriculum. These initiatives were accompanied by projects to produce new teaching materials and national tests in literacy and numeracy. The need for further research was recognised through a proposal for a new National Research Centre. It was recognised that there were weaknesses in the teaching of ABS resulting from an under-skilled workforce. The result was a call for specialist qualifications for trainee ABS teachers and a programme of continuing professional development for existing teachers.

National Standards for adult literacy and numeracy

QCA published a set of National Standards at three levels (Entry, Level 1 and Level 2) for adult numeracy and literacy in 2000 (QCA 2000). The National Standards were designed to bear a relationship to ABS curricula, the proposed qualifications framework, diagnostic and assessment tests and the qualifications framework for teachers of ABS. The production of the Standards was informed by sources such as the National

Literacy and Numeracy Strategies for schools, the National Curriculum and the requirements of Key Skills qualifications.

A common problem with standards is that, if interpreted too literally, they can be inflexible and provide a poor response to individual needs. This is problematic for those writing standards because an attempt to cover all possible needs would result in very large, unmanageable documents. QCA emphasised that potential learners may not correspond to the major groups addressed by the standards, for example, they may have pre-entry or special learning requirements. Furthermore, they indicated that the standards could be interpreted by curriculum designers to take learners' particular circumstances and experience into account.

A clear relationship between the National Standards and the NQF was required to ensure that progression routes between and from the different levels were clear, individuals had confidence that they were achieving at a nationally recognised level and that duplication of qualifications already held was not an issue. Table 5.3 shows the relationship between the NQF and levels relating to the Literacy and Numeracy Standards, Key Skills and the National Curriculum.

Literacy covers the ability to:

■ speak, listen and respond

■ read and comprehend

■ write to communicate.

Numeracy covers the ability to:

■ understand and use mathematical information

■ calculate and manipulate mathematical information

■ interpret results and communicate mathematical information.

TABLE 5.3 The relationship between the levels for Literacy and Numeracy Standards, the National Curriculum, Key Skills and the National Qualifications Framework (*Source*: adapted from QCA 2000: 5)

Literacy and Numeracy Standards level	National Curriculum level	Key Skills level	National Qualifications Framework level
Level 2		Level 2	Level 2 (equivalent to GCSE grades A* to C or NVQ Level 2)
Level 1	Level 5 Level 4	Level 1	Level 1 (equivalent to GCSE grades D to G or NVQ Level 1)
Entry 3	Level 3		
Entry 2	Level 2		Entry
Entry 1	Level 1		

The National Standards are available from the QCA website (see 'Useful websites' at the end of this chapter), but it's useful to consider the relationship between the different levels and to understand in outline their requirements. Tables 5.4 and 5.5 have been adapted to provide such a summary.

The Standards break a particular skill into capabilities and include descriptors that describe the level of performance required to address each level. For example, the Level 1 standards for speaking and listening are provided in Table 5.4.

From 2004, ICT will become a basic skill in response to the White Paper *21st Century Skills: realising our potential: Individuals, employers, nation* (DfES 2003). The White Paper recognised the potential role of ICT in enabling those in need of basic skill support to access learning via e-learning materials. QCA have published National Standards for ICT (QCA 2004) in order to commit adults to gain ICT skills as a third skill for life. The agenda proposed in the White Paper was supported by funding of £200 million to be allocated by the LSC over three years.

Discussion points

1 What are the strengths and weaknesses of defining a set of national standards for any curriculum area?

2 Given that standards are used to produce a curriculum, what are the challenges facing curriculum planners (those from awarding bodies, for example) in translating knowledge and skill requirements into a curriculum framework?

3 What factors need to be considered when devising a course based on an awarding body specification?

TABLE 5.4 Extract from the National Standards for literacy to Level 2 (*Source*: adapted from QCA 2000: 14)

Entry level			[Level 1]	[Level 2]
[Entry 1]	[Entry 2]	[Entry 3]	[Level 1]	[Level 2]
Speaking and listening **At this level, adults can:**	**Speaking and listening** **At this level, adults can:**	**Speaking and listening** **At this level, adults can:**	**Speaking and listening** **At this level, adults can:**	**Speaking and listening** **At this level, adults can:**
listen and respond to spoken language, including simple narrative, statements, questions and single-step instructions	**listen and respond** to spoken language, including straightforward information, short narratives, explanations and instructions	**listen and respond** to spoken language, including straightforward information and narratives, and follow straightforward explanations and instructions, both face-to-face and on the telephone	**listen and respond** to spoken language, including information and narratives, and follow explanations and instructions of varying length, adapting response to speaker, medium and context	**listen and respond** to spoken language, including extended information and narratives, and follow detailed explanations and multi-step instructions of varying length, adapting their response to speaker, medium and context
speak to communicate basic information, feelings and opinions on familiar topics	**speak to communicate** information, feelings and opinions on familiar topics	**speak to communicate** information, feelings and opinions on familiar topics, using appropriate formality, both face-to-face and on the telephone	**speak to communicate** information, ideas and opinions adapting speech and content to take account of the listener(s) and medium	**speak to communicate** straightforward and detailed information, ideas and opinions clearly, adapting speech and content to take account of the listener(s), medium purpose and situation
engage in discussion with another person in a familiar situation about familiar topics	**engage in discussion** with one or more people in a familiar situation to establish shared understanding about familiar topics	**engage in discussion** with one or more people in a familiar situation, making relevant points and responding to what others say and to reach a shared understanding about familiar topics	**engage in discussion** with one or more people in familiar and unfamiliar situations, making clear and relevant contributions that respond to what others say and produce a shared understanding about different topics	**engage in discussion** with one or more people in a variety of different situations, making clear and effective contributions that produce outcomes appropriate to purpose and topic

TABLE 5.5 Extract from the National Standards for numeracy to Level 2 (*Source*: adapted from QCA 2000: 16)

Entry level				
[Entry 1]	[Entry 2]	[Entry 3]	[Level 1]	[Level 2]
Understanding and using mathematical information	**Understanding and using mathematical information**	**Understanding and using mathematical information**	**Understanding and using mathematical information**	**Understanding and using mathematical information**
At this level, adults can:	**At this level, adults can:**	**At this level, adults can:**	**At this level, adults can:**	**At this level, adults can:**
read and understand information given by numbers and symbols in simple graphical, numerical and written material	**read and understand** information given by numbers, symbols, simple diagrams and charts in graphical, numerical and written material	**read and understand** information given by numbers, symbols, diagrams and charts used for different purposes and in different ways in graphical, numerical and written material	**read and understand** straightforward mathematical information used for different purposes and independently select relevant information from given graphical, numerical and written material	**read and understand** mathematical information used for different purposes and independently select and compare relevant information from a variety of graphical, numerical and written material
specify and describe a practical problem or task using numbers and measures	**specify and describe** a practical problem or task using numbers, measures and simple shapes to record essential information	**specify and describe** a practical problem or task using numbers, measures and diagrams to collect and record relevant information	**specify and describe** a practical activity, problem or task using mathematical information and language to make accurate observations and identify suitable calculations to achieve an appropriate outcome	**specify and describe** a practical activity, problem or task using mathematical information and language to increase understanding and select appropriate methods for carrying through a substantial activity

The adult literacy, numeracy and ESOL Core Curricula

While standards specify exactly what should be achieved within a given subject or skill area and ensure consistency, they do not provide curriculum developers, awarding bodies and teachers with a route to enable learners to reach the standards. The *Adult Literacy Core Curriculum* and *Adult Numeracy Core Curriculum* (Basic Skills Agency 2001a, b) provide such a route. It should be emphasised that the Core Curriculum is not a qualification in its own right, but it can be used to inform the development of qualifications in line with the NQF.

The Core Curricula enable teachers to devise diagnostic tools to assess learners' needs, provide a learning plan to meet those needs, produce resources to meet learning objectives and incorporate assessment instruments to measure progress and final achievement. The Core Curricula reiterate each National Standard and provide descriptors identifying the skills required to meet each standard. Additionally, there are examples of tasks, activities and advice on appropriate teaching methodologies. A strength of the Curricula in their current form is that they are not prescriptive on the routes to be taken to achieve the Standards. This is critical as adults in need of basic skill support are extremely diverse in terms of their experience, age, gender and cultural background. Furthermore, learning and other disabilities may need to be addressed. It is therefore essential that flexibility exists in order to adapt the Curricula to meet individual needs.

Adaption to meet the needs of diverse learners is crucial in the case of ESOL (English for Speakers of Other Languages), since ESOL classes probably comprise the most disparate group of learners in terms of their educational, cultural, linguistic and economic backgrounds. Consequently, it is a challenge to devise inclusive teaching and learning strategies. The *Adult ESOL Core Curriculum* 'defines the detail, skills, knowledge and understanding that non-native English speakers need to demonstrate achievement of the National Standards' (Basic Skills Agency 2001c: 7).

The Adult ESOL Core Curriculum relates to the Adult Literacy Standards and the EFL (English as a Foreign Language) curriculum as recommended in the *Breaking the Language Barriers* report (DfEE 2000a). The Curriculum is intended to have similar uses to the Literacy and Numeracy Curricula described above, although the intended learners are from settled communities, refugees, migrant workers and spouses or partners of foreign nationals. In contrast with the *Adult Literacy Core Curriculum*, the ESOL Curriculum separates the skills of speaking and listening to reflect the tendency for ESOL learners to understand more than they can speak.

While adults with learning difficulties and/or disabilities may be included in programmes offering qualifications based on the Core Curricula described above, there are many ways in which such programmes fail to meet the needs of these learners. These issues were addressed in the *Freedom to Learn* report (DfEE 2000b). The working group remit included an appraisal of issues faced by learners with hearing or visual impairment, physical disabilities, mental health difficulties, dyslexia and learning disabilities. The key barriers to progress among these learners were found to be low self-esteem and confidence, problems with transport, timetabling and equipment availability and, most significantly, the lack of suitably trained and experienced staff. Where suitable staff were available, there was often a lack of support assistants. The learners were often found to be below Entry level, consequently, qualification frameworks failed to meet their needs. The report recommended that a pre-entry core curriculum should be produced and that alternative ways of demonstrating achievement should be available. Additional investment in training was also a major recommendation, not only for teachers, but also support staff. The need to provide a form of training for community workers (social workers and health workers, for example) was also recognised since there are many opportunities for learning to take place in community settings. The report resulted in the Basic Skills Agency producing the *Adult Pre-entry Curriculum Framework for Literacy and Numeracy* (DfES 2001).

Adult literacy and numeracy qualifications

QCA have developed a series of basic skills qualifications based on the Core Curricula, which are offered by awarding bodies such as Edexcel. Certificates in Basic Skills are available for learners over 16 at Entry levels 1, 2 and 3 and Levels 1 and 2. The Entry level assessment is paper-based and on-demand, with an 80 per cent pass mark; re-takes are available after two weeks and certification can be achieved for components or the full qualification. The Level 1 and 2 tests are the same as the Key Skills tests, but without the portfolio. These are available online. Associated 'Skills for Working Life' qualifications have been developed in a range of curriculum areas, including business, health and social care and hospitality and catering.

The assessment and related courses for the adult qualifications are free, with full fee remission for providers from the LSC. This includes employer and franchised provision. Taster sessions and diagnostic tests are also funded. Other sources of funding include the Standards Fund, the Learner Support Fund to provide childcare for learners. Funding is also available from European sources such as the European Social Fund, the European Regional Development Fund and the European Union Socrates and Leonardo da Vinci programmes.

Reflective questions

1   How do your learners' literacy and numeracy skills affect their ability to engage in learning? What strategies could you adopt to support the development of your learners' literacy and numeracy skills?

2   If you are a basic skills teacher, how do you assess the individual needs of your learners and what are the mechanisms for supporting these needs in terms of an individualised curriculum? What further strategies could you adopt to ensure that individual needs are met?

Key Skills

The concept of encouraging individuals to reach a prescribed level in skills that enable them to engage in social and work-related activity with a view to personal development has been with us for some time. Initiatives such as the Adult Literacy Campaign and the BBC television series *On the Move* in the mid-1970s marked a significant increase in government involvement. However, these were voluntary models that required adults to attend sessions run by voluntary tutors (75,000 were trained between 1975 and 1978) or watch television programmes, assuming that those in most need had access to televisions. Since these initiatives, these 'generic' skills have been seen as a priority area for targeting resources in order to enhance social integration and economic competitiveness.

This section addresses the development of the current Key Skills model and sets it in the context of the basic skills agenda. The focus is on the English model, however the ACAC (the Qualifications Curriculum and Assessment Authority for Wales), the CCEA (Northern Ireland Council for the Curriculum, Examinations and Assessment) and the SQA (Scottish Qualifications Authority) can provide information on regional variations (see 'Useful websites' for the relevant websites).

The traditional 'Common Skills' units have been important components of National and Higher National Diploma and Certificate courses. These have many features in common with the current Key Skills. Briefly, the components of Common Skills are:

- Managing and developing self
- Working with and relating to others
- Communicating
- Managing tasks and solving problems
- Applying numeracy
- Applying technology
- Applying design and creativity.

Evidence for these skills is normally sought from assignments completed as part of the main qualification (such as National Diploma in Computing, or Higher National Certificate in Early Childhood Studies). The amount of support provided for Common Skills is variable and the rigour of the internal assessment process can be questioned. However, the range of skills covered and the close link with subject content has enabled the model to stand the test of time. This is a significant test as for well over a hundred years, reports (more recently, those of Bullock, Newbold and Cockcroft) on the communication and numeracy skills of employees in industry have been critical of the provision provided by vocational and work-based training and lamented the poor skills of new entrants.

One of the most significant reports addressing the issue of generic skill development in recent years is the Dearing Report (Dearing 1996). The report led to the Curriculum 2000 initiative and has been the subject of much criticism (see below). Nonetheless, significant recommendations were made for the integration of generic skills within the post-16 curriculum. These recommendations resulted from views expressed by various stakeholders, including employers, 16–19-year-olds, schools, colleges and universities. All contributors felt that the numeracy and literacy skills of those leaving compulsory education were too low, indeed 30 per cent of students entering FE were regarded as having poor skills in these areas. In contrast, IT skills were considered to be satisfactory.

Employers valued the development of additional skills such as problem solving and working with others, though young people did not consider that these were critical.

After so many years of criticism, it's difficult to identify the reason for persistent poor skill levels, but Dearing suggests that the overloaded National Curriculum was to blame, with 10 subjects, resulting in a marginalisation of literacy and numeracy skills. Recent reductions in the extent of mandatory subjects and the introduction of the National Literacy and Numeracy Strategies (websites relevant to the National Curriculum and Literacy and Numeracy Strategies are provided under 'Useful websites') may serve to ameliorate some of these difficulties. Furthermore, the lack of reinforcement of generic skills post-16, particularly in the academic routes, is likely to be a major contributory factor. Dearing recognised that recent initiatives had reduced the problem, including the spelling, punctuation and grammar components of GCSE examinations and 'A' Level coursework, the separate oral result in GCSE English and the integration of Communications, Application of Number and IT units within General National Vocational Qualification (GNVQ), NVQ and Modern Apprenticeship courses.

Dearing recognised that imposing the study of numeracy, literacy and IT post-16 would be too demanding. The solution proposed was to review 'A' Level subject cores with a view to incorporating these key skills and significantly, to introduce an optional AS (Advanced Subsidiary) Level Key Skills qualification. An element of external testing to improve rigour was also proposed for key skills associated with GNVQs and National Diplomas and Certificates.

Key Skills have been defined as: 'a range of essential generic skills that underpin success in education, employment, lifelong learning and personal development' (DfES/LSC/QCA 2002: 3). The current Key Skills are:

- Communication
- Application of number
- Information technology (IT)
- Problem solving
- Working with others
- Improving own learning and performance.

The last three are called 'Wider Key Skills'. These are not quoted on the National Qualifications Framework and as such are not formally regarded as qualifications.

The specifications and guidance for Key Skills are available from the QCA website (see 'Useful websites'). New specifications are available from September 2004. The current expectation is that post-16 learners should achieve Level 2 in Application of number, Communication and IT if they haven't already achieved that level (grades A* to C) during their GCSE programme (Modern Apprenticeship requirements are similar, but do not include IT and Level 1 is expected for those on Foundation programmes). Those on Level 3 programmes such as Vocational Certificate of Education (VCE) and

General Certificate of Education (GCE) should aim for at least one relevant Key Skill at Level 3. This latter objective has been marginalised by the already demanding nature (in terms of content and assessment) of Level 3 programmes and the lack of recognition of Key Skills by higher education institutions. The key point here is that these expectations are *entitlements* established in the Green Paper *14–19: extending opportunities, raising standards* (DfES 2002) and are funded by the LSC as an 'entitlement package'; the significance of this is that funding continues once the qualification has been achieved if support structures (such as tutorials) and enrichment activities are still in place.

Key Skills are assessed by external test and a portfolio of evidence (except the Wider Key Skills, which are assessed by portfolio only). Encouraged by QCA, awarding bodies have been increasing the frequency of assessment opportunities with the aim of 'assessment on demand'; to this end, online testing has been an important development.

Table 5.3 illustrated the comparability between Key Skills levels and those for the Literacy and Numeracy Standards (basic skills), but they are closely aligned in terms of content too. However, the Literacy and Numeracy Standards tend to focus more on the knowledge and understanding required. An important difference between Key Skills and basic skills assessment is that basic skills qualifications only use the external Key Skills tests; a portfolio is not required.

Inspection of Key Skills provision is carried out by Ofsted or ALI, depending on the setting. Full details of the inspection criteria can be found on the relevant website (see 'Useful websites'). Briefly, the corresponding Key Skills are inspected with mathematics, English or IT and the Wider Key Skills as part of the main qualification. Factors such as attendance, participation and achievement are considered and judgements are based on the quality of initial guidance, learner support, inclusivity, diversity of delivery methods and integration with learners' main programmes. This last point clearly indicates that an integrated model of delivery is favoured in which evidence for portfolios is obtained from activities associated with the main course. Tests may be supported by timetabled sessions or workshops. This contrasts with a model in which assignments are devised in order to provide the necessary evidence, irrespective of the main qualification. The latter model tends to disengage learners as they usually fail to see the relevance of the (often contrived) assignments. Consequently, attendance and achievement suffer.

Discussion points

1 Consider the challenges provided for the curriculum planner and teacher in order to deliver the integrated model of Key Skills delivery described above.

2 How do the characteristics of the adult literacy and numeracy and Key Skills programmes reflect the nature of their intended participants (for example adults and post-16 in full- or part-time education)?

Reflective questions

1 Describe your experience of generic skills accreditation programmes such as Key or Common Skills. Suggest which of the delivery models was used and consider how your teaching methods could be adapted to provide improved support.

2 Review your organisation's strategic plan with regard to Key Skills. What is the involvement of your current role in the strategy and what professional development would enable you to fulfil your role more effectively?

Learning difficulties and disabilities

'I am blind, I have always been blind and always will be. I don't mind people knowing that: in fact I want them to know it. What I do not want is their pity or condescension. And what I do want is to be able to learn the same kind of things as sighted people learn.'

The Tomlinson Report (FEFC 1996: 4)

In 1995 The Widening Participation Committee (chaired by Helena Kennedy QC) reported (FEFC 1997), the aim of which was to improve learning opportunities for all, regardless of learning difficulties and/or disabilities. The issue was further explored by Tomlinson, who felt that these 'special educational needs' students were underachieving, with some not fully aware of how to access the wide and varied curriculum, while others appeared to be lacking in confidence through having apparently 'failed' at school. As a consequence a national strategy to widen participation was put in place, which was to ensure that all students over the age of 16 could have equal access to further and higher education. The objective was to create new learning opportunities for employment and personal/professional development purposes. New systems of student financial support were also to be introduced to recognise the need for the provision of childcare, discretionary awards, travel and transport, for example.

Historically individuals with learning difficulties and/or disabilities were excluded from mainstream education. Statistics (FEFC 1996: 3) have shown that they appear to have failed to achieve academically, perhaps because they felt excluded and viewed their exclusion as a failure on their part to be accepted as a member of the learning group. The result was a feeling of marginalisation and being on the fringes of society, thereby compounding and exacerbating their feelings of inadequacy. This type of exclusion had an impact on the culture of the organisation, creating a segmented and isolated cohort. Tomlinson believed that 'the burden of a disability and/or learning difficulty placed on individuals was socially constructed – the result of attitudes and attributions of those who deem themselves without disability or able to learn normally' (FEFC 1996: 4). However, with the passage of time these 'marginalised' students are slowly finding their way into mainstream education, with, Tomlinson stating that 'the focus (*should be*) on the capacity of the educational institution to understand and respond to the individual learner's requirement' (FEFC 1996: 4).

The report made recommendations that Further and Higher Education Funding Councils and education establishments should publish their own disability statements containing information about facilities, with open access for the disabled student to ensure that equality was 'a right for all' regardless of age, gender, ethnicity or disability. It was hoped that with the focus on 'inclusive learning', the quality of teaching and learning for students with difficulties and/or disabilities would undergo radical and necessary reform.

Certainly there has been considerable development in the area of education for those with learning difficulties and/or disabilities over the past decade, but it is a true vision of a learning society that all citizens are able to participate in education and training that will lead to a more integrated society.

It is this message conveyed by Tomlinson that will pave the way forward for those who have been marginalised by society, thus 'demanding equality for all'. The emphasis should not be placed on the disability, but on what it means for the way that person can be helped, or be helped to learn more effectively.

Support for basic skills in FE initial teacher training programmes

The drive to improve literacy and numeracy standards in the UK has involved an increased emphasis on developing these skills in the workplace, as part of other qualifications via Key Skills and through wider availability of direct support to adults, including English for Speakers of Other Languages (ESOL). The result has been a shortage of suitably qualified teachers in ABS. For many years it has been clear to managers in FE that some teachers of ABS lacked the appropriate specialist knowledge to adequately support their learners. These observations prompted Ofsted to survey ABS provision across a wide range of sectors (Ofsted 2003).

One of the difficulties of monitoring ABS provision lies in the diversity of the organisations involved. The Ofsted report examined ABS and ESOL in general and specialist FE colleges, sixth form colleges, community organisations, adult education institutions, provision for the long-term unemployed, work-based provision, Learndirect and prisons. In relation to achievement and standards, the report identified weaknesses in monitoring progress, achievement and retention and absenteeism among learners was considered a significant barrier to success. Although achievement of qualification aims was found to be as low as 30 per cent in some cases, those who did achieve improved their skills, not only in literacy and numeracy, but in ICT and communication.

The best providers achieved high standards in the quality of education and training. These high standards were rare though and criticism focused on initial assessment, screening, diagnostic assessment and the lack of effective individual learning plans. The quality of feedback to learners on their progress was variable and the standard of literacy and numeracy of a minority of tutors was a cause for concern. Tutors were uncertain of the qualifications required to teach numeracy and literacy and this was compounded by a shortage of suitable training courses. Prisons and young offender institutions suffered from poor behaviour management procedures and inadequate plans to manage movement between institutions.

Although effective partnership arrangements were identified, there were a number of shortcomings in the leadership and management of ABS courses. Quality assurance was considered weak, or non-existent in some work-based providers. Good practice was rarely shared to improve the quality of courses and significant deficiencies in the promotion of equal opportunities policies were identified. Those with learning difficulties and disabilities such as dyslexia received inadequate support, particularly in prisons and with work-based providers.

The key recommendations of the report focused on an immediate need to improve tutors' literacy and numeracy skills and also their teaching skills. A solution in the form of short courses was proposed. These would focus on the skills needed to remedy the shortcomings of the system such as target setting, learning theory and assessment. The intention was that all tutors would complete the course before starting work. Recommendations were made to improve the literacy and numeracy skills of tutors in vocational subjects and that the relevance of ABS courses to learners' vocational needs should be improved. Improvements to quality assurance mechanisms and the development of strategies to improve the sharing of best practice were recommended. Provision for those in prisons and young offender institutions, the unemployed and those engaged in work-based learning was singled-out as in need of significant improvement.

Responding to the need for FE teachers to be able to support their learners' basic skills needs on vocational programmes particularly, FENTO has published minimum core standards for FE initial teacher training courses (FENTO 2004a) and guidance on how the necessary skills might be included in training programmes (FENTO 2004b). One of the factors influencing the development of the core was that many learners with poor basic skills are reluctant to engage in specialist support. The minimum core emphasises the need to understand personal and social factors in developing learners' literacy and numeracy skills. The core is organised as follows:

Language and literacy

Part A Knowledge and understanding

A1 Personal, social and cultural factors influencing language and literacy learning and development

A2 Explict knowledge of the four skills

a. Productive skills – speaking and writing

b. Receptive skills – listening and reading

Part B Personal language skills

B1 Productive skills – speaking and writing

B2 Receptive skills – listening and reading

Numeracy

Part A Knowledge and understanding

A1 Personal and social factors

Part B Personal numeracy skills

FENTO (2004a: inside cover)

The intention is that FE teachers should have skills in relation to literacy and numeracy at least on a par with their learners and that they should be able to recognise their own personal development needs. FENTO emphasise that the core is a minimum specification and that teachers should be encouraged to develop their skills further.

Most teacher training courses will need to be modified to include the core and it is anticipated that specialist tutors will be needed to deliver some aspects. The requirement for particular skills in addition to subject knowledge is also emphasised. These include effective initial assessment of learners' basic skills needs and an ability to conduct a skills audit of their course in order to determine the skills needed to access the necessary learning. There was recognition that many FE teachers do not have sufficient under-standing of the needs of learners with learning difficulties and disabilities and the skills to produce suitably differentiated lessons. Knowledge of appropriate sources of support and guidance was also identified as a priority area in addition to developing the skills needed to communicate with diverse learners.

Many providers of FE initial teacher training courses will offer qualification routes for those interested in specialising in pre-entry, literacy, numeracy or ESOL. These qualifications provide opportunities to develop subject-specific skills to Level 4. Subject specifications for adult literacy and numeracy at Level 4 (DfES/FENTO 2002a) and ESOL (DfES/FENTO 2002b) have been published and these form the basis of modules developed in conjunction with the Basic Skills Agency to support providers of training programmes.

Summary

- The level of basic skills competence within the adult population is critical to ensuring social, cultural and economic prosperity.

- The Moser Report (DfEE 1999) was seminal in emphasising the need for improved basic skills provision in order to meet national targets for literacy, numeracy and ESOL.

- A set of National Standards developed by QCA laid the foundations for improving basic skills provision.

- The National Standards for adult literacy and numeracy have been used to devise Core Curricula in adult literacy, numeracy and ESOL at Entry, Level 1 and Level 2.

- In order to improve provision for learners with disabilities, an adult pre-entry curriculum framework for literacy and numeracy has been produced.

- The Core Curricula have been used to develop qualifications in ABS, which are aligned to the NQF.

- The Dearing Report (Dearing 1996) resulted in the Curriculum 2000 initiative which formalised the integration of Key Skills within the post-16 curriculum.

- The development of Key Skills qualifications has led to progress and tensions in the post-16 sector.

- New opportunities for those with learning difficulties and disabilities focus on integration supported by a responsive curriculum delivery to meet individual needs.

- The rapid progress towards a formalised ABS curriculum in the UK has resulted in a significant need to improve the skills of existing ABS teachers and to ensure that ITT programmes for post-compulsory education have enhanced basic skills content and specialist literacy, numeracy and ESOL pathways.

- The FENTO Teaching and Learning Standards relating to supporting basic skills for life are shown in Figure 5.3. Full details of these standards are available at the FENTO website (see 'Useful websites').

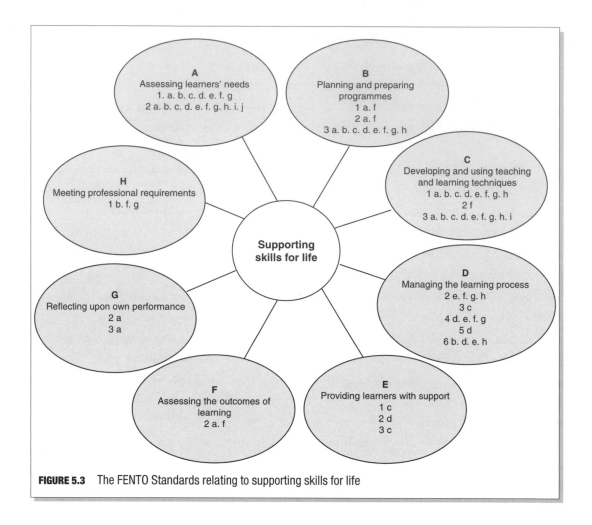

FIGURE 5.3   The FENTO Standards relating to supporting skills for life

Useful websites

www.acac.org.uk/english.html
The Qualifications Curriculum and Assessment Authority for Wales (ACAC)
Last accessed 7 May 2004

www.ali.gov.uk
The Adult Learning Inspectorate (ALI)
Last accessed 7 May 2004

www.basic-skills.co.uk
The Basic Skills Agency (BSA)
Last accessed 7 May 2004

www.bbc.co.uk/skillswise
Interactive learning support for literacy and numeracy
Last accessed 7 May 2004

www.ccea.org.uk
The Northern Ireland Council for the Curriculum, Examinations and Assessment (CCEA)
Last accessed 7 May 2004

www.dfes.gov.uk/readwriteplus
Information and advice on implementing the Skills for Life agenda produced by the Adult Basic Skills Strategy Unit.
Last accessed 7 May 2004

www.fento.ac.uk
The Further Education National Training Organisation (FENTO) website
Last accessed 7 May 2004

www.lancs.ac.uk/wbsnet
The Workplace Basic Skills Network
Last accessed 7 May 2004

www.learndirect.co.uk
Computer-based courses, including basic skills qualifications
Last accessed 7 May 2004

www.literacytrust.org.uk
A charity with the aim of developing a literate nation
Last accessed 7 May 2004

www.nc.uk.net
The National Curriculum website
Last accessed 7 May 2004

www.niace.org.uk
The National Institute of Adult Continuing Education (NIACE): the Institute aims to increase inclusion and participation among adult learners.
Last accessed 7 May 2004

www.ofsted.gov.uk
The Office for Standards in Education (Ofsted) website
Last accessed 7 May 2004

www.qca.org.uk
The Qualifications and Curriculum Authority (QCA) website
Last accessed 7 May 2004

www.sqa.org.uk
The Scottish Qualifications Authority (SQA) website
Last accessed 7 May 2004

www.standards.dfee.gov.uk/literacy
The National Literacy Strategy
Last accessed 7 May 2004

www.standards.dfee.gov.uk/numeracy
The National Numeracy Strategy
Last accessed 7 May 2004

References

Basic Skills Agency (2001a) *Adult Literacy Core Curriculum*. London: Basic Skills Agency.

Basic Skills Agency (2001b) *Adult Numeracy Core Curriculum*. London: Basic Skills Agency.

Basic Skills Agency (2001c) *Adult ESOL Core Curriculum*. London: Basic Skills Agency.

Dearing, R. (1996) *Review of Qualifications for 16–19 Year Olds*. Middlesex: School Curriculum and Assessment Authority.

DfEE (1999) *Improving Literacy and Numeracy: a fresh start*. The report of the working group chaired by Sir Claus Moser. London: DfEE.

DfEE (2000a) *Breaking the Language Barriers*. London: DfEE.

DfEE (2000b) *Freedom to Learn: basic skills for learners with learning difficulties and/or disabilities*. London: DfEE.

DfEE (2001) *Skills for Life: the national strategy for improving adult literacy and numeracy skills*. London: DfEE.

DfES (2001) *Adult Pre-entry Curriculum Framework for Literacy and Numeracy*. London: DfES.

DfES (2002) *14–19: extending opportunities, raising standards*. London: DfES.

DfES (2003) *21st Century Skills: realising our potential. Individuals, employers, nation*. London: DfES.

DfES/FENTO (2002a) *Subject Specifications for Teachers of Adult Literacy and Numeracy*. London: DfES/FENTO.

DfES/FENTO (2002b) *Subject Specifications for Teachers of English for Speakers of Other Languages*. London: DfES/FENTO.

DfES/LSC/QCA (2002) *Key Skills Policy and Practice*. London: DfES.

FEFC (1996) *Inclusive Learning*. Coventry: FEFC.

FEFC (1997) *Learning Works – Widening Participation in Further Education*. Coventry: FEFC.

FENTO (2004a) *Addressing Language, Literacy and Numeracy Needs in Education and Training: defining the minimum core of teachers' knowledge, understanding and personal skill*. London: FENTO.

FENTO (2004b) *Including Language, Literacy and Numeracy Learning in all Post-16 Education: guidance on curriculum and methodology for generic initial teacher education programmes*. London: FENTO.

OECD (1997) *Literacy Skills for the Knowledge Society*. Paris: OECD.

Ofsted (2003) *Literacy, numeracy and English for speakers of other languages: a survey of current practice in post-16 and adult provision*. London: Ofsted.

QCA (2000) *National Standards for Adult Literacy and Numeracy*. London: QCA.

QCA (2004) *Draft Standards for Information and Communication Technology*. London: QCA.

Entitlement, quality and inclusiveness

6

Managing diversity in the classroom

Debra Wilson

Introduction

THIS CHAPTER AIMS to explore and highlight the key issues surrounding disaffection and consequent underachievement in post-16 education.

In 1998 a comprehensive research study carried out by the Further Education Development Agency (FEDA; Martinez and Munday 1998) on student persistence and drop-out drew attention to a variety of reasons for why some young people become 'disaffected' and consequently marginalised in society. A series of recurring and interrelated themes were identified including: dysfunctional family relationships, emotional and behavioural difficulties, educational failure, homelessness, drug and/or alcohol abuse and criminal activity. Several authors have addressed related issues, including the lack of role models, peer pressure to conform to a culture of unemployment and vulnerability to crime and vandalism, both as victims and perpetrators.

Blair (2002) in his keynote speech on tackling poverty and social exclusion recognised the complexity of the situation, but argued that in addressing social and structural barriers to opportunity there is a reciprocal responsibility on the part of the young person:

> if we give our young people a decent start – hope and education – then we are in a position to turn round and ask for responsibility in return. It is a simple equation – we give opportunity, we demand responsibility, and that's how we build strong communities.

This reciprocal compact between the state and young citizens involves all young people staying on into the sixth form or undertaking a Modern Apprenticeship with the objective of having improved job prospects. The culture of personalised learning would be structurally created through 'every secondary school having the resources, skills, and ambition to develop the talents of its students, whatever their starting point or aspiration'.

While the political ambition is to create an environment in which structural barriers are removed and youngsters develop the capability and confidence to challenge barriers, it is clear from the FEDA research that ambition has first to engage with reality. Consequently, the focus of this chapter will be centred on research related to the themes identified here before moving on to suggest how policy and practice might work to provide tenable solutions. In addition, given the nature of young offender profiles, the role of young offender education will be considered as an arena for providing possible solutions to mainstream problems.

Managing disaffected learners

Now it is easy to decry these young people, many of whom have had really bad educational experiences, but we have to realise their needs are different and very individual. They don't always fit neatly into a school setting, and they can't always easily cope with the demands made on them by school. In some ways they are set up to fail.

(FEFC 1997: 56)

The Further Education Funding Council (FEFC) in June 1997 published the Kennedy Report *Learning Works – Widening Participation in Further Education*. This highlighted the need for change in the Government's strategic approach to teaching and learning, with recommendations put forward to incorporate learning in the welfare system, to take education to the learners and to make the fullest use of information technology. The report described the disaffected learner as being 'socially and economically disadvantaged'.

Martinez and Munday (1998) collated the views of some 9,000 students and staff in 31 colleges in their study of student persistence and drop-out in the UK. They identified that learners are more likely to drop-out if they:

- do not feel they have been placed on the most appropriate course
- applied to college late
- find it difficult to make friends
- find it difficult to settle in at the beginning of their course
- are less satisfied (than current students) that their course is interesting
- are less satisfied with the quality of teaching
- are less satisfied with their course timetable
- are less satisfied with help either to get a job or to go to university
- are male
- have difficult financial circumstances (older students) or family circumstances (younger students)
- have their fees waived or reduced.

(Martinez and Munday 1998: 7)

The study reinforced the perception that reasons for drop-out are multi-factorial. Definitive conclusions applicable across the UK were difficult as there was considerable variation in the responses from students and staff from different colleges, though the work supported the notion that students use a cost-benefit approach to making decisions on their future. Socio-economic factors were significant, though once again the picture was complex; older learners, for example, were more susceptible to withdrawing for these reasons. This extensive study reinforced the findings by the FEFC and highlighted important issues on appropriateness of courses, late registrations to colleges and student motivation.

The Government's Green Paper *14–19: extending opportunities and raising standards* (DfES 2002a) also acknowledged 'disaffection' as a major challenge for teachers, schools and meeting government education targets. The Green Paper recommended that the National Curriculum should constitute a basic entitlement, but that from the age of 14 there will be more opportunities to combine vocational, academic and work-based programmes according to individual needs, aptitude, ability and preferences. The emphasis on vocational rather than academic qualifications may make a significant contribution towards meeting the needs of disaffected learners, many of whom have failed academically and may respond to a more individualised curriculum incorporating work-based experience together with learning opportunities provided by employers, colleges and private training providers. The core purpose was identified as promoting social justice, improving economic competitiveness and providing opportunities for young people to reach their full potential.

Elliot *et al.* (1981) dispute the tendency to define disaffection through behavioural indicators such as truancy and disruption. They advocate instead a conceptualisation of disaffection as a lack of subject engagement, whereas Willis (1977) speaks of the 'counter-school' culture, where young people withdraw in favour of developing their own identity, away from the formal, conformist, institutionalised constructs of the class-room. Willis emphasised the structural features of society that produce and reproduce class cultures:

> The non-conformist culture is a vital tool with which to think through the nature of other pos-
> itions. Any classroom situation is a complex combination of elements: acceptance, opposition,
> legitimacy, and the particular way in which the teacher inhabits the educational paradigm.
>
> (Willis 1977: 85)

This bespoke style can create a solid foundation on which to build confidence in order to enable the learner to progress at a rate and level appropriate to academic and intellectual ability, thus working towards their goals by creating meaningful personal objectives.

Roche and Tucker (1997: 1) commented on the problematisation of youth: 'Generally *"youth"* tends to be seen as a problem: young people are beset by predominantly nega-tive images and are seen as either a source of trouble or in trouble.' This said, Roche and Tucker create a picture in which there is a real need to promote 'critical reflection' with regard to youth and society by looking at the changing images and perceptions experienced by the young, together with embracing the positive contributions that these people can make to their local communities with support and positive criticism.

The social construction of youth is a significant area for further investigation in order that we may further understand the psycho-social basis for disaffection. Griffin (1993) researched the concepts of 'youth', 'identity' and 'adolescence'. Her views resonate with Blair (2002), Willis (1977) and Roche and Tucker (1997):

> 'Youth' is . . . treated as a key indicator of the state of the nation . . .: it is expected to reflect the cycle of booms and troughs in the economy; shifts in cultural values over sexuality, morality and family life; and changes in class relations, concepts of nationhood, and in occupational structures. Young people are assumed to hold the key to the nation's future, and the treatment and management of 'youth' is expected to provide the solution to a nation's 'problems', from 'drug abuse', 'hooliganism' and 'teenage pregnancy' to inner city 'riots'.

Griffin (1993: 17)

Reflective questions

1   Research data on retention and achievement in your institution. This will be available from internal reports and inspection data, for example.

2   Compare the institutional data with historical data for your programme(s).

3   Consider the factors that produce the patterns of retention and achievement observed, particularly in the light of information provided here.

4   Use your institution's strategic plan to identify how it is responding to retention and achievement issues and consider how you may contribute to the objectives stated.

5   What additional staff development do you need in order to fulfil your answer to point 4?

Discussion points

1   Consider Griffin's assertion that youth is treated as 'a key indicator of the state of the nation'. How does your perception of 'youth' as evidenced from your institution support or refute this assertion?

2   Discuss the relative importance of educational structures influencing the state of 'youth', when compared with the ways in which 'youth' influence educational structures.

Exclusion: age, gender, ethnicity

Social exclusion has been considered by many workers as a root cause of the disengagement of young people from education and training. Social exclusion has been defined as:

a multi-dimensional process, in which various forms of exclusion are combined: participation in decision making and political processes, access to employment and material resources, and integration into common cultural processes. When combined, they create acute forms of exclusion that find a spatial manifestation in particular neighbourhoods.

(Madanipour *et al.* 1998: 22)

The Social Exclusion Unit (SEU; see 'Useful websites') was established in 1997 to devise measures to prevent social exclusion and to re-integrate those already excluded. A significant co-ordination role was anticipated to ensure the continuity of mainstream provision.

Bridging the Gap (Social Exclusion Unit 1999) was an early report produced by the Unit. The report highlighted to criticality of the age of 16 in determining an individual's future destiny; over 9 per cent of 16–18-year-olds were disengaged from education, training or work for long periods. These young people were from the most disadvantaged backgrounds and often suffered from personal, family, financial or drug-related problems. The report recommended planning for local delivery of support services with an aim for 16-year-olds to remain in education, training, or work with a significant training content. In common with the White Paper *Learning to Succeed: a new framework for post-16 learning* (DfEE 1999a), the establishment of the 'Connexions' youth support service was proposed, in conjunction with providing financial support through the Education Maintenance Allowance (EMA) scheme. EMAs pay 16+ learners up to £30 per week and a bonus of up to £100 for remaining on their course (see 'Useful websites' for further information).

The European Commission (1997) concurred that poverty was a critical factor in social exclusion, but identified the rights of individuals in relation to housing, education, health and provision of social services as important. People living in rural and urban areas were considered particularly at risk given the prevalence of discrimination and segregation in these areas. The authors considered that this 'emphasizes the weakness in the social infrastructure and the risk of allowing a two-tier society to become established by default' (European Commission 1997: 1).

The 'weaknesses in social infrastructure' identified emphasise the multifaceted nature of social exclusion, with reference to the 'exclusionary process' and 'policy failure' together with an endorsement of the rights of the individual to a basic standard of living and to participate in the major social and occupational institutions of society. Therefore, one can conclude that social exclusion occurs when an individual is denied basic social rights. This issue has been addressed by the Social Exclusion Unit (2004) in their report *Tackling Social Exclusion: taking stock*. The following is a summary of the main points highlighted within their policy document:

- *Individuals not realising their educational potential*: a teenager from a deprived neighbourhood is five times more likely to go to a failing school and less likely to achieve good qualifications compared to their peers (see also Social Exclusion Unit 2001).

- *Higher risks of unemployment*: adults with poor basic literacy and numeracy skills are up to five times more likely to be unemployed or out of the labour market than those with adequate skills (see also DfEE 1999b).

- *Poorer physical health*: men born into the bottom social class are likely to live seven years less than those born in the professional classes. Poorer diets, lack of opportunities for exercise, and higher rates of smoking and drug use are seen among deprived groups of people (see also DoH 1999).

- *Crime and fear of crime both disproportionately affect the most deprived communities*: the sale of drugs, with the associated crime and antisocial behaviour that underpins drug use, adds to the decline of communities and social exclusion.

The summary of the report states that:

> Social exclusion has complex and multi-dimensional causes and consequences, creating deep and long lasting problems for individual families, for the economy, and for society as a whole. It can be passed from generation to generation: children's life chances are strongly affected by their parents' circumstances, such as their income and the place they live.
>
> (Social Exclusion Unit 2004: 1)

Since 1997 these issues have been addressed by investing in early years' education, by introducing 'Sure Start' projects, whereby a strategic framework was established to engage with disadvantaged young families to combine increased availability of childcare with education in the community in an attempt to improve cognitive and social outcomes (see 'Useful websites'). The investment in early years' education is regarded as pivotal in securing the future of the economy and the strategic direction of the UK as a whole. In moving the political agenda from 'policy and place' towards 'person, process and purpose' the emphasis has firmly shifted toward inclusiveness, thereby tackling some of the most severe and intractable forms of disadvantage, with teenage pregnancy showing a 9·4 per cent reduction in the number of conceptions (Office for National Statistics 2004) and a 22·5 per cent reduction in the number of juveniles re-offending (Jennings 2003).

The Prince's Trust (see 'Useful websites') contributes to reducing social exclusion by offering support for young people between the ages of 14 and 30 who have been excluded for a variety of reasons, but particularly those who have been unemployed for long periods, are leaving care or have committed offences. The charity can provide mentors to assist young people to integrate with the community. Financial assistance of up to £500 is provided for education or training and the 'Prince's Trust Team' involves groups of 12 to 15 young people in community-based projects, work experience, teambuilding activities and a residential week in a 12-week programme. Similarly, the 'New Deal' initiative (see 'Useful websites') is at the centre of the Government's welfare to work policy. The scheme provides an assessment of individual needs for the unemployed in several different categories, namely: aged 18 to 24; aged 25+; aged 50+;

musicians; the disabled; lone parents and partners. Subsidised employment, work experience, training and basic skills support can be provided as well as short courses and interview practice in order to facilitate return to work.

The report (Social Exclusion Unit 2004) concluded that investment in educational attainment and skills at an early age will boost the life chances of those from a wide range of backgrounds and promote equality of opportunity.

Indicative task

Use the Social Exclusion Unit website to explore resources relevant to your learners. Which of the issues raised above are particularly pertinent? Critically analyse the strategies by comparing their relative effectiveness at promoting inclusion. Which relevant issues are not addressed by these strategies?

Responding to learning styles: differentiation

Learning style approaches have been discussed in detail in Chapter 4. This section seeks to explore the wider context of learners' needs, particularly in relation to effects on disaffection. Teachers need to adapt and modify their teaching styles to support, nurture and encourage the individual so that we can facilitate, enable and promote active learning to take place (see Maslow 1970; Rogers 1969).

Teachers are exposed to many policy documents imbued with rhetoric on strategies designed to engage the disaffected learner, emphasising that the economy needs all citizens regardless of age, gender or ethnicity, to play an active and meaningful part in education. The Kennedy Report (FEFC 1997) recognised that positive discrimination is required in order to enable non-traditional learners to reach their potential, in contrast with successful learners who are aware of the benefits of learning.

Change is, therefore, at the heart of education and more especially teaching and learning with greater emphasis firmly placed on student-centred learning. Extensive research has already been undertaken in this area, with contributions including: Kolb's 'Experiential Learning' (Kolb 1984); Honey and Mumford's 'Learning Styles' approach (Honey and Mumford 1982); and Carl Rogers' theories on 'Humanistic Learning' (Rogers 1969). 'A quiet revolution is underway in almost every field. It holds the promise of moving us forward to a more human, more person centred world' (Rogers 1969: 290). It is the need for differentiation in order to address preferred learning styles that may pave the way towards a more inclusive and integrated education system.

Every stage of the post-16 curriculum has a critical role in responding to the needs of the disaffected learner. The induction process in schools and colleges can enable and support the integration of the learner into the unfamiliar and somewhat daunting learning environment with comprehensive support mechanisms firmly in place to ensure an understanding of the organisational structure, its culture, and support agencies. This is essential in order that individual preferences are met. Maynard and Martinez (2000) interviewed teachers on courses with both high and low retention rates. A key finding was the need for more comprehensive induction programmes to promote positive and collaborative behaviour thereby engaging the learner. However, this induction process may not always be seen positively by the disaffected as the focus is often on conformity and organisational structures.

Disaffected young people may have negative perceptions of the school environment and thus the teaching and learning methodologies used. Traditionally the distinction is often made between approaches applicable to teaching children (pedagogic approaches) and those for teaching adults (andragogic approaches: Knowles 1990). Andragogy encourages a proactive approach to learning in which enquiry and autonomy feature predominantly. However, pedagogy and andragogy should be seen as parallel rather than opposing models (Quinn 1995) as ultimately both concern the process and the method of learning. This is supported by Knowles (1990) who also acknowledges that both models may be appropriate for children and adults, dependent on their individual circumstances, for example when a learner is first exposed to a new or unusual learning situation.

The 'adult' environment of FE and related andragogic philosophy is often seen as preferable for the disaffected as it has the flexibility to respond more effectively to individual learning preferences. However, developing Quinn's view, a robust assessment of preferences is required at the induction stage to ensure that appropriate methods are employed in order that young people are not set up to fail.

Synergogy is a model developed by Mouton and Blake (1984). It attempts to capitalise on the best features of andragogy and pedagogy by making the most of expert knowledge and encouraging active involvement of the learner. Synergogy has three main principles that can be applied to disaffected learners:

- the use of learning materials that give direction without inhibiting self-development

- group work, peer support and shared experiential learning, which are very important parts of fostering vocational education rather than a more structured academic construct, thereby contributing significantly to encouraging and supporting the disaffected learner

- an holistic approach that the whole is greater than the sum of its parts: the aim is to ensure a sharing of knowledge, understanding and experiences.

Taking all this into account it is imperative that the 'disaffected learner' is seen not as part of an homogeneous group, but as an individual, whose development is different; whose needs are and will be different from their peers. For the teacher it means an attempt to develop the learner's autonomy, to empower and not to control.

Reflective questions

1 Given the characteristics of pedagogy, andragogy and synergogy described above, how could you identify which approaches would be most successful at motivating your learners?

2 How could you modify your teaching in order to satisfy the needs identified?

The models described here are about approaches to *teaching*. Respected theorists have developed approaches to *learning* (but see 'Discussion points' below). When several theorists have consensus on a theory, they are sometimes called a 'school'. It is common to talk of the humanistic school, or the behaviourist school, for example. The theories proposed by these schools have messages for those needing to engage disaffected learners. Learning theory is also addressed in Chapter 4.

The humanistic school emphasises the role of thoughts, feelings and experiences in the learning process. Maslow (1970), a major exponent of the humanistic approach, developed a hierarchy of needs, in which he stated that we strive to reach self-actualisation (to realise one's potential), but in order to achieve this, we must meet other needs first as illustrated in Figure 6.1. In order to progress up the hierarchy, the need below must be met. Petty (1998: 46) provided an excellent summary of the consequences of Maslow's hierarchy to the learner.

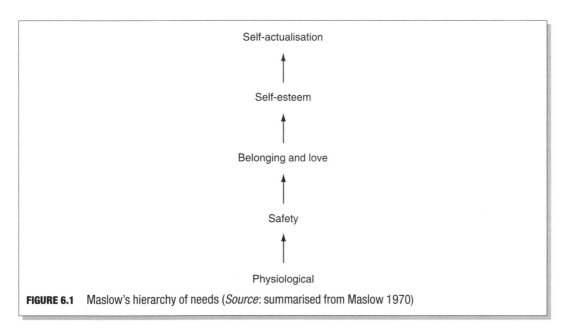

FIGURE 6.1 Maslow's hierarchy of needs (*Source*: summarised from Maslow 1970)

Maslow believed that the purpose of education is to assist the individual to achieve their goal, or as Maslow put it 'help the person become the best that he is able to become'. The significance of the hierarchy of needs to the disaffected is that issues relating to their personal life can seriously inhibit their ability to learn. In practical terms it is therefore essential that learning support needs are identified and provided in a way that is acceptable to the learner. The traditional institutionalised response may not be appropriate. For example, mentors can be an effective way of reaching learners and providing targeted help.

Rogers (1969), another leading advocate of the humanistic school, developed an approach called client-centred therapy; a student-centred approach to learning. The main assumptions that Rogers made was that all humans have a natural potential to learn, and that significant engagement takes place when the subject matter is relevant and appropriate to the individual and their learning needs are met. What we can conclude, therefore, is that the role of the facilitator should be based on the sharing of knowledge, supporting, encouraging and empowering the learner. The relationship is that of symbiosis and not one of power. The implication for the tutor is that their perceived power is a barrier to the student's learning.

Hertzberg (1966) developed the concept of motivators and hygiene factors. He saw motivators as factors that encourage the learner to participate, feel good about their learning, and have a sense of achievement, recognition and responsibility. This would lead to personal advancement, achievement and development. In contrast the hygiene factors, for example the learning environment, can create a sense of dissatisfaction. The inference here is to ensure the learner is motivated to learn and to continue to learn by the use of positive feedback, reinforcement, appropriate praise and constructive rather than destructive criticism. One needs to ensure the presence of motivators to maintain learning and the absence of hygiene factors to achieve positive results thereby engaging and motivating the learner.

Carl Rogers considered that the most socially useful learning is the learning of the process of learning, in other words to learn how to learn (see also Chapter 4, in which a discussion of informal learning is also relevant). Developing the skill and knowledge necessary to deal with differentiation in the classroom requires nothing short of what Rogers has described as a 'cultural and industrial renaissance'. He considered that weaknesses in our education system make such a renaissance extremely difficult to achieve (Rogers 1969).

Discussion point

Is the distinction between theories relating to *teaching* and those relating to *learning* a valid distinction? Clearly there is a link between the processes of teaching and learning, but are they really different facets of the same thing? In other words, is it possible to formulate a theory of learning without encompassing teaching?

Indicative task

1 There are no 'quick fixes' to the problem of disaffection. The issues are so diverse that it isn't possible to produce a checklist applicable to all.

2 Use the results of Martinez and Munday's (1998) research study provided at the beginning of this chapter and the discussion on disaffection to produce a 'disaffection action plan' targeted to the needs of your own learners.

3 Implement the plan and evaluate its success.

Prison education

The prison education system

Over 58 per cent of former prisoners re-offend within two years. The cost of one offender going through the criminal justice system is around £65,000 and it costs about £37,500 a year to keep an offender in prison. One of the key strategies for dealing with the increasing prison population, reducing recidivism and thereby the costs of the prison system, is to improve the quality of prison education and ensure that the system meets the needs of individual learners such that they can play an active role in society.

Offenders have poor basic skills, with 80%, 65% and 50% having skills in writing, numeracy and reading, respectively, below those of an 11-year-old. Over 52% of males and 71% of females in custody have no qualifications. The response has been to focus resources on schemes designed to reduce recidivism. Most 'return to work' schemes including New Deal and Prince's Trust Teams are applicable to the rehabilitation of offenders. Individual prisons have schemes to promote education and training. Her Majesty's Prison (HMP) Reading has a day release programme to train offenders in forklift truck driving, which has significantly reduced re-offending. HMP Leeds has a high turnover with an average stay of 12 weeks (the unpredictability of when prisoners will have to move is a major barrier to progress in education), nevertheless, all prisoners receive targeted education and training, including basic skills and dyslexia testing. These data and examples have been taken from the *Reducing Re-offending by Ex-prisoners* report (Social Exclusion Unit 2003). This report influenced the development of the National Rehabilitation Strategy designed to improve support for ex-offenders.

The Prisoners' Learning and Skills Unit (PLSU) is part of the Department of Education and Skills and has a remit to improve the quality of prison education in partnership with the Home Office and the Prison Service. The *'Improving Offenders' Learning and Skills* report (DfES 2003) identified improved funding and an expansion of the PLSU role to cover areas such as probation as key elements of their improvement strategy. The report supported the strategies proposed in the *Skills for Life* (DfEE 2001) and *Success for All* (DfES 2002b) reports relating to improvements in literacy, numeracy and language provision and the reform of FE and training, respectively, and the National Skills Strategy to reduce by 40 per cent the number of adults lacking a Level 2 qualification. Proposals were made to improve partnerships: over 18 organisations are involved in prison education, including the DfES, the Qualifications and Curriculum Authority and the Learning and Skills Council, for example. Learning and Skills Advisors were introduced to support individual prisoners, recommendations were made to improve participation among under-represented groups and spread good practice. The report described a strategy with three key aims:

- *Increased supply* of resources for prison education
- *Building capacity* by improving the infrastructure
- *Delivering learning, targets and improving quality* particularly of basic skills and vocational education and the role of Ofsted and the Adult Learning Inspectorate.

The Prison Reform Trust has produced a revealing report on prisoners' views on prison education (Prison Reform Trust 2003). The report identified barriers to participation in learning in prison and recommended further investment based on the following views of prisoners:

- a lack of places on courses leading to vocational and skills qualifications
- an inconsistent approach between prisons and a wide variation in curriculum provision causing problems when prisoners are moved
- timetables that result in a need for choices between different activities
- low pay for attending courses
- poor initial assessment and advice and guidance.

Prison education is franchised through a bidding process, for example one college in the Black Country delivers training and education to nine penal institutions in the East and West Midlands. The curriculum is not dissimilar to that on offer through other FE colleges, but there is an emphasis on basic, social and life skills together with ICT.

Young offenders often have a poor perception of education, often resulting from historical role models and negative experiences. Short-term gains often appear more attractive than the risk of repeating past failures. Other barriers to learning can include low self-esteem, lack of confidence, peer and family group pressures, with the 'family' imposing their beliefs and values on the young offender resulting in a shrouded view that learning new skills will not have any impact on their future employability. This downward spiral can prejudice their learning with worries over a lack of control of external issues and lead to anxiety, depression and, in extreme cases, suicide.

The curriculum within the Prison Service is accredited through one of the following examination boards: City & Guilds, Open College Network (OCN), Oxford, Cambridge and RSA examination board (OCR), Edexcel and Assessment and Qualifications Alliance (AQA) with provision available for Accreditation of Prior Learning (APL). Owing to the nature of prison education comprehensive lesson planning and preparation has to be undertaken by the teacher as learners move in and out of education and have a wide range of academic ability. Subject delivery is based on a unitised model with short programmes covering a wide range of subject areas including Key Skills.

Holism and prison education

Capra (1997) considered that an holistic approach to prison education is at the centre of penal reform, whereby it is considered imperative to support, encourage and engage the learner. Learning does not and should not happen in a vacuum, therefore in order for prison education to be meaningful and worthwhile this holistic approach to teaching and learning must be adopted.

Foucault commented that:

> The delinquent is to be distinguished from the offender by the fact that it is not so much his act as his life that is relevant in characterising him. The penitentiary operation, if it is to be a genuine re-education, must become the sum total existence of the delinquent, making of the prison a sort of artificial and coercive theatre in which his life will be examined from the top to the bottom.

(Foucault 1977: 251)

The institutionalised model for learning is therefore constrained. Education in order to succeed in such an environment must be relevant, current and relatable to what learners are doing, so a prescriptive curriculum needs to be on offer. Consequently, the disaffected inmate is given an individual learning plan at the initial assessment, incorporating learning aims and objectives, with the opportunity to progress onto further and indeed higher education should they so wish.

Following release from prison, either on parole or on completion of sentence, an individual 'care plan' is drawn up to ensure that learning continues in a structured, supportive and positive environment, with information being disseminated across all sectors, including the Probationary Service.

Prison education throws into sharp relief many of the issues highlighted above. In drawing from this model, it might be argued that a 'captive environment' is a more productive one, as criminality is seen, in part, about alienation from mainstream society where the institutional focus is on education, rehabilitation and reintegration back into the community. With lessons learnt it appears that the disaffected student needs to be placed firmly at the heart of curriculum planning and delivery. However, for this process to be meaningful and successful we must develop our listening capabilities together with the ability to respond to the issues raised.

Discussion points

1 Compare and contrast the challenges faced when planning a curriculum involving disaffected youth with those of planning the prison education curriculum.

2 Evaluate the effectiveness of the approaches to reforming prison education described above.

Indicative task

1 Research the role of your institution, or a neighbouring institution in prison education.

2 Interview members of staff involved in the programme to determine their views on the problems faced by the prison education system and the improvement initiatives.

3 Analyse the results and evaluate them in the light of the above discussion.

Summary

- The causes of disaffection are complex, with socio-economic and personal circumstances having a significant influence.

- The academic/vocational divide marginalises participation, resulting in barriers to access.

- The problematisation of youth by society may result in disaffection.

- Social exclusion is a significant issue in disengaging youth from education and training.

- A learning style approach can identify the individual preferences needed to promote learning.

- Teaching and learning theory can inform strategies to reduce disaffection.

- Teaching and support strategies need to plan to motivate the disaffected learner.

- Offenders have low levels of literacy and numeracy and poor qualifications.

- Education is seen as central to strategies to reduce recidivism.

- Strategies to improve prison education involve partnership, expanding capacity and improving quality.

- The FENTO Teaching and Learning Standards relating to managing diversity are shown in Figure 6.2. Full details of these standards are available at the FENTO website (see 'Useful websites').

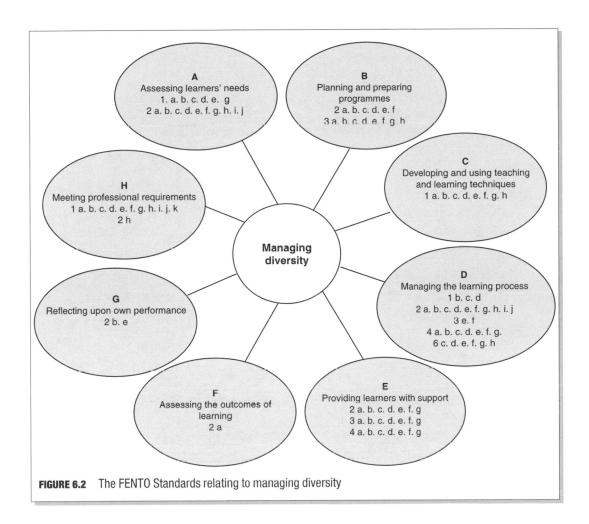

FIGURE 6.2   The FENTO Standards relating to managing diversity

Useful websites

www.des.gov.uk/financialhelp/ema
Information on the Education Maintenance Allowance (EMA) Scheme
Last accessed 8 August 2004

www.fento.ac.uk
The Further Education National Training Organisation (FENTO) website
Last accessed 7 May 2004

www.newdeal.gov.uk
Part of the Government's scheme to get people back into work.
Last accessed 7 May 2004

www.princes-trust.org.uk
Offers advice and information on the Prince's Trust: practical solutions for young people to get their lives working.
Last accessed 7 May 2004

www.prisonreformtrust.org.uk
Research, education and information about the Prison Reform Trust
Last accessed 7 May 2004

www.socialexclusionunit.gov.uk
The Social Exclusion Unit (SEU) website
Last accessed 7 May 2004

www.surestart.gov.uk
The Sure Start Programme website
Last accessed 7 May 2004

References

Blair, T. (2002) speech on tackling poverty and social exclusion (18.09.2002). http://www/number10.gov.uk/print/page1726.asp – Accessed 19/03/04.

Capra, F. (1997) *The Web of Life: a new synthesis of mind and matter*. London: Flamingo (an imprint of HarperCollins).

DfEE (1999a) *Learning to Succeed: a new framework for post-16 learning*. London: DfEE.

DfEE (1999b) *Improving Literacy and Numeracy: a fresh start*. The report of the working group chaired by Sir Claus Moser. London: DfEE.

DfEE (2001) *Skills for Life: the national strategy for improving adult literacy and numeracy skills*. London: DfEE.

DfES (2002a) *14–19: extending opportunities, raising standards*. London: DfES.

DfES (2002b) *Success for All: reforming further education and training*. London: DfES.

DfES (2003) *Improving Offenders' Learning and Skills*. London: DfES.

DoH (1999) *Saving Lives – Our Healthier Nation*. London: DoH.

Elliott, J., Bridges, D., Ebbutt, D., Gibson, R. and Nias, J. (1981) *School Accountability*. London: Grant McIntyre.

European Commission (1997) *Evaluating EU Expenditure Programmes: a guide*. Brussels: European Commission.

FEFC (1996) *Inclusive Learning*. London: HMSO.

FEFC (1997) *Learning Works – Widening Participation in Further Education*. Coventry: FEFC.

Foucault, M. (1977) *Discipline and Punish: the birth of the prison*. Harmondsworth: Peregrine.

Griffin, C. (1993) *Representations of Youth: the study of youth and adolescence in Britain and America (feminist perspectives)*. Cambridge, MA: Polity Press.

Herzberg, F. (1966) *Work and the Nature of Man*. Cleveland, OH: World Publishing.

Honey, P. and Mumford, A. (1982) *Manual of Learning Styles*. London: P. Honey.

Jennings, D. (2003) *One Year Juvenile Reconviction Rates, 1st Quarter Cohort.* London: Home Office.

Knowles, M. (1990) *The Adult Learner: a neglected species.* Houston, Texas: Gulf Publishing.

Kolb, D. A. (1984) *Experimental Learning: experience as the source of learning and development.* Englewood Cliffs, NJ: Prentice-Hall.

Madanipour, A., Cars, G. and Allen, J. (1998) 'Social exclusion in European cities', in Madanipour, A., Cars, G. and Allen, J. (eds) *Social Exclusion in European Cities, Processes, Experiences and Responses,* 279–88. London: The Stationery Office.

Martinez, P. and Munday, F. (1998) *9,000 Voices: student persistence and drop-out in further education.* London: FEDA.

Maslow, A. H. (1970) *Motivation and Personality.* New York: HarperCollins.

Maynard, J. and Martinez, P. (2000) *Pride or Prejudice? College teachers' views on course performance.* London: Learning and Skills Development Agency.

Mouton, J. S. and Blake, R. (1984) *Synergogy: a new strategy for education, training and development.* San Francisco: Jossey-Bass.

Office for National Statistics (2004) *Under 18s – conception rates data 1998–2002 for top tier local authorities.* London: Office for National Statistics.

Petty, G. (1998) *Teaching Today.* Cheltenham: Stanley Thornes.

Prison Reform Trust (2003) *Time to Learn: prisoners' views on prison education.* London: Prison Reform Trust.

Quinn, F. (1995) *The Principles and Practice of Nurse Education.* Cheltenham: Stanley Thornes.

Roche, J. and Tucker, S. (1997) *Youth in Society.* London: Sage.

Rogers, C. (1969) *Freedom to Learn.* Ohio: Merril.

Social Exclusion Unit (SEU) (1999) *Bridging the Gap: new opportunities for 16–18 year olds not in education, employment or training.* London: SEU.

Social Exclusion Unit (2001) *Preventing Social Exclusion.* London: SEU.

Social Exclusion Unit (2003) *Reducing Re-offending by Ex-prisoners.* London: SEU.

Social Exclusion Unit (2004) *Tackling Social Exclusion: taking stock.* London: SEU.

Willis, P. (1977) *Learning to Labour: how working class kids get working class jobs.* Farnborough, Hants: Saxon House.

Widening participation and lifelong learning

Anthony Coles

Introduction

'WIDENING PARTICIPATION' IS a commonly used phrase in post-compulsory education circles; sometimes it is used as a general term for increasing recruitment. This was far from the intention of those engaging in the debate during the 1990s, including John Tomlinson and Helena Kennedy, authors of influential reports in the area (FEFC 1996 and 1997a respectively). The significance of widening participation is effectively summed up in Kennedy's quotation 'If at first you don't succeed . . . you don't succeed' (p. 21). The emphasis is on improving participation specifically among under-represented groups and non-traditional learners and the critical role of the FE sector in this process.

Definitions of widening participation focus on improvement. For example, 'a reduction of barriers to inclusion, resulting in greater equality of opportunity' is one possible definition. Kennedy used 'access, achievement and progression for those groups often under-represented in further education' (FEFC 2000c: 4) and the Higher Education Funding Council (HEFC) used 'activities to target the individual groups that Higher Education Institutions have identified as under-represented and to ensure their success' (HEFC 2001: 1). This chapter will focus on widening participation in post-16 FE, though – as the latter quote indicates – this is also a priority in HE given government targets of 50 per cent participation in this sector.

The entitlement to learning for all is a surprisingly recent notion. The Education Act (1944) discriminated between learners who were 'educable' and those who were not; essentially making education an entitlement only for the 'educable'. The 'ineducable' were segregated to training centres and hospitals under the requirements of the Mental Deficiency Act (1913). The need for inclusive learning, with those not traditionally (at the time) part of mainstream education was recognised in law as late as the Education Act (1981), which specified initial assessment of learning needs and integration of those with learning difficulties and disabilities within mainstream provision; essentially recognising that education is for all and fostering the tenet of inclusive learning. The 1981 Act was in response to a recommendation made in the Warnock Report (HMSO 1978).

This discussion implies that widening participation is only about including those in the greatest need; those with particular difficulties and disabilities. The debate is much wider than that. If those with the greatest difficulties cannot participate, then there is little chance for those who are excluded for other reasons. If legislation to make inclusion a statutory right was enacted as recently as 1981, then it is understandable that there is still a long way to go to devise an equitable system.

Who are excluded?

The terminology associated with widening participation usually refers to the need for greater inclusion of 'non-traditional' or 'under-represented' learners. The problem with the term 'non-traditional' is that it implies that there is such a person as a 'traditional' learner. These terms tend to be used interchangeably, though they do have different implications. 'Non-traditional' refers to those learners who do not normally engage in learning; the term can be qualified to specify learning within a particular discipline, or location, for example. Typically, women could be regarded as non-traditional learners in the construction sector. Under-represented learners may, or may not be traditional. They may be learners from social, ethnic or gender groups for example, who normally participate, but who are prevented from doing so for a particular reason due to local or personal circumstances. When considering these definitions and analysing data, it is also important to clarify 'participation'. Does this mean 'enrolment', 'retention', 'achievement', or a combination of these?

The purpose of this discussion, which may at first seem rather pedantic, is to emphasise that whether someone participates or not is a complex issue. When discussing widening participation, it is easy to label particular groups – mature learners, for example – as having high or low participation rates. The reality is that factors influencing participation form a multi-layered web, which can restrict access to learning for a multitude of reasons.

The FEFC report *Widening Participation and Raising Standards* (FEFC 2000c) identified the following groups as having particularly high withdrawal and/or low achievement:

- adults in receipt of benefit and entitled to remission
- adults on literacy, numeracy or ESOL courses
- all minority ethnic groups
- some full-time male students (when compared with female)
- those on lower-level courses in general (apart from construction)
- those aged 19 to 24 in relation to older students
- those from deprived postcode areas
- those in receipt of additional support.

Some of these categories give a false impression of the situation as there are considerable local variations. This has resulted in the 'lottery of learning': essentially a postcode lottery resulting from variations in local distribution of funding in relation to need. Kennedy (FEFC 1997a) recognised the difficulty of categorising participants according to criteria such as age and ethnicity for this reason. She considered it more relevant to use prior experience, income or locality, since these were the criteria that provided a more consistent pattern. A further reason for using these criteria is that they are based on information available. Postcodes and prior experience are usually identified on enrolment and postcode can be used as an indicator of possible income. These might seem rather 'blunt instruments' to use for making such important deductions, after all, effective future planning depends upon accurate up-to-date demographic information. Herein lies one of the core problems of addressing the issue of widening participation, namely that data collection has been *ad hoc*, particularly in the case of part-time students who comprise significant numbers in the under-represented groups identified above.

With regard to ethnicity, it is worth noting that Further Education Funding Council data (FEFC 1997c) indicated that minority ethnic groups had higher participation rates in FE in relation to their proportion in the population (Table 7.1). These data illustrate the complexity of the situation and emphasise the need for caution as there is clear evidence that some minority groups are under-represented. The reason for this is that locality or level of study is not taken into account. The number of students with

TABLE 7.1 Participation in further education for different ethnic groups in 1995–96 in the UK (*Source*: FEFC 1997c: 28)

Ethnicity	Participation in FE (%)	Representation in whole population (%)
Bangladeshi	0·7	0·3
Black African	1·5	0·4
Black Caribbean	2·0	1·1
Black other	0·6	0·4
Chinese	0·5	0·3
Indian	2·4	1·8
Pakistani	2·0	1·0
White	87·6	93·8
Other – Asian	0·8	0·4
Other	1·8	0·6
Total	100	100

learning difficulties and disabilities enrolled in FE increased threefold between 1985 and 1995, however 40 per cent of the disabled population had no qualifications, compared with 11 per cent of the non-disabled (FEFC 1996).

Table 7.2 illustrates the situation in 1997–98 with regard to age and gender. For the under-16 age group there was a bias towards males at higher qualification levels. Between 16 and 18, more females were enrolled at Levels 1, 2 and 4 + 5, with fewer at Level 3. More males were enrolled at all levels apart from 4 + 5 in the 19–24 age group and more males at all levels for the 25+ group, with a particular discrepancy at Level 3.

These data are provided to emphasise the complexity of carrying out this sort of analysis and producing meaningful results that can lead to effective policy change. Poor data gathering and a significant delay in data publication exacerbate the situation.

Indicative task

Research the data relating to participation in your area. Consider factors such as unemployment rates, percentage of postcodes defined as 'deprived', achievement at Level 2 (e.g. GCSE grades A*–C), the proportion of students studying at Level 1, employment prospects in the area, retention and achievement rates compared with the national average. Possible sources of information include Local Learning and Skills Council (LLSC) annual reports, the Government statistics site (see 'Useful websites'), your organisation's annual report, recent inspection reports and the 'Social Trends' survey (see 'Useful websites').

Reflective questions

Consider your course management (marketing, for example) and teaching strategies. Which factors mitigate against recruiting and retaining under-represented groups? What steps could you take to reduce these effects?

TABLE 7.2 Students enrolled on FEFC-funded provision in 1997–98 by gender, age and qualification level (*Source*: Adapted from FEFC 2000a: 6)

Qualification level	Males aged (000s)				Females aged (000s)			
	Under 16	16–18	19–24	25+	Under 16	16–18	19–24	25+
Level 1	2·6	41·2	81·8	470·3	2·6	42·9	60·4	341·0
Level 2	1·8	88·2	74·2	330·3	1·3	97·0	60·6	241·2
Level 3	0·5	190·0	65·5	226·9	0·3	166·1	54·3	132·4
Level 4 + 5	0·0	2·5	11·5	44·6	0·0	2·8	14·4	42·3

Note that data for unspecified qualification level and age have not been included.

Progress since Kennedy

Learning and Skills Council (LSC) data collected from colleges between 1997 and 2000 from Individual Student Records (ISRs) have revealed some interesting trends in participation (LSC 2002). The data relate to students who are eligible for additional funding via widening participation initiatives. The proportion of students in this category rose from 25·1 to 33·1% during this period. Greater London had the highest number resident in a 'deprived area' at 47·8%, while 30% of all students fell into this category. The key points are summarised below, together with the relevant charts:

- Participation rates for students in areas designated for increased funding for widening participation purposes has increased at all levels (see Figure 7.1).

- The West Midlands demonstrates the greatest increase in widening for students' participation over the two periods, with the East Midlands and South East showing the greatest decline in participation among these learners (see Figure 7.2).

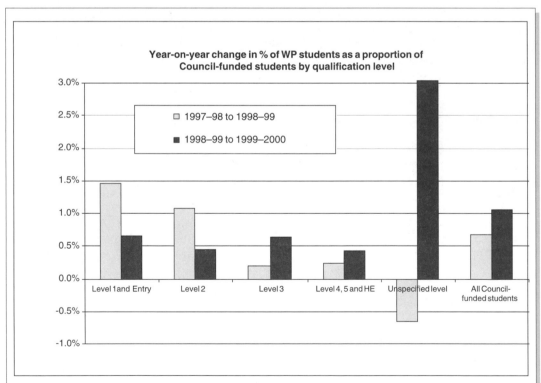

FIGURE 7.1   Percentage of widening participation students as a proportion of total LSC-funded students at each qualification level for 1997–99 and 1998–2000 (*Source*: LSC (2002))

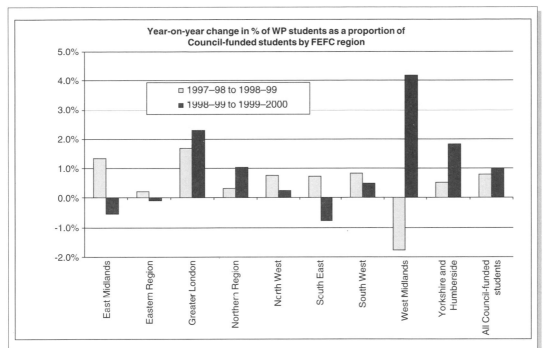

FIGURE 7.2   Percentage of widening participation students as a proportion of total LSC-funded students by FEFC region for 1997–98, 1998–99 and 1999–2000 (*Source*: LSC (2002))

- Colleges designated for the receipt of increased funding for widening participation purposes showed the greatest increase in recruitment of designated students. General FE and specialist colleges (horticulture, for example) showed relatively small increases, while sixth form and external institutions showed a slight fall in the number of these students (data not shown).

- Part-time students in the widening participation category increased by around 11 per cent during the period, though the full-time data showed a discrepancy between full time (full year) and other full-time students. Full time full year (there are several definitions here, but 16 hours per week will suffice) showed little change, while other full time showed a decrease of around 1·5 per cent (data not shown).

- The ethnicity data (see Figure 7.3, based on students' self-assessment) indicated that Black Caribbean participation increased by around 6%, Indian and 'other' by around 3%, though there was a decrease in participation among Bangladeshi and Black African by 3·5 and 2%, respectively.

The impression is that progress is being made in some areas, but not others. The percentage changes are relatively small in some cases, so it is difficult to tell, at least over the time period during which these data were gathered, whether they are significant or not in the longer term.

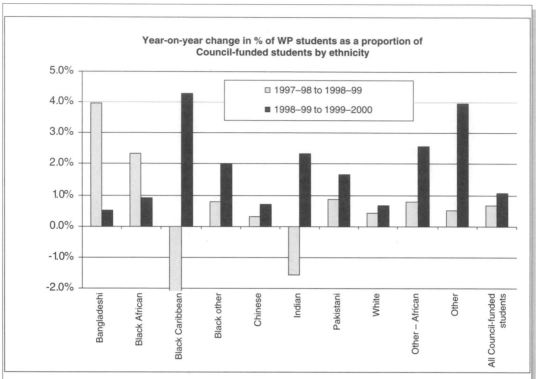

FIGURE 7.3   Percentage of widening participation students as a proportion of total LSC-funded students by ethnicity for 1997–98, 1998–99 and 1999–2000 (*Source*: LSC (2002))

Discussion points

1   Examine the data provided above. Can you think of factors likely to result in the trends shown?

2   How significant do the trends seem and is there any other information that you would need in order to make more credible deductions?

Barriers to participation

Just as the pattern of participation is complex, the barriers to participation are complex too. The term 'barrier' relates to factors mitigating against participation. Thomas (2001) categorised barriers as follows:

■   features of the education system itself

■   economic factors relating to the labour market and unemployment

■   social and cultural factors

■   'deficits' of the individual.

Features of the education system

For many years FE has been a 'Cinderella' service. Government, the public and private sector and the public at large have had a poor understanding of its role. Yet the reality is that it has been crucial in maintaining a semblance of coherence to the post-16 education system. The introduction of an education market as colleges became incorporated and thus independent financial entities resulted in a competitive environment in which decisions were made in order to maximise funding, rather than widen participation. With funding attached to achievement, the focus was on recruiting students most likely to be successful against the benchmarks of the day. This 'commodification' (the notion that education can be bought and sold in common with other goods and services) of education had strengths and weaknesses, but the general view is that it mitigated against widening participation. Expensive provision leading to greater participation, such as outreach, became less attractive against courses able to recruit large numbers of students with low delivery costs.

The perceived benefits of the market approach were that competition would lead to improvements in the quality of provision. The problem was that there was a discrepancy between indicators of quality that would attract students and those that would ensure high standards of teaching and learning. With the market approach came efforts to discover what students (or customers) wanted from the course through market research. The results of student satisfaction surveys tend to focus on factors such as car parking and catering as important, rather than the quality of teaching. The natural response was to focus resources on areas that would improve student satisfaction.

Paradoxically, independence brought greater accountability to funding bodies and a requirement to attain benchmark targets for retention and achievement, for example. While there are strong arguments in favour of target-setting and accountability, the result can be a focus on factors most likely to favour meeting targets; the assumption being that the targets are appropriate and that those setting them have an understanding of their implications. For example, there is no incentive to recruit someone to a course if they are unlikely to achieve the benchmark standard, although they may gain considerably from the experience and may ultimately achieve, albeit over a longer period. Hence the value of appropriate pre-entry advice and guidance; this person should be counselled onto a course that would be likely to result in achievement in the benchmark period. The assumption is that there will be sufficient numbers for the course to run.

Given the argument that widening participation initiatives need to take local circumstances into account, the change in funding body from the FEFC to the LSC, with Local LSCs (LLSCs) determining local funding priorities through Strategic Area Reviews, has gone some way to ameliorating the inability of providers to satisfy local need as a result of national funding strategies. For example, it was not uncommon for there to be sufficient local demand for a course, but because potential students were spread between different institutions, there were insufficient numbers to offer the course at any one location. Currently, LLSC have responsibility to select institutions to run particular courses according to their strengths and local need. Munn *et al.* (1993) found that collaboration between departments in the same institution, between institutions of the same and different sectors and between institutions and employers was a critical factor in promoting and maintaining participation.

The notion that the definition of 'participation' is contentious has been discussed above with regard to how participation may be measured. A similar difficulty exists with one of the key factors involved in participation, namely progression. There are two definitions worth noting here: **progression** is a learner-centred concept that relates to the movement of learners between different components of the education system; **articulation** refers to the design of the curriculum such that progression is possible. Tett (1996) identified three different kinds of progression:

- non-participation to participation, usually involving under-represented groups
- sideways progression from one subject or institution to another
- upward progression to a higher level in the system.

For any form of progression to take place, it is essential that programmes are articulated; that it is possible, according to learners' preferences, skills and aptitude, to move from one part of the system to another. Responsibility for articulation resides at many different levels within the system. Curriculum planning bodies such as QCA must ensure that credit accumulation and transfer are possible, while awarding bodies must be sufficiently co-ordinated to enable learners to transfer from one to another. LLSCs and individual institutions must ensure that there is provision to enable appropriate progression to meet local needs and characteristics of learners. Tett makes the point that, while participation has been increasing, the new participants are from skilled or professional groups with positive views of education. The unskilled, unemployed or women with dependent children, for example, remain sidelined.

The role of education professionals in facilitating participation cannot be ignored. While much of the teaching in FE is recognised to be of a high standard, many reports have commented that there are weaknesses in some areas; these areas are often those in the front line of widening participation. For example, the Moser Report (DfEE 1999) recognised that the quality of provision in adult basic skills was variable and that it relied on part-time teachers with little training. A lack of co-ordination of inspection was also cited as an issue. The Office for Standards in Education (Ofsted) reported on the quality of teaching and learning on literacy, numeracy and English for Speakers of Other Languages (ESOL) courses and came to similar conclusions. The result was recommendations for the incorporation of basic skills at Level 3 into initial teacher training courses and specialist training routes in each of the key areas (Ofsted 2003).

Maynard and Martinez (2002) reported on teachers' views on college performance, particularly in relation to the characteristics of teachers associated with courses having high or low retention and achievement.

Teachers on courses with high levels of retention and achievement generally took a positive view of their own professional development, being reflective and prepared to engage in staff development. They motivated and supported their students with effective induction programmes, tutorials designed to identify those at risk and action plan students' progress. These teachers acted upon information such as course evaluations and responded to resource shortage with creativity.

In contrast, teachers on courses with low levels of retention and achievement were complacent about their role, considered team morale to be low and that change for the better was beyond their control. They tended to stereotype students and blame them for their lack of achievement. Negative attitudes about the institution prevailed and they complained of a lack of time to focus on improvement, often citing poor management as a contributory factor.

Course-related factors identified by college staff as impacting upon retention have included:

- weak induction
- poor group cohesion
- limited alternative modes of study
- gaps in student timetables
- reduced contact time
- insufficient practical work
- issues related to GNVQ course structure, language and assessment
- the jump between intermediate- and advanced-level courses
- poor independent learning skills
- poor basic skills.

(Martinez and Munday 1998: 85)

While there are clearly issues relating to the 'match' between institution and staff expectations and students' expectations and needs, many colleges have devised innovative programmes in order to widen participation. Some of these strategies are summarised in the 'Good practice' and 'Case studies' sections later in this chapter. Chapter 6 'Managing diversity in the classroom' also considers a range of issues relating to disaffection, retention and achievement.

Discussion points

Here is a quotation from the Kennedy Report that sums up many of the issues discussed above:

> The hallmark of a college's success is, as it should be, public trust, satisfaction of the stakeholders and esteem rather than profitability. These colleges do not see their students as consumers, or learning merely as training. They see education as being more than the acquisition of knowledge and skills. In a system so caught up in what is measurable, we can forget that learning is also about problem-solving, learning to learn, acquiring the capability for intelligent choice in exercising personal responsibility. It is a weapon against poverty. It is the route to participation and active citizenship.
>
> (FEFC 1997a: 4)
>
> Do you agree with the sentiments expressed here? Can there be disadvantages in placing so much credibility on the 'measurable'?

Economic factors

Economic factors clearly have some bearing on levels of participation, but once again, this factor cannot be considered in isolation from the others. Many students attempt to reduce economic effects by working part time. This can result in institutional, personal and social tensions. Indeed, economic factors can operate on different levels. There may be immediate financial difficulties in funding travel to college, childcare, IT equipment, books and tuition fees for those on low pay or in part-time work; these factors may result in a lack of motivation to engage in learning, or result in early withdrawal. A distinction needs to be made between the direct and indirect costs of education. The direct costs are those associated with funding different aspects of the course, the indirect costs relate to lost opportunities for part-time work. There are many ways in which the curriculum can be adapted to enable part-time work (see below), however difficulties arise when poor timetabling creates spare time that cannot be used for part-time work (for example when a course has one day with two hours timetabled at lunchtime). Seasonal working may be an issue in some localities and courses may need to be planned to take this into account.

At a different level, employment prospects can also influence participation in complex ways. Gray *et al.* (1993) investigated the relationship between staying-on rates and the prevailing labour market conditions. They did not find a relationship between these two factors, recognising that the motivation to learn in different employment climates is complex. For example, school leavers may not continue in education post-16 in order to be available to seek work in a competitive employment environment. Equally, they may remain in education owing to a lack of any alternative, but drop out because of poor motivation (Martinez and Munday 1998). The latter study also found that courses with low retention rates did not have a large number of students with financial problems and that these courses didn't have particularly high levels of dissatisfaction among students.

The relationship between the benefits system and tuition fees is a significant issue in further and higher education. The present structure is complex and inaccessible to potential students. Often guidance staff are unsure of the appropriate advice to give in particular circumstances. Funding mechanisms can influence the advice given by colleges; the distinction between Schedule 2 (leading to accreditation) and non-Schedule 2 (not leading to accreditation) is a case in point, with colleges often enticing those on recreational evening classes to take programmes leading to accreditation for financial reasons. The introduction of tuition fees and student loans (this is not just a university issue as much higher education takes place in FE colleges and there are implications for access courses) has resulted in more caution among students in FE when considering progression to higher education courses (Knowles 2000). The 'part-time rule' under which students are considered to be part time (and consequently lose financial benefits) has also been a significant issue (see also Chapter 11). While the structure of public funding of FE can have a significant effect on participation, so can the considerable amount of investment in education and training provided by employers. This tends to be targeted towards relatively narrow socio-economic groups.

Social and cultural factors

According to the work of Martinez and Munday (1998), students from under-represented groups are less likely to agree that it was easy to make friends at college, or that they were supported by teachers during their induction period. Equally, those withdrawing from courses were less likely to have felt treated as an equal or to have considered that they got on well with other students on the course. Though paradoxically, they were more likely to have felt secure in the college environment. The explanation for this could have been that one of the most common likes was the social and learning environment. There is some contradiction here though as Martinez and Munday noted that this was also one of the most common dislikes. These results point to the heterogeneity of the so-called 'widening participation' group and the dangers of trying to apply solutions without first understanding the possible effects on sub-groups.

So far it has not been suggested that the onus for widening participation lies anywhere else than with the education system. The assumption has been that under-represented groups actually want to participate, but are prevented from doing so for various reasons. There is however an argument that some groups are self-excluded and that they have ample opportunity to participate if they so wish. For example, males have the opportunity to enrol on health and social care courses, indeed equal opportunities initiatives may positively encourage it, but they do not do so as a result of social conditioning; the possibility is not part of their experience. This describes the concept of Pierre Bourdieu's 'habitus'. Habitus refers to socially conditioned preferences that determine future actions and can relate to particular cultures or social classes, for example (Bourdieu and Nice 1992). It is the case for some cultures and social classes that formal education post-16 is not part of their experience and that this in itself constitutes a barrier.

Bourdieu further considered that the educational elite – those in positions of power to determine what is acceptable in educational terms – possess 'cultural capital' in that they have the ability to exclude those of different cultures or social class. He considered that, far from being a means of empowering the working classes, the education system was a means for particular social classes and cultures to subjugate them. The conspiracy, he considered, was extended to employers who are themselves products of the system controlled by the dominant hegemony. The result being that those subjugated by the system attach less value to learning, since it appears to confer little advantage.

Returning to the Kennedy Report, the relevance of social and cultural factors is summed up as follows:

> A special effort is necessary to encourage the most disadvantaged members of society to seek advice and guidance. These may be people who are in part-time or low-skilled jobs, who are unemployed or whose first language is not English. They may have poor educational attainment and no previous family history of benefit from education. Their common characteristic is a lack of confidence in approaching any formal provision that is connected with education or officialdom.
>
> (FEFC 1997a: 95–6)

'Deficits' of the individual

Thomas (2001) drew attention to the tendency to 'problematise' the individual, essentially to regard the individual as the source of the problem of particular groups being under-represented. Specific factors mitigating against participation were identified as individuals having low aspirations, poor motivation and being in possession of insufficient information on the availability of learning opportunities. All these factors can be addressed by implementing inclusive strategies central to widening participation. Hence 'deficits' are in inverted commas in this chapter because the implication of the word is that there are characteristics inherent to individuals that reduce the tendency to participate. One could argue that these factors could be ameliorated by implementing programmes designed to raise aspirations, addressing the socio-cultural causes of poor motivation and using methods of information dissemination designed to reach all members of the community.

Discussion points

1 Thomas' (2001) notion of individual 'deficits' suggests that particular characteristics of individuals result in non-participation. Is this a tenable concept given the influence of socio-cultural experience on predisposition to learning (see also Chapter 4)?

2 The 'nature or nurture' debate is relevant here. 'Nature' refers to characteristics resulting from our heritable genetic make-up, including eye and hair colour, for example. 'Nurture' refers to the environment that influences our development. What effect, if any, could these factors have on the predisposition to participate?

Good practice

A number of particularly useful documents relating to widening participation strategies have been published. The 'Itslifelonglearning' website (see 'Useful websites') has widening participation checklists for teachers and organisations, together with widening participation resources and links. Martinez (1997) also provides some useful strategies.

The FEFC (FEFC 2000c) published a report on widening participation in the FE sector, with a focus on progress since the Kennedy Report. The features of successful colleges were identified. These included:

- retention, achievement, attendance and progression strategies monitored and implemented by senior managers and governors, with named responsibilities;

- quality assurance systems that identify strengths and weaknesses and inform action planning and target setting;

- varied modes of study and wide curriculum provision targeted towards under-represented groups using inclusive teaching methods, community-based provision and individual learning plans;

- effective initial assessment and support for at-risk students provided through a robust tutorial and referral system; and

- clear preparation for progression to other courses or employment.

The LSC has published a very useful review of widening participation strategies, which includes case studies and related statistics, examples of good practice and a literature review (Taylor 2003).

Martinez and Munday (1998: 108) provided a summary of problems and solutions relating to reasons for students leaving their course. The key problem areas are identified below with several suggested solutions (the reader is referred to the original report for a more comprehensive list):

- incorrect or inappropriate expectations by the student
  - improved publicity; taster sessions

- inappropriate parental guidance or influence
  - parental involvement in open days and interviews

- low self-esteem and poor motivation
  - peer mentoring; confidence building exercises

- incorrect course placement
  - use of initial assessments and diagnostics; taster programmes

- withdrawals between application and enrolment
  - buddy schemes; effective tracking and follow-up

- feelings of isolation or not belonging
  - use of recreational and social activities and group learning exercises

- early problems settling in
  - effective induction, peer support and teambuilding
- early difficulties with coursework
  - structured work with progressive difficulty; integration of practical and theoretical work
- problems with progress on the programme
  - regular review and action planning; review of timetabling and amount of free time; development of study and time-management skills
- basic skills problems
  - early screening and diagnostics and basic skills support integrated within main provision
- personal and financial difficulties
  - referral to specialist support, including childcare and financial assistance with travel and course materials

Case studies

Case studies can provide models to evaluate the effectiveness of a range of different widening participation strategies. The FEFC published a collection of case studies (FEFC 2000b), two of which are summarised below.

Case study 1

Knowsley Community College is in an area with high unemployment and 75% of students from postcode areas identified as highly deprived. Just 23% of students achieved GCSE grades A–C and 60% of students were studying at Level 1. Several particular challenges were identified, including preparing students for progression to work, lower than average retention rates on some courses (though overall retention and achievement were above the national average) and improving progression rates from Level 1.

Some of the strategies adopted by the college in response to these issues were:

- Governors regularly monitor widening participation targets and progress towards meeting growth of outreach provision and recruitment of students from particular groups.
- A senior manager has responsibility for widening participation.
- New initiatives are supported by appropriate staff development.
- Quality improvement groups have responsibility for particular widening participation issues.
- External funding is secured for projects designed to support disadvantaged students.

- Teachers complete a self-assessment checklist with 31 items relating to widening participation. The process is linked to appraisal and course reviews.
- There is detailed analysis of retention, achievement and progression rates of learners from disadvantaged postcode areas, followed by target setting and action planning.
- Initiatives are used to enhance the curriculum, including induction and developing learner–employer links.
- There is flexible delivery of community-based provision, including multiple start dates, modular programmes and 'catch-up' learning packs.
- There is establishment of an open learning centre on an industrial site and a home-based IT scheme for students with disabilities.
- There are over 90 community-based centres that respond to local needs.
- New courses are developed to attract non-traditional participants such as an army preparation course.
- Progression is encouraged by short taster courses and information provision encourages progression from community centres to the college main site.
- Introductory courses are designed to raise the confidence and self-esteem of students from under-represented groups and former students are used as positive role models.
- Guidance staff are thoroughly trained to assess the most appropriate courses for prospective students.
- 'Right choice' reviews are carried out six weeks after the beginning of a course.
- Diagnostic screening is used for basic skills.
- Students' attendance and progress is rigorously tracked and followed-up using the tutorial system.
- Students' successes are celebrated across the college.

Case study 2

Hackney Community College serves one of the most deprived areas of the country, with 97 per cent of students coming from postcode areas described as highly deprived. One third of the population consists of refugees and migrants with ESOL needs. Half the students come from minority ethnic groups.

Strategies to support widening participation include:

- rigorous monitoring and follow-up of attendance, retention and achievement
- tutorials for part-time students
- repeat sessions
- individual target setting
- close monitoring of the quality of community-based provision

- provision for under-represented groups including those with mental health difficulties, Jewish organisations and people with disabilities from ethnic minorities

- high quality accommodation and services for students

- extensive community provision in targeted areas such as refugee hostels

- delivery of non-Schedule 2 work in partnership with community and voluntary organisations

- routes for progression from non-Schedule 2 to Schedule 2 (leading to accreditation), e.g. IT for the profoundly deaf

- students' own cultural background and literature are used to support ESOL classes and drop-in classes are offered for those who cannot attend regularly

- extensive childcare facilities operating from several sites offering evening availability and care up to the age of 14

- awards ceremonies to celebrate achievement.

Reflective question

You may have identified some weakness in your institution's widening participation policy in the Indicative task at the beginning of this chapter, or you may be aware of weaknesses as a result of reading this chapter. Which of the above strategies could be useful for dealing with the weaknesses? If you can't find any, use the sources suggested to explore alternatives.

Lifelong learning

The concept of 'lifelong learning' is closely related to the widening participation debate. Lifelong learning is about adults taking responsibility for engaging in learning that serves to develop their social, cultural and professional awareness. The issue with regard to widening participation is that adults have particular difficulties with taking part in learning due to the pressures of work, family and social life. Many of the strategies discussed above are relevant to ensuring that adults achieve their learning goals. Financial constraints need to be addressed; distance and e-learning approaches together with sensitive timetabling are needed; effective advice and guidance is required in addition to comprehensive support packages; modular approaches and credit-transfer can be particularly beneficial. See Stock (1996) for a review of issues relevant to lifelong learning.

The stimulus for lifelong learning has not been solely for the benefit of the individual. The climate is one of a competitive global learning economy in which continuing personal and professional development is critical to maintaining a competitive advantage. The result has been a shift in priorities from learning in community-based settings for recreational purposes (see Chapter 1 for a discussion of 'liberal education' and the role of organisations such as the Workers' Educational Association and university extension programmes) to work-related training for professional development purposes. The era of growth of adult education in the first half of the twentieth century will be remembered by many as a period of personal enrichment; the idea that one was learning for learning's sake, rather than for economic gain. The system was largely organised on a local basis and funded though the LEA. The advantage was that a response could be made to local need, but the result was inequalities across the country in terms of levels of funding according to LEA priorities.

The curriculum tended to be determined by demand and the expertise of individual tutors. The *ad hoc* nature of the system was also seen in the 'amateur' status of tutors, who rarely had any formal training. Nevertheless, the system proved inspirational to many and was the envy of European neighbours. The 1970s saw a professionalisation of the adult education system, with the Venables Report (1976) emphasising the importance of continuing vocational education. Adult education initiatives started to focus on the development of skills, including basic skills (with voluntary adult literacy schemes, for example) and latterly IT skills have featured among the most popular courses. IT is interesting because there is a polarity between the motivation for taking the subject, with some learners doing it out of general interest and some for professional development. With changing career patterns and 'portfolio' careers involving several part-time jobs, the idea of 'recurrent education'; that one would return to learning as and when required by one's career, became appealing (Van der Zee 1996).

Staff development in the workplace has also become much more purposeful. Several work-based schemes have received recognition, including those from Unipart, Motorola and the Ford Employee Development and Assistance Programme (EDAP). EDAP is a collaborative venture between Ford and several unions. It has been running since 1989 and has been the model for many work-based education programmes, to the extent that these have often been generically called 'EDAP' programmes. The scheme offers advice, guidance, support and financial assistance for employees to take part in training in their own time. Courses range from the academic to those involving technical and practical skills. Creative subjects and general interest courses such as bricklaying and plastering are also included. During the launch of the scheme's cybercafé, John Crew, Operations Manager of Ford Dagenham commented that: 'Nowadays, competitive advantage comes not from facilities or product so much as people. People who are committed to lifelong learning know how to deal with change, know how to upgrade their skills.' Alan Tuckett, Director of the National Institute of Adult Continuing Education (NIACE) considered that: 'The scheme shows that people who develop confidence in learning pass that confidence on to their family' (reported by Ingram 2004). This last point is crucial. Kennedy commented that 'learning parents create learning families' (FEFC 1997a: 73). So the value of lifelong learning permeates beyond the individual and can influence generations to come.

The EDAP scheme is a good example of one aspect of a 'learning organisation'. Senge defined the learning organisation as:

> organisations where people continually expand their capacity to create the results they truly desire, where new and expansive patterns of thinking are nurtured, where collective aspiration is set free and where people are continually learning how to learn together.
>
> Senge (1990: 3)

Garvin (1994) produced a concise justification for learning organisations:

> The need (for learning organisations) is due to business becoming more complex, dynamic, and globally competitive. Excelling in a dynamic business environment requires more understanding, knowledge, preparation, and agreement than one person's expertise and experience provides. Continuous improvement requires a commitment to learning.
>
> Garvin (1994: 19)

Senge described five 'disciplines' as the means of building learning organisations, namely:

- *systems thinking*, involving identifying interrelationships between processes, rather than simply cause and effect;
- *personal mastery*, in which our personal vision is deepened and clarified, resulting in 'creative tension';
- *shared vision*, involving the ability to conceive shared 'pictures' of the future;
- *mental models*, essentially being able to reflect on our own thinking and open our thoughts to scrutiny by others; and
- *team learning*, which involves developing the arts of dialogue and discussion.

The need for 'learning organisations' has arisen from the development of the 'knowledge economy' in which information and knowledge are the currency. Figure 7.4 illustrates the succession of 'currencies' over the last few hundred years. While 'information' might be the currency, the way in which the currency is used is critical. Van der Zee remarked that 'an information society is not an informed society' (Van der Zee 1996: 164). He commented on the current influences on teaching and learning and concluded that:

> a preferred score would provide room for a variety of initiatives to renewal, without justifying every proposal beforehand and so circumventing the need to choose. Rather it would act as a common source of inspiration. The metaphor of a *learning society* has the potential to meet this need.
>
> (Van der Zee 1996: 164)

He went on to identify five criteria for a learning society, namely:

- a broad definition of learning as a dimension of society
- redirection of the goal of learning from growth towards completeness

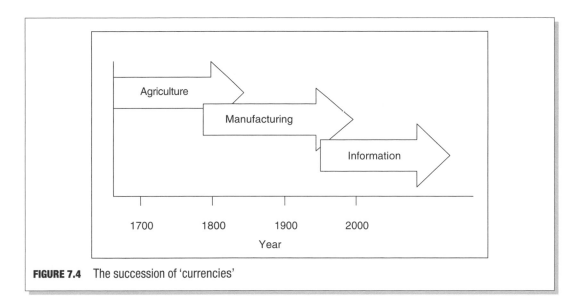

FIGURE 7.4   The succession of 'currencies'

- surpassing learning and instruction to increase collective competence
- fostering autonomy in learning
- the right to learn – a political approach to learning.

Kennedy should have the last word here as her 1997 report (FEFC 1997a) still has substantial relevance to current widening participation issues. She used the phrase 'sustainable learning' to convey the notion that learning should be seen as a continuing process to support an individual's personal development. The purpose of the widening participation agenda is to ensure that learning is sustainable for all.

Summary

- When describing issues affecting participation, it is necessary to define participation in terms of enrolment, retention or achievement. Similarly, terms such as 'non-traditional' or 'under-represented' need to be set in context.
- Identification of under-represented learners by age, ethnicity or gender fails to take account of local circumstances. Using prior experience, income or locality provides a more consistent pattern.
- The level of qualification must be considered when analysing participation rates. For example, the situation with regard to gender and age varies considerably with qualification level.
- Barriers to participation have been categorised under four headings: features of the education system itself; economic factors relating to the labour market and unemployment; social and cultural factors and 'deficits' of the individual.

- A key feature of the education system has been the 'commodification' of education and the resulting effects of competition.

- Economic factors include the cost of travel, childcare, IT facilities, books and stationery. Those on low pay and in part-time work are particularly affected as they may not qualify for fee remission. Employment prospects can have a complex effect on participation.

- Bourdieu's notions of 'habitus' and 'cultural capital' (Bourdieu and Nice 1992) imply that the education system is biased towards an elite who perpetuate the *status quo* in order to subjugate others.

- Many examples of good practice involve comprehensive information collection followed by targeted support, a relevant curriculum and opportunities for progression.

- Case studies can provide a useful basis for devising widening participation strategies.

- Promoting lifelong learning involves many of the issues relating to widening participation. Lifelong learning has relevance to issues such as the knowledge economy, learning organisations and the learning society.

- The FENTO Teaching and Learning Standards relating to widening participation and lifelong learning are shown in Figure 7.5. Full details of these standards are available at the FENTO website (see 'Useful websites').

Useful websites

www.fento.ac.uk
The Further Education National Training Organisation (FENTO) website
Last accessed 7 May 2004

www.itslifejimbutnotasweknowit.org.uk/index.htm
The 'itslifelonglearning' website: resources for teachers, trainers and instructors in the Learning and Skills sector
Last accessed 7 May 2004

www.statistics.gov.uk
Links to sites containing statistics on participation such as the 'Social Trends' survey
Last accessed 7 May 2004

www.wpsw.co.uk
The Widening Participation South West website with many useful links and resources
Last accessed 7 May 2004

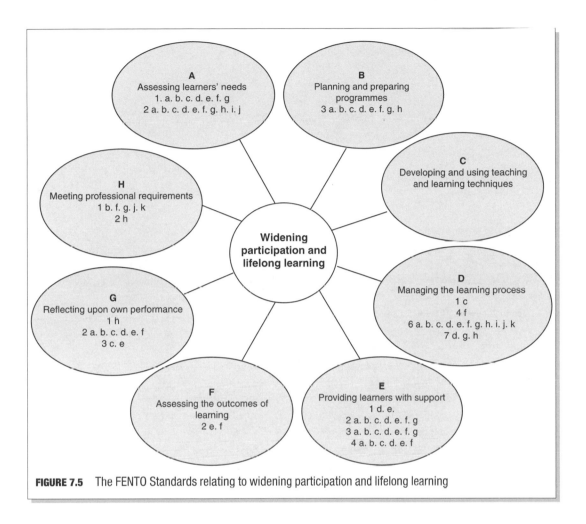

FIGURE 7.5 The FENTO Standards relating to widening participation and lifelong learning

References

Bourdieu, P. and Nice, R. (1992) *The Logic of Practice*. London: Stanford University Press.

DfEE (1999) *Improving literacy and numeracy: a fresh start*. The report of the working group chaired by Sir Claus Moser. London: DfEE.

Education Act (1944). London: HMSO.

Education Act (1981). London: HMSO.

FEFC (1996) *Inclusive Learning*. Coventry: FEFC.

FEFC (1997a) *Learning Works: widening participation in further education*. Coventry: FEFC.

FEFC (1997b) *How to Widen Participation: a guide to good practice*. Coventry: FEFC.

FEFC (1997c) *Widening Participation in Further Education: statistical evidence*. London: The Stationery Office.

FEFC (2000a) *Widening Participation in Further Education: statistical evidence*. London: The Stationery Office.

FEFC (2000b) *Widening Participation and Raising Standards: colleges' case studies*. Coventry: FEFC.

FEFC (2000c) *Widening Participation and Raising Standards*. Coventry: FEFC.

Garvin, D. (1994) 'Building a learning organization', *Business Credit* **96**(1), 19–28.

Gray, J., Jesson, D. and Tranmer, M. (1993) *Boosting Post-16 Participation in Full-time Education: a study of some key factors*. England and Wales Youth Cohort Study Report 20. London: DfEE.

HEFC (2001) *Strategies for Widening Participation in Higher Education: a guide to good practice*. London: HEFC.

HMSO (1978) *Special Educational Needs*. Report of the committee of enquiry into the education of handicapped children and young people (Warnock Report). London: HMSO.

Ingram, R. (2004) *Ford's EDAP adds a Cybercafé*. http://www.lifelonglearning.co.uk/iln6000/iln6001.htm – Last accessed 10/05/04.

Knowles, J. (2000) 'Access for few? Student funding and its impact on aspirations to enter higher education', *Widening Participation and Lifelong Learning* **2**(1) 14–23.

LSC (2002) *Widening Participation in Further Education – Statistical Evidence 1997–98, 1998–99, 1999–2000*. London: LSC.

Martinez, P. (1997) *Improving Student Retention: a guide to successful strategies*. London: FEDA.

Martinez, P. and Munday, F. (1998) *9,000 Voices: student persistence and drop-out in further education*. London: FEDA.

Maynard, J. and Martinez, P. (2002) *Pride or Prejudice? College teachers' views on college performance*. London: LSDA.

Mental Deficiency Act (1913). London: HMSO.

Munn, P., Tett, L. and Arney, N. (1993) *Negotiating the Labyrinth: progression opportunities for adult learners*. Edinburgh: SCRE.

Ofsted (2003) *Literacy, numeracy and English for speakers of other languages: a survey of current practice in post-16 and adult provision*. London: Ofsted.

Senge, P. (1990) *The Fifth Discipline: the art and practice of the learning organization*. London: Doubleday.

Stock, A. (1996) 'Lifelong learning: thirty years of educational change', in Raggatt, P., Edwards, R. and Small, N. (eds) *The Learning Society: challenges and trends*. London: Open University/Routledge.

Taylor, S. (2003) *Widening Adult Participation: ways to extend good practice*. London: LSC.

Tett, L. (1996) 'Education and the marketplace', in Raggatt, P., Edwards, R. and Small, N. (eds) *The Learning Society: challenges and trends*. London: Open University/Routledge.

Thomas, L. (2001) *Widening Participation in Post-compulsory Education*. London: Continuum.

Van der Zee, H. (1996) 'The learning society', in Raggatt, P., Edwards, R. and Small, N. (eds) *The Learning Society: challenges and trends*. London: Open University/Routledge.

Venables, P. (1976) *Report of the Committee on Continuing Education*. Milton Keynes: The Open University.

The 14–19 sector: responding to change

Tricia Le Gallais

Introduction

THIS CHAPTER SEEKS to offer some insights into the major changes occurring in the 14–19 sector. It combines summaries of the various pertinent government papers together with responses from education stakeholders and links these with case study examples of increased vocational opportunities for 14–16-year-olds.

The debates surrounding the 'new vocationalism' in the UK are introduced. Following a discussion of issues relating to the 14–19 curriculum, the implications of exchanges of staff and pupils between schools and FE colleges are identified. Three case studies relating to the implementation of the Increased Flexibility Programme (IFP) in schools and colleges are presented and finally the future direction of 14–19 education is discussed in the light of lessons from Curriculum 2000 and proposals from the Working Group on 14–19 reform.

The 'new vocationalism'

International league tables rank us 25th out of 29 among developed nations for participation of 17-year-olds in education and training. Behind such worrying statistics lies one of the most persistent shortcomings of our education system: the weakness of our vocational offer . . . learning a trade has still to become a truly valued option.

(DfES 2003a: 4; Executive Summary)

The term 'new vocationalism' has been used with reference to the increased emphasis being placed by government upon the importance of vocational training and qualifications. This was largely a result of high youth unemployment in the 1970s and the resulting expansion of youth training in the 1980s and a shift from what has been described as 'vocationalism for some' to 'enterprise for all' (Coles and MacDonald 1996). The key message from documents such as the Green Paper *14–19: extending opportunities, raising standards* (DfES 2002a) and in the DfES response to the Green Paper

14–19 Opportunity and Excellence (2003a), is a commitment to achieving parity of esteem between vocational and academic qualifications. Such a drive is welcomed by many stakeholders, including the Learning and Skills Development Agency (LSDA): 'At long last there is recognition that there is a problem with a system that devalues vocational education, focuses exclusively on formal qualifications and writes off a significant proportion of young people at 16' (Burnette 2002: 3).

Other organisations, such as The Association of Teachers and Lecturers (ATL 2002), the Trades Union Congress (TUC 2002) and The National Institute of Adult Continuing Education (NIACE 2002) also welcome the Green Paper's acknowledgement of the importance of vocational qualifications, not least for the part such qualifications play in the economic prosperity of the country.

NIACE does, however, suggest that, contrary to the aspirations of the Government to achieve increased staying-on rates by proposing a 'vocationalising' of the 14–19 curriculum, the Green Paper may well encourage young people to move towards employment rather to university. Experiencing what may seem to many young people a more relevant and work-oriented curriculum may result in increased numbers joining trades or entering the workplace in preference to extending their education in schools, colleges or higher education (HE). Would this automatically exclude them from further learning? There is a need for clear learning pathways in the workplace and incentives for employers to embrace the lifelong learning agenda.The emphasis on young people *'staying on'* in education until they are 19, might be better applied to young people *'continuing'* their education, whether this be in the workplace or an educational establishment.

There is a long history of vocational qualifications being perceived as low status (see also Chapter 1). For example, research for this chapter has indicated a widely held presumption among many teachers that the IFP (an initiative to provide vocational courses in FE colleges for post-14 pupils) is for *'those kinds of students'* (East Midlands Learning and Skills Research Network 2002). Inferred by this comment is the belief that the less able, the disaffected and the disapplied are the most suitable candidates for the more vocational courses, while others should pursue 'academic' qualifications. As Estelle Morris, the then Minister of State for Education and Skills, commented in her foreword to the Green Paper that 'For too long vocational studies and qualifications have been undervalued . . . We must introduce qualifications . . . that are not a sink option for failed students' (DfES 2003a).

The 'sink option' described above, in which young people with aptitude in vocational areas are undervalued and channelled into a sequence of 'schemes' rather than robust training programmes, must be challenged. Until this is successful, the 'new vocational-ism' is in danger of reinforcing negative stereotypical views concerning the status and importance of vocational education and training.

Discussion points

1 What are your views concerning the issue of 'staying on' in education?

2 How might the Government ensure that young people are encouraged and enabled to access further study, whether in an educational institution or in the workplace?

3 How might your proposals impact upon the status of vocational education and training?

Indicative task

Use the arguments above and further reading from the sources indicated to arrive at a definition of the 'new vocationalism' that is relevant to your setting. This definition would be a useful start to an assignment based on vocational education.

14–19 opportunities

This section contains an analysis of the Government's Green Paper *14–19: extending opportunities, raising standards* (DfES 2002a) together with responses from a range of stakeholders. The format matches that of the Green Paper.

The vision

'Sixteen has been a traditional cut-off point in education. We need to transform it from a point at which young people divide into those who stay on and those who leave into a point where every young person is committed to continue learning' (DfES 2002a: 1). The challenges of technological and economic change in the twenty-first century make reform of the present education system an imperative. The Green Paper proposes to introduce new vocational qualifications and incentives to stay on beyond 16, such as the Education Maintenance Allowances (EMAs). These are means-tested payments to post-16 learners designed to encourage them to remain in education and training. The broader curriculum aims to increase students' future employability.

The 14–19 phase

The Government's aim of shifting the focus from 16 to 19 for the completion of a young person's education features strongly throughout the Green Paper and is regularly reinforced through ministerial speeches. It is clear, for example, from Prime Minister Tony Blair's speech at the Labour Party spring conference in Manchester in February 2004 that he wishes to see young people staying on until the age of 18 or 19 and to 'make irrelevant the school leaving age of 16' (BBCi 2004).

The end of Year 9 will see the start of the 14–19 phase with a review of a young person's progress and achievement. An individual learning plan (ILP) will be drawn up to aid the monitoring and reviewing of the pupil's progress throughout the 14–19 phase. Qualifications at 16 will form a progress review rather than being an endpoint for many students.

The Key Stage 4 curriculum will contain a core of compulsory subjects, which all pupils should study, namely mathematics, English, science and ICT, citizenship, religious education, careers education, sex education, physical education and work-related learning. In addition pupils would have 'a new statutory entitlement of access to a subject within each of modern foreign languages, design and technology, the arts and the humanities' (DfES 2002a: 9). More vocational qualifications and new 'hybrid' qualifications combining traditional general subjects with their vocational applications are planned. Modern Apprenticeships will form an important part of a 14–19 vocational pathway. All 16- to 19-year-olds will have the entitlement to study literacy, numeracy and ICT to at least Level 2. The strategy aims to achieve a four-year pathway for students with greater flexibility in the pre-16 curriculum to emphasise the importance of personal, vocational and work-related learning.

The new award

The Green Paper proposes the introduction of a new qualification to be awarded at age 19, which would recognise key skills, all academic and vocational qualifications and cover participation in wider activities.

Pace and progression

The intention is to create greater flexibility with regard to allowing young people to develop at a pace consistent with their abilities, allowing some of them increased time to reach the required standard and allowing others to 'fast-track'.

Advice, guidance and support for young people

The Green Paper stresses the increased importance of ensuring that young people receive independent advice, guidance and support with careers advice starting in Key Stage 3 in order to cope with the wider range of choices available at age 14. Financial support for young people will be available through EMAs.

Drivers and support for change

Targets and performance tables are seen to be key drivers in raising standards. Changes are proposed to school performance tables to recognise differing rates of progress at age 16, and to school and college performance tables to reflect national achievement targets. Chapter 7 of the Green Paper (DfES 2002a: 60) details these targets. The fact that school performance tables are to include vocational qualifications as well as GCSEs is indicative of the Government's drive to achieve parity between vocational and 'academic' qualifications.

Implementation

The implementation of the 14–19 proposals is to be phased in over several years with consultation concerning changes to the curriculum, qualifications, regulations and guidance. The Government's anticipated funding allocation of £60 million in 2002–2004 is an indication of its commitment to these proposals.

Next steps

The DfES carried out extensive consultation with regard to the proposals in the Green Paper. The general consensus of opinion from a range of stakeholders was that the proposals had real potential to make a difference to 14–19 education but that they did not go far enough (LSDA 2002, ATL 2002).

In January 2003 the DfES published its response to the Green Paper, in which it set out the arrangements for the setting up of a Working Group led by Mike Tomlinson to consider 14–19 reform. Tomlinson's interim report (DfES 2004) provides the focus for the final section in this chapter 'Future models for an integrated learning approach post-14'.

Discussion points

1 What implications do the above proposals have for staffing in schools and colleges?
2 What difficulties might ensue from these proposals for both staff and 14–16 pupils?

The FE college perspective

The 14–19 proposals are likely to have a major impact upon the culture and ethos of FE colleges. While there have been arrangements with Local Education Authorities (LEAs) for colleges to accept certain pupils under 16 (those with learning difficulties and disabilities, for example), the vast majority of college clientele have been over the age of 16. Since the introduction of the IFP, which brought with it funding to aid implementation, the number of 14–16-year-olds in colleges has increased dramatically.

In conjunction with the introduction of Vocational GCSEs, the IFP provided opportunities for Year 10 pupils to gain additional support for their vocational programme as a result of partnerships between their school and predominantly FE colleges, but occasionally universities or training centres. Links with colleges enabled young people to take qualifications other than Vocational GCSEs such as Business and Technician Education Council (BTEC) First and National Vocational Qualifications (NVQs). Progression to Foundation and Advance Modern Apprenticeships was also possible. The scheme included an extended period of work placement and was funded through the Learning and Skills Council (LSC).

For most colleges the influx of 14–16 students has provided considerable challenges, with many staff feeling ill-prepared to cope with the different characteristics of these learners and with the new regulations concerning supervisory arrangements and Criminal Records Bureau (CRB) checks for staff acting *in loco parentis*.

Fortunately, in December 2003 the LSC produced a comprehensive booklet for FE colleges, *Guidance for FE Colleges Providing for Young Learners* (LSC 2003). This guide contains a detailed list of legal requirements with regard to young people's equal access to learning, child protection vetting and health and safety, for example.

The diversity in the stakeholders involved in 14–19 initiatives such as the IFP has resulted in a need for extensive partnerships to share expertise. As one would expect with the stress on vocational learning there is a strong emphasis on the involvement of local business partnerships and employers as well as schools, colleges, the local LSC, the Connexions Service and the LEA. FE colleges are considered well placed to build upon their existing links with local employers from their experience of programmes such as the Modern Apprenticeship (MA) and to encourage wider employer involvement with learner support activities such as mentoring.

A major issue arising from the 14–19 proposals is that of parity of pay between FE colleges and schools. NIACE (2002) welcomed the strengthening of the position of vocationally oriented education but stressed the need for parity of funding with 'academic' education. This includes addressing the disparity of pay and working conditions between schools and colleges. ATL (2002) supported this concern and also raised a further serious issue for FE, namely the need for staff to be trained to teach the wider age range:

> Differentials in pay, qualifications and conditions of service between the school, college and work-based sectors need urgently addressing . . . One further issue is the need for teaching staff to be trained to deal with the different qualifications to be delivered to a wider age range.

This issue is particularly significant in the case of FE teachers involved in supporting vocational programmes in schools (such as the Vocational GCSE). It is therefore particularly important for FE colleges to access relevant training for their staff to ensure they can best accommodate these younger learners.

Schools receive significantly more funding per capita than colleges for providing the same programme. This situation has arisen as a result of historical differences in the funding mechanisms, with schools being funded via the LEA and colleges via the LSC. This is a serious issue for FE colleges as their achievement rates will inevitably be compared with those in schools and they are expected to provide the equivalent service with lower levels of funding.

The school perspective

Schools are expected to play a key role in ensuring that their partner college(s) comply with the regulations appertaining to collaborative programmes involving the 14–16 age range. This is highly significant as learners will be placed in a range of different settings in order to gain vocational experience, including the workplace. Most important, however, is the acknowledgement that the schools still retain the primary duty of care for their pupils while at college. The statutory regulations for the care of 14–16 students in colleges and other establishments are the same as those applied in schools. Therefore, the schools are ideally placed to advise and oversee educational provision to young learners in colleges and places of work.

Some schools have selected students to take part in the IFP in terms of their low ability or difficult behaviour, which has led college teachers to complain that they are having students 'dumped on them' (East Midlands Learning and Skills Research Network 2002). Other schools genuinely seek to offer their students increased opportunities, thereby helping them to explore their potential and experience the world of work and vocational training. Unfortunately, where schools show a reluctance to allow their brighter students to take part in the IFP, it is serving to reinforce young people's perceptions that only the less bright follow vocational pathways.

Schools have much expertise to share with colleges in terms of their 14–16 experience and much to learn from them with regard to the wide range of vocational courses available in colleges. Schools need to be looking towards creating a comprehensive Continuing Professional Development (CPD) programme in order to develop their staff's knowledge and understanding of vocational qualifications and to identify how they can reinforce their students' college learning within the school. The LSC offers customised and in-house training and a range of resources to support colleges and schools in responding to the challenges of the IFP.

Discussion points

Why may some schools be reluctant to involve more able pupils in 14–19 initiatives? How could this be resolved?

Training teachers for 14–19 education

Background

The strength of the FE sector – its diversity of teachers, trainers, learners and settings – makes the creation of a coherent teacher training programme a challenging one. Unlike schools, where most teachers train pre-service and full time, only a minority of FE lecturers follow this path. Most train in-service and part time. Chapters 2 and 3 also contain relevant information on this topic.

The Office for Standards in Education (Ofsted) have carried out a survey inspection of teacher training provision (Ofsted 2003). Good practice was identified, however, significant issues were highlighted:

- the diverse needs of FE teachers and the lack of data concerning the trainees' prior learning and present needs, which need to be identified and addressed via an ILP

- the importance of support with regard to their practical teaching and for the teaching of their subject specialism, for which the provision of workplace mentors is recommended

- the wide ability range and experience of trainee teachers. It was found that about one third of all trainees in the inspection lacked Level 2 qualifications in literacy and numeracy

- the lack of integration of initial teacher training (ITT) with an organisation's professional development programme

- the lack of independent scrutiny and monitoring in the sector to ensure agreed standards are covered within ITT.

Ofsted stressed the need to link standards within the learning and skills sector with those in schools. This is particularly relevant in the light of the 14–19 strategy, which requires greater partnerships between schools and colleges with staff from both sectors becoming involved in the education of 14–19-year-olds.

Until 2001 when Ofsted became responsible for the inspection of FE teacher training, there was no national requirement for FE teachers to hold a teaching qualification. From September 2001 all new entrants to FE teaching have to obtain a teaching qualification based on national standards drawn up by the Further Education National Training Organisation (FENTO). This must be done within two years of a suitable course being available for full-time staff and four years for part-time staff.

Following on from *Success for All* (DfES 2002b), which launched the Government's reform strategy for the FE and training sector, the DfES published *Consultation on ITT in FE* (DfES 2003b) a document concerned with the future of initial teacher education for the learning and skills sector. This document contains detailed responses to the concerns expressed by Ofsted with regard to the training of teachers in the learning and skills sector.

In particular the DfES sought to respond to the criticism of specialist subject support by introducing the concept of subject-specific mentoring. Additionally, a full initial assessment of trainee teachers to ensure individual needs are known was recommended, thereby enabling an ILP to be produced. Support will be available to ensure trainees achieve agreed literacy and numeracy levels.

The Government's vision for ITT in the learning and skills sector can be summarised as follows:

- Teachers are to be 'well-grounded in generic pedagogy alongside the specific skills of teaching their subject' (DfES 2003b: 4); able to teach across the 14–19 and adult range; teach students with learning difficulties or disabilities; be competent in literacy, numeracy, ICT and ESOL and be committed to lifelong learning and CPD.

- Teachers are entitled to professional formation leading to qualified status and encompassing initial training and workplace development, and to an ILP and mentoring support from experienced, qualified teaching staff. A professional record will be kept to record progress and achievements and to form a basis for the trainee's CPD. Trainees should experience a breadth of teaching and learning contexts to prepare them for the sector, in which they are to teach.

- The endorsement of teacher training courses will be linked to a three-year cycle of inspection and funding available to support the 14–19 reforms.

- Teacher educators should have a minimum of a Cert Ed and preferably a first degree or Masters qualification together with recent experience of teaching in the learning and skills sector.

While the Government's proposals address college teacher education specifically, it is intended that the reforms will eventually encompass teacher and trainer training across the learning and skills sector. The need to create linkages with school and HE teacher training is also acknowledged in order to raise the status of FE teachers. To this end there is the intention to award a qualification, possibly named the Qualified Teacher of Further Education (QTFE) or the Qualified Teacher of Learning and Skills (QTLS) to those teachers who achieve a Level 4 Stage 3 qualification and successfully complete their workplace development.

The implementation of the proposals for initial teacher training in FE

Prior to the introduction of the FENTO Standards (FENTO 1999) there was no formal way to measure the consistency and quality of teacher training across the sector. These standards are at present under review by FENTO, the Lifelong Learning Sector Skills Council (LLLSSC) and the DfES.

Endorsement and inspection

The Government proposals for the endorsement and inspection of courses build upon the improvements achieved through the requirement for initial teacher education to be endorsed by FENTO. The endorsement process will be strengthened through checks to ensure that:

- an ILP is in place following an initial assessment of each trainee teacher
- the trainee is maintaining a Professional Development Record
- there is a formalised mentoring system in place
- minimum observation time is upheld
- moderation procedures are appropriate
- there are clear links between the theoretical and practical and the generic and subject-specific elements of the course
- teacher educators themselves are suitably qualified to carry out their role.

The education of learning and skills sector teachers in England

Unlike the system for educating teachers to work in schools, where the Teacher Training Agency (TTA) and the General Teaching Council (GTC) for England have the responsibility for advising the Secretary of State concerning standards for Qualified Teacher Status (QTS) and funding issues, the learning and skills sector involves many different organisations. It is anticipated that the LLLSSC will facilitate a more holistic approach to the training of teachers in the sector.

The Institute for Learning (IfL)

It is mandatory for schoolteachers to register with the GTC for England, which sets professional standards, is responsible for teachers' CPD and offers teachers a sense of professional identity. Consideration is being given to making membership of the IfL mandatory for teachers in the sector.

Discussion points

1 How might the above proposals support greater equality of status between school-teachers and learning and skills sector teachers and trainers?
2 What are the possible benefits to the sector of the proposals?

Case studies of current practice: the Increased Flexibility Programme

This section briefly describes three differing models of IFP implementation.

Case study 1

This is the case of a tertiary college model where the IFP is thriving. Kempis College (the names of institutions and staff have been altered to ensure anonymity) is a tertiary (sixth form) college. Prior to the implementation of the IFP in September 2002, the college's involvement with the 14–16 age range was on a small scale. However, having strong links with local schools, from where their 16–19 students originate, it was a natural progression to explore the potential of offering a range of courses to younger learners.

The funding attached to the IFP was a significant factor in the college's decision to embrace the programme. It is, however, important to stress the belief stated by Paul, Senior Tutor in charge of 14–16 provision, that offering school students the opportunity to experience college life within the supportive framework of the IFP encourages young people to continue their studies beyond 16. He believed this to be particularly important for students working at Level 1, who would, through the IFP, have the chance to familiarise themselves with college life and would be less anxious about moving on to further education post-16.

Paul attributed the college's success with their 14–16 programme to their status as a tertiary college. Their core business is in the 16–19 age range, thereby providing them with more experience of younger learners than many FE colleges, which have students with a wider age range.

Anticipated problems with poor behaviour among the 14–16 cohort have not been realised. In a recent college survey the students described themselves as feeling more grown-up and they rate the opportunity to undertake work-related learning, which they consider more relevant to their future aspirations, very highly.

Most schools work with Kempis College to ensure the right student is selected for the right course. Unfortunately, some schools send students on inappropriate courses or select troublesome students for the programme. In order to stop such a situation occurring in future, the college has now tightened its selection procedures. These will include the requirement for individual learning agreements to be set up with Key Stage 3 targets for students to achieve prior to acceptance by the college.

Case study 2

This is a study of how an 11–16 Birmingham comprehensive, Hollybank School, has responded in an innovative way to the IFP by creating its own Construction Academy. Through sheer determination on the part of the school staff and with the support of the local LSC and a national construction company, the school opened the Construction Academy in September 2003. This was in response to the dearth of quality vocational training within the immediate area and the local and national skills shortage in construction trades.

Talking with Maurice, the construction teacher, it is clear why the course is proving a success. He comes from a construction background and can create a realistic work environment within his workshop. Raising of the students' self-esteem is very important to Maurice. The majority come without any aspirations or hope of success on the course. His most frequently uttered sentence is 'You *can* do it.' Maurice uses his own poor educational experiences to show how much he has achieved from a low base and that they can do it too.

Maurice uses every opportunity to draw parallels between real-life situations and the simulations in the workshop. One young person could not see why he needed to take his boots off to access a room across a carpeted area in the centre. Maurice helped him to realise that his future reputation as a craftsman would not be solely dependent upon his trade skills, but upon his courtesy and the way he took care of his clients' property. In this way Maurice aims to help students apply their theoretical knowledge through practical work and to ensure they appreciate the relevance of what he teaches for the world outside the school, regardless of the students' future occupations.

The success of the Construction Academy has encouraged the school to expand its IFP within the school environment to include hairdressing, horticulture and hydroponics for local 14–16 students. These facilities are available to the local community too, thereby encouraging lifelong learning for all.

Case study 3

This is a study of an LSDA action research project aimed at improving the 'customer' experience of 14–16 students in Motor Vehicle Maintenance at Riverford College. Prior to the implementation of the IFP this general FE college accepted 14–16-year-olds on an informal basis through personal contacts. Consequently there were many organisational issues to be addressed. For example, there was very little formal documentation and lines of communication were informal, breaking down if key personnel were absent.

Such a situation could not continue with the increased numbers involved via the IFP. The new 14–16 manager utilised the structure of the LSDA action research project (see LSDA in 'Useful websites' for details of these projects) to identify the key areas of need. It was clear that there were insufficient communication channels between the college and the feeder schools' staff, students and parents. To this end a range of procedures were set up, which included contracts between the college and schools, students and parents, newsletters and an awards programme.

Through using a systematic action research approach to evaluate the ongoing development of the IFP, the team were able to identify issues quickly and use the data provided by their research to trial different approaches. An example of this was the decision to trial lesson reports to enable the team to gain an overview of an individual student's progress and of the level and type of work being covered. This was in response to concerns about the work being too theoretical for the ability level of the students and to the expression of concern by lecturers concerning students' attitudes and behaviour patterns. By regularly completing these lesson reports the liaison/support worker was able to identify students with specific educational or other needs, which had not been reported by their schools, and to set up individual support programmes. The lesson reports also highlighted students who consistently showed commitment to their studies. The report system was welcomed by the schools for the ongoing and detailed information it offered with regard to learners' progress.

The IFP has brought a range of issues to the fore, such as the concern expressed by lecturers about the legal implications of having the 14–16 students in the college.

Involvement with the LSDA research projects has proved beneficial for Riverford College by encouraging a more proactive and reflective approach. Networking with other colleges involved in the awards has been an excellent way of achieving collegial support. Sharing good practice and discussing problems with others in similar situations has given the project team the confidence to address problems more openly.

Indicative tasks

1 Evaluate the strengths and weaknesses of the approaches taken in the three case studies provided here. Use the information on 14–19 issues provided to help you.

2 Research the approach taken by your institution to meet the needs of younger learners.

3 How does your institution's approach compare with those described here and what improvements can you suggest?

Future models for an integrated learning approach post-14

The 'Curriculum 2000' reforms were implemented following the Dearing Report (Dearing 1996) and *Qualifying for Success* (DfEE 1997). This followed a long period of stability with GCSE and 'A' Levels representing a well-understood system. Curriculum 2000 sought to broaden the post-16 curriculum and enhance the parity of esteem between academic and vocational qualifications. The proposals involved devising a 'National Qualifications Framework' (NQF), which would enable a comparison to be made between different qualifications with regard to level (see Chapter 5). The broader curriculum was achieved by encouraging the study of four 'AS' subjects in Year 12, reducing to three 'A2' subjects in Year 13. Key Skills qualifications (see Chapter 5) were introduced and Advanced GNVQ was re-named 'Vocational "A" Level'. Problems followed though as candidates were overwhelmed with assessments and awarding bodies struggled to manage the workload. Following problems with the marking of coursework in 2002, Mike Tomlinson was asked to report on the difficulties (DfES 2002c) and form a working group to respond to issues raised with a view to further reform of the post-16 curriculum.

Mike Tomlinson's interim report concerning 14–19 Reform (DfES 2003c) offers very clear indications for the future shape of 14–19 education in the UK. The working group identified key weaknesses, which need to be tackled. These include:

- low post-16 participation and achievement rates
- restrictive curriculum and assessment regimes
- confusing vocational qualifications
- a failure to acknowledge the importance of generic skills, knowledge and personal attributes.

The Diploma

Tomlinson proposed a diploma to replace the vast array of qualifications at present on offer to the 14–19 age range. The Diploma is expected to have four levels, namely Entry, Foundation, Intermediate and Advanced. The stress will be placed upon individual progression through these levels according to ability and personal choice on the part of the learner not age. Each Diploma shares a common core which forms the major part of the learner's programme.

Acknowledgement is made of the importance of mathematics, communication and ICT by incorporating these into the core of each level of the Diploma. The core also seeks to address the present lack of recognition given to achievements outside formal education by including the requirement for young people to undertake an 'extended project or personal challenge' (DfES 2003c: 22). Also emphasised is the need for the development of personal skills and attributes, for involvement by young people in their local community and for the undertaking of personal planning aided by an ILP.

Main learning is concerned with individual subjects and areas of learning important for the young person's progression into work or further study. Stress is laid upon the need to support such specialised learning as selected by the young person.

It is envisaged that there will be two types of Diploma: specialised and open. The latter would offer a mixed selection of subject areas, while the former would be orientated towards providing the knowledge and skills necessary for specific employment or further learning.

It is anticipated that eventually Modern Apprenticeships will be fully integrated into the reformed diploma framework, thereby also responding to the Green Paper's stress on parity of esteem for vocational training.

The timeframe for the introduction of Tomlinson's 14–19 Reform

It is important to note that the timeframe for these implementations is identified to be 10 years, a fact welcomed by those stakeholders responding to the Working Group's progress report published in July 2003. All too often in the past major educational reforms have been implemented without sufficient time for consultation.

According credibility to the Diploma

'A key problem with new qualifications in the past has been the credibility gap between the qualification and the worth attached to it by employers, HE and society in general'

(DfES 2003c: 40). Tomlinson is keen to address this issue by ensuring that the Diploma offers all the information necessary for selection for employment or further study.

Creating a valid and reliable assessment regime

Tomlinson stresses the importance of ensuring that the assessment of the Diploma meets stringent criteria by being relevant, non-burdensome for both teachers and students and flexible in response to the differing programmes of study.

Tomlinson: conclusions

In selecting the key words, which encapsulate the message of 14–19 Reform as envisaged by the interim report, *inclusiveness*, *challenge*, *quality* and *choice* are described by Tomlinson as characterising features of the proposed 14–19 phase. The various levels of diplomas and the breadth and depth of learning opportunities available should ensure that students of all abilities are encouraged to participate and to stretch themselves to their full potential.

That such educational reform is timely cannot be in doubt as evidenced by the reference in the report to the 20 to 25 per cent productivity gap between the UK and its competitors, reputedly caused through inadequate skills to meet the needs of the 'knowledge economy' (DfES 2003c: 9). The imperative for young people to embrace change with transferable skills, a broad knowledge base and appropriate, vocationally specific training is all too evident if the UK is to achieve a competitive edge in the global economy of the twenty-first century.

Discussion points

1   How do these proposals seek to enhance the status of vocational qualifications?

2   Given the evidence provided from current practice, evaluate the strengths and weaknesses of the proposals for 14–19 reform.

Summary

- The challenges of the twenty-first century demand the innovative reform of our education system.

- The Green Paper *14–19: extending opportunities, raising standards* (DfES 2002a) seeks to respond to these challenges through the creation of a 14–19 phase and the increased profile of vocational education.

- The Tomlinson Report (DfES 2003c) details the shape of the new phase and outlines how it will function.

- In conjunction with the Ofsted report (Ofsted 2003) on teacher education in the learning and skills sector, the DfES have set out detailed entitlements for trainee teachers, together with regulations concerning teacher educators.

- The IFP has brought challenges to both schools and colleges in terms of differing expectations and regulations. It has also made a positive difference to many young people, offering them a range of vocational and workplace experiences.

- The FENTO Teaching and Learning Standards relating to the 14–19 sector are shown in Figure 8.1. Full details of these standards are available at the FENTO website (see 'Useful websites').

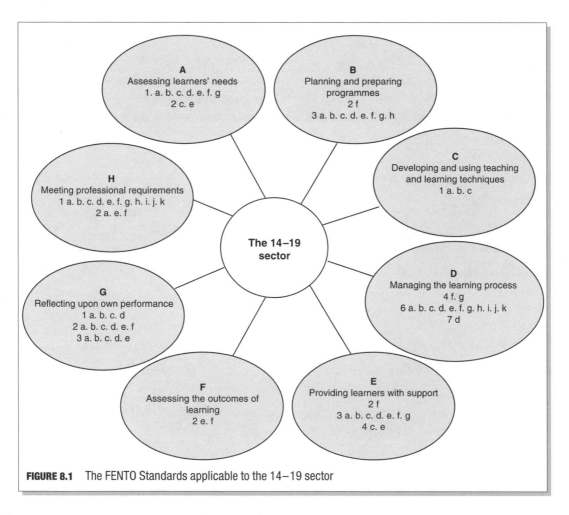

FIGURE 8.1   The FENTO Standards applicable to the 14–19 sector

Useful websites

www.dfes.gov.uk/qualifications/
The Increased Flexibility Programme (IFP) for 14–16-year-olds
Last accessed 7 May 2004

www.fento.ac.uk
The Further Education National Training Organisation (FENTO) website
Last accessed 7 May 2004

www.lsda.org.uk
Learning and Skills Development Agency (LSDA) with details of the action research programme and information on a range of 14–19 issues and initiatives.
Last accessed 7 May 2004

www.s4s.org.uk
Support for Success Quality Improvement Programme: information on action research projects taken in further education to improve students' retention and achievement.
Last accessed 7 May 2004

References

ATL (2002) *Response to the Green Paper: 14–19: extending opportunities, raising standards*. London: ATL.

BBC i (2004) *Blair Urges Students to Stay On*. http://news.bbc.co.uk/go/pr/fr/-/1/hi/uk_politics/3508214.stm – Accessed: 18/03/04.

Burnette, J. (2002) 'Opportunities for change: thoughts on the government's proposals for 14–19s'. *LSDA Briefing* May 3.

Coles, B. and MacDonald, R. F. (1996) 'From new vocationalism to the culture of enterprise', in Edwards, R., Sieminski, S. and Zeldin, D. (eds) *Adult Learners, Education and Training*. London: The Open University/Routledge.

Dearing, R. (1996) *Review of Qualifications for 16–19 Year Olds*. London: School Curriculum and Assessment Authority.

DfEE (1997) *Qualifying for Success: a consultation paper on the future of post-16 qualifications*. London: DfEE.

DfES (2002a) *14–19: extending opportunities, raising standards*. Consultation document. London: DfES.

DfES (2002b) *Success for All: reforming further education and training*. London: DfES.

DfES (2002c) *Inquiry into A Level Standards: final report*. London: DfES.

DfES (2003a) *14–19 Opportunity and Excellence*. London: DfES.

DfES (2003b) *Consultation on ITT in FE*. London: DfES.

DfES (2003c) *14–19 Reform Progress Report*. (DfES/ 0489/2003). London: DfES.

DfES (2004) *Interim Report of the Working Group on 14–19 Reform*. London: DfES.

East Midlands Learning and Skills Research Network (2002) *My Mates are Dead Jealous 'Cause They Don't Get to Come Here*. LSDA funded project. London: LSDA.

FENTO (1999) *Standards for Teaching and Supporting Learning in Further Education in England and Wales*. London: FENTO.

LSC (2003) *Guidance for FE Colleges Providing for Young Learners*. Coventry: LSC.

LSDA (2002) *Response: 14–19: extending opportunities, raising standards*. London: LSDA.

NIACE (2002) *14–19: extending opportunities, raising standards*. Leicester: NIACE.

Ofsted (2003) *The Initial Training of Further Education Teachers*. London: Ofsted.

TUC (2002) *Response to the DfES Green Paper*. Press release issued 1 July 2002.

Reflective practice and scholarship

Reflection and critical reasoning in educational contexts

Glynis Worrow

Introduction

THE PURPOSE OF this chapter is to introduce practising tutors to ways in which thinking skills, critical reasoning, argument and reflection could be used with their students. The chosen and referenced texts give the reader an idea of what they mean in an educational context and some of their uses in practice. The reader will need to understand that there is an enormous amount of literature on this subject and what is used here is deemed by the author to be the most relevant and explicit material for a beginner in this field.

Critical, creative and analytical thinking skills

'Learning how to think is, surely, what education is all about', the first line of Cowley's (2004) book sets the scene for this section on thinking skills. Clearly 'thinking' is a critical aspect of the learning process, yet it is rare that time is devoted to developing skills associated with using thinking processes for critical analysis and creativity. This chapter describes some of the skills required to apply critical thinking in the classroom.

The foundation for exploring the application of thinking skills was the vision of Socrates over 2,500 years ago. He devised a method of using probing questions that would seek evidence, examine reasoning and assumptions, analyse basic concepts and trace out implications, not only of what is said but also what is done. This method of questioning is now known as Socratic questioning; a process of critical thinking designed to question common beliefs and explanations in order to distinguish beliefs that are reasonable and logical from those which lack adequate evidence or foundation.

Plato and Aristotle suggested that things are often very different from what they appear to be and that only the trained mind can distinguish appearance from reality. The purpose of much academic writing is to use previous literature to formulate arguments to support or refute a theory. The skill is to identify relevant arguments and to compare and contrast these to develop a debate.

What are thinking skills? Some basic principles and definitions

According to Rochelle, thinking skills are ways of assessing and developing how we think and how we argue (Rochelle 2000). When we ask questions it is the use of thinking skills that helps us resolve whether answers are valid, invalid, possible, impossible, useful or useless. Rochelle points to three ways of thinking: **logically**, **laterally** and **illogically**; these are not mutually exclusive.

Logical thinking

Logic (including critical reasoning) infers conclusions from reasons and has two main types. **Deductive logic** establishes valid (true) conclusions from true reasons, for example:

- if it is raining the streets will be wet
- it is raining
- therefore the streets will be wet.

Inductive logic establishes probable inferences from evidence, for example:

- crow 1 is black
- crow 2 is black
- crow 3 is black
- therefore all crows are black
- therefore the next crow I see will be black.

Lateral thinking

Lateral thinking (see for example de Bono 1968) tries to accommodate the 'Imaginative Leap', in the sense that it aims to provide a solution (usually to a clear a practical problem) and can be roughly divided into three types: **insight thinking**, in which the process of thinking is not always apparent and the solution is arrived at suddenly; **sequential thinking**, in which the solution is reached by following a sequence of mistakes, improvement, modification and ideas; and **strategic thinking**, in which there is an attempt to find a directional policy, a definite solution is not the main aim. An example of strategic thinking could be:

- I need to stop the streets getting wet when it rains.
  Solution 1 – cover the streets with plastic
  Solution 2 – stop it raining

This can be productive (in that solutions are arrived at) but may not be helpful (the solution may be impracticable, useless etc.).

Illogic

According to Rochelle, illogic is an 'anything goes' system more often used by a persuader than a 'valid reasoner', for example:

- we need to change our employment laws to ensure unemployment will not rise
- tell everyone that without these changes millions will be unemployed
- everyone will then support the new laws.

Illogical arguments can carry much emotional force.

Reflective questions

1   Consider a recent problem that you had to solve. This could have been at work or at home. Reflect on how you solved the problem and categorise your method according to the ways of thinking described here. Would the solution have been more or less valid, possible or useful if you had used an alternative method?

2   Consider a problem that you have set for your learners. How did they approach a solution? You could set them a problem and ask them to describe the thoughts that they have in order to solve the problem. Could you improve their problem-solving skills by suggesting strategies based on the principles described here? One possibility is to devise some structured questions to guide their problem solving. This works well with the 'sequential thinking' method in which the 'prompt' questions are used to record mistakes and suggest ideas, improvements and modifications.

Critical reasoning, argument and evaluating reasoning

Thompson (1996) described critical reasoning as:

> centrally concerned with giving reasons for one's own beliefs and actions, analysing and evaluation of one's own and other people's reasoning, devising and constructing better reasoning. Common to these activities are certain . . . skills . . . and the ability to use language with clarity and discrimination.

Thompson justified the need for argument in order to 'persuade others to accept the truth of a statement, and one way of doing this is to offer them reasons or evidence in support of this statement. This is the essence of argument' (Thompson 1996: 6).

Rochelle (2000) considered that when we read, think or listen to words that are written or spoken, we need to consider their 'implicit truth'. Such 'truth' emerges from reasons or evidence offered in support. Common words that are used in this process are: therefore, so, thus, should, must, hence, cannot. These are usually referred to as **argument indicator** words or **conclusion indicators**. It is important to identify these as they inform us that reasoning processes are in action. **Reason indicator** words such as 'because' or 'since' can also be sought to identify where justifications for arguments are being made.

When assessing whether an argument is being presented, Thompson (1996) suggests using the following stages:

- Search for conclusion indicator words.

- There may be additional information providing a conclusion (leading to an assumption).

- If there's no explicit or implicit conclusion, then there is no argument.

- Try re-writing the passage with the conclusion at the end preceded by 'So' to convince yourself that an argument is present.

Here are some simple examples of argument – the indicators can be implicitly inferred or explicitly stated. In the following the indicators could be stated or not stated and are written in italics (if inferred, then an **assumption** must be made).

- The train is late. (*therefore*) It must have broken down.

- There are no students on the campus. (*therefore*) They must be on holiday.

Indicative task

Read these passages and consider whether they constitute an argument:

1 Achievement improves when ICT is used for teaching mathematics, so ICT must enhance students' learning.

2 Attendance at communication classes has improved this term. This has not been the case with numeracy.

From these examples the argument or reason may not be false but they are not necessarily the correct explanation for the observation; there is not necessarily a **causal** relationship between them, yet it is common to encounter spoken and written arguments that attempt to draw valid conclusions. Identifying these flaws in spoken arguments takes practice, however, looking through written documents and texts is more straightforward. Thompson (1996) identifies four ways in which arguments can be flawed:

- General conclusions may be drawn from an isolated example, although the evidence is strong (for example, a neighbour's car has broken down, therefore all cars of that make will break down).

- The argument may be based on insufficient evidence.

- Because two things occur together, there is an assumption that one has caused the other (the road is slippery, so it must have rained recently).

- An inappropriate analogy may be drawn (for example, children who play video games demonstrate poor concentration in class).

Once conclusions have been identified (whether explicit, or implicit), they should be evaluated against the points above to determine if they constitute valid conclusions and therefore whether the argument is valid. In order to make this judgement, you may rely on your experience (comments based on your experience must be justified with evidence) and the provenance of the information; what are the qualifications, reputation and experience of the people or organisations making the statements? If you identify a flawed argument, the reasons for the flaws must be stated in your evaluation.

The summary in Table 9.1 provides a very useful framework for analysis and evaluation.

TABLE 9.1 Summary framework for the analysis and evaluation of an argument (*Source*: adapted from Thompson 1996: 99/100)

Analysing	Evaluating
1. Identify the conclusion and reasons using conclusion and reason indicators.	5. Evaluate the truth of reasons and assumptions and seek further information if necessary.
2. Confirm what the passage is trying to ask me to accept or believe.	6. Assess the provenance of the information.
3. Identify the reasons and evidence provided in order to persuade me to believe this.	7. Is there any additional evidence which strengthens or weakens the conclusion?
4. Identify unstated assumptions.	8. How plausible is the explanation?
	9. How appropriate are the comparisons made?
	10. Can you draw conclusions from the passage and do these reveal any false reasoning by the author?
	11. Are general (well-accepted) principles involved? If so, comment on the applicability of these.
	12. Is the conclusion well supported by the reasoning? If so how? If not, in what way is it flawed?

Indicative task

Look at a report, in three different newspapers, on an important issue that has been written by different reporters but all looking at the same issue.

As you read try to find words, such as 'so', 'should' etc., that the authors have used to argue their case and/or conclude their reports.

1   What evidence have they given to support their conclusions?

2   Is their evidence logical? State why you believe this is the case giving reasons.

3   Is their evidence illogical? State why you think this is the case giving reasons.

4   If you have time, try to apply the framework illustrated in Table 9.1 and comment on the validity of each article in terms of the arguments stated.

The challenge is to incorporate these critical thinking skills into classroom practice. Blagg *et al.* (1988) suggest that thinking skills are linked to cognitive resources; before critical thinking can take place, students need to have an understanding of and practice in three domains, namely concepts, skills and knowledge and verbal tools. Here are some examples:

- **Concepts**

    colour

    shape

    volume

    number

    size

    metaphor

    simile

    analogy

- **Skills and knowledge**

    working precisely and accurately

    recognising and interpreting clues and reference points

    labelling, coding and abbreviating

    understanding universal codes and conventions

    following instructions accurately

    describing, comparing and classifying

    being able to consider differing viewpoints and feelings

    understanding the nature of bias and prejudice

    knowing techniques to aid memorising, like visualising, rehearsing, elaborating and mnemonics

■ **Verbal tools**

> possessing the precise verbal tools to name things we observe, experience and feel.

> (Blagg 1988: 12–13)

Reflective questions

1 Think of examples of where you enable your students to practise and demonstrate these skills.

2 List the possible places within your lessons that this takes place.

The premise here is that there will be certain prerequisites to enable your learners to develop their thinking skills. For example, it is difficult to present an argument for and against a particular business strategy unless the learner has an understanding of the basic economic principles (the **concepts**) involved, the ability to interpret and classify information for and against the argument (**skills and knowledge**) and the **verbal tools** to be able to bring relevant experience to the problem.

A possible starting point for the development of thinking skills is to make an assessment of the concepts, skills and knowledge and verbal tools required and then to assess the competence of your learners in these areas. If deficiencies are identified, these need to be remedied before progressing to the next stage.

Although 'thinking' appears to be a very abstract exercise, it is nonetheless a skill that can be broken down into different components. Stiggins *et al.* (1988) provided a framework in which to develop the process of critical thinking. The framework can be used as a planning tool for lessons, or with some modifications to take into account the background of the learners and the discipline, as a teaching resource. The framework requires tasks to be completed in relation to five components, namely recall, analysis, comparison, inference and evaluation. Table 9.2 (adapted from Stiggins *et al.* 1988) demonstrates how the framework can be used for developing the critical analysis of learning theory. The 'Bloom categories' mentioned in Table 9.2 refer to Bloom's taxonomy of educational objectives (Bloom 1956).

Indicative task

1 Study Table 9.2 to clarify the definitions of the five components.

2 Use the sample trigger words (or alternatives if appropriate) to plan a lesson designed to develop the critical thinking skills of your learners in relation to a particular topic.

3 Complete the 'sample questions and tasks' appropriate to developing each component.

4 Devise teaching resources to support your learners with appropriate tasks for each component.

TABLE 9.2 A framework for the critical analysis of learning theory (*Source*: adapted from Stiggins *et al.* 1988)

Category	Recall	Analysis	Comparison	Inference	Evaluation
Description	Remembering, recognising or repeating key facts and definitions from previous class notes or other information that has already been provided	Understanding the relationship between the whole and its component parts and between cause and effect; understanding how things work and how the parts of something fit together; getting notes from other sources. Analysis means structuring knowledge in new ways	Being able to explain how things are similar and how they are different. Simple comparisons are based on a small number of obvious attributes. Complex comparisons require an examination of a more extensive set of attributes. Comparisons start with the whole/part relationships and then carry them a step further	Being able to reason and explain evidence both inductively or deductively. In deductive tasks students reason from generalisations to specific instances and are asked to recognise or explain the evidence. In inductive tasks students are given the details or evidence and they are then required to relate and integrate the information and come up with the generalisation	Expressing and defending opinion. Evaluation tasks require students to judge quality, credibility, worth or practicality using established criteria and explain how the criteria are met or not met
Sample trigger words	Define List Label What When Identify Who	Analyse How it works How is it used? Give an example	Compare Contrast How are things different? How are things alike? Distinguish	Synthesise Use evidence Create Predict Conclude Apply	Judge Justify Evaluate Defend Best solution

Sample questions and tasks				
Define behaviourist, cognitivist and humanistic principles List the characteristics of each of the above schools When is learning theory beneficial to a teacher? What is learning theory? Identify some learning theorists relevant to your teaching Who is the theorist known for their theory of Person Centred Education?	Analyse humanistic theories of learning in their application to your own learning and teaching environment Give an example of how the humanistic theory affects your teaching Repeat this exercise for the behaviourist school	Compare and contrast the uses of both humanistic and behaviourist schools of thought in a teaching and learning situation What are the similarities and differences between these theories?	Using your lesson plan and rationale for teaching, predict the outcome of using behaviourist and humanistic principles within your lessons Apply these theories of learning from these schools in an observed/peer-group teaching session Having taught this lesson, what are your conclusions regarding the value of these principles to teaching and learning?	First justify the use of humanistic and then behaviourist principles in your teaching What are the strengths and weaknesses of using teaching methods based on these principles? Defend the tenet that 'humanistic principles are inherently more valuable in teaching than behaviourist principles'
Corresponding Bloom categories				
Knowledge Comprehension	Analysis	Analys s	Application Synthesis	Synthesis Evaluation

Myers (cited in Brookfield 1987: 82) demonstrates the use of critical thinking skills with adult learners. He suggests that students should be exposed to 'critical teaching', where the tutor could 'begin each class with a problem, followed by creative silence periods used for reflection and to ponder new perspectives'. He goes further to suggest that this time might also be used for learners to discuss their feelings and anxieties and for tutors and students to recognise that all members of the group will need to be involved in this process, however the outcome may be uncertain. These uncertainties may dissuade many teachers from using this technique in practice, however there are times in the course of a programme of study where tutors could and should expose their students to using thinking skills and reflection to aid their learning.

Ginnis (2002) also shows, through teachers' practice, how tutors might explicitly demonstrate their uses of thinking and other skills that are to be developed in a lesson. He describes lessons, in a school environment, using specific topics and indicating the areas of thinking, emotional intelligence, fun, independence, interdependence etc. together with what he describes as 'particulars', that show whether students will be working individually, listening, looking, reading or doing group work etc. This simplistic yet important way of logging what is to be covered during a lesson is something that tutors of students of all ages could benefit from.

Reflection in an educational context

The importance of an individual's personal experience to the learning process has been emphasised above. Many assignments for teacher training or professional development programmes require theory to be set in the context of practice. The theory can be obtained from taught sessions and resources, but the practice is very personal and can only be discussed following a consideration of past events (see for example Moon 1999). Given that remembering specific details of events can be difficult, it's useful to have a framework within which to record and discuss past experience. The starting point for this is usually to have a means of recording experiences; these data will form the evidence for the writing of reflective accounts. The evidence could be in the form of a video, or an audio tape of a conversation, but more commonly it involves keeping a reflective diary. This should be a regular record of events, accordingly; a small notebook is particularly useful so that entries can be made whenever time is available.

The problem is deciding what to reflect upon and how to express the issues. Commonly, reflective diaries submitted as part of an assessment tend to focus on daily activities and be highly descriptive of events, rather than evaluative. Try to focus on 'critical incidents', for example. These don't have to be crises, but incidents or problems that result in the formulation of a strategy to deal with them. For example, a group may have difficulty following a particular activity. Comments in the reflective diary could focus on what the signs of difficulty were, what possible strategies could be adopted to remedy the situation, which you chose and why and what the learning points are from the incident to inform future practice. Record events producing discomfort, dissatisfaction or uncertainty (Boud *et al.* 1985). The 'experience of surprise' described by Schon (1992) in his seminal work can be useful to record. Schon considered that there was insufficient focus on process (how an end is achieved, rather than the end itself) and that research was too often divorced from practice.

Although the emphasis here is on teachers reflecting on their own practice as a means of professional development, reflection can be a very useful tool in the classroom. The critical role of experience in the learning process is discussed in Chapter 4; encouraging the use of reflective techniques is central to integrating experience within learning.

Brookfield (1995) suggests that there are four 'critical lenses' that teachers should use for reflection. These are:

- by their autobiographies as teachers and learners
- through their students' eyes
- their colleagues' perceptions
- the theoretical literature.

Reflective question

If you have completed some reflective writing, read it again and consider whether have you addressed these different lenses? Make a note in your reflective diary to address these perspectives when making entries.

To be able to reflect, self-awareness enables learners to analyse their feelings. It is only at the point where there is a recognition of what 'caused' a problem or critical incident and the affect that this has had on them, together with their part in it, that changes in future practice can be addressed. Boud *et al.* (1985) suggest that reflection can be used as a learning tool, however before this can begin students should be given the skills to reflect. These identified skills are a knowledge of self-awareness, description, critical analysis, synthesis and evaluation. In the context of reflection, these terms can be defined as follows:

- **Self-awareness** constitutes an appreciation of one's own strengths and weaknesses, preferred learning styles and relationship with individuals and the community.
- **Description** involves being able to describe what actually happened in an objective way. It is suggested that learning through reflection can only take place by writing down or verbalising observations.
- **Critical analysis** then requires students to look at each component of the situation in an objective way. Look at the issues and explore alternative actions or strategies.

- **Synthesis** is looking for new knowledge to add to what was previously known. It requires students to be imaginative and creative, so developing new perspectives.

- **Evaluation** is the making of judgements. These judgements should be made using the description, critical analysis and synthesis to form a new perspective.

Using a reflection process as an aid for developing practice

The above discussion identifies features and prerequisites of the reflection process. Reflective accounts are very common in FE teacher training courses, so it is often necessary to recount reflections on practice. Using a **model of reflection** helps to structure reflective accounts and can be a very useful tool to inform the reflection process itself. The models have similarities and differences, but it's worth choosing a model that fits the characteristics of your setting. Begin your account by justifying your choice of model and summarise its features. Nurse education has been particularly proactive at devising models and these are all applicable to education contexts.

There are various sources of evidence for your account. Use evidence from your learners: observe their reactions in class; use their responses to written activities; speak to them; use their course evaluations. Consider how you're feeling about their reactions. Schon (1992) called this process **reflection-in-action**; essentially considering events as they happen. This is in contrast with his **reflection-on-action**; considering events after they have happened. He considered this particularly useful for developing as a 'reflective practitioner'.

Consider other sources of evidence to help with reflective accounts: ask peers for constructive comments regarding your teaching; video yourself teaching; observe other teachers teaching. When you watch yourself, what were you doing? At the same time what were the students doing? Consider others as sources of evidence including your line manager, other stakeholders, your tutor and external moderators.

Johns' model of reflection

This model (adapted from Johns 1993) provides a particularly useful framework for structuring a reflective account:

- Phenomenon – cue questions to describe the experience
  - Describe the positive/negative experience.

- Causal
  - What were the factors that contributed to it?

- Context
  - What was the history or background to the experience?
  - What are the processes for reflection in the experience?

- Reflection
  - What was I trying to achieve?

- What actions did I take?
- Why did I intervene as I did?
- What were the consequences of my actions for myself, my learners and others?
- How did I feel during the process? How did my learners and others feel? How did I know how they felt?
- Why did it work/not work so well? Make an objective list of factors.
- What external factors influenced your decision?
- What sources of knowledge should or did influence your decision?

■ Alternative actions
- How could I have acted differently?
- What consequences would these actions have had?

■ Learning
- How do I feel about it now?
- What did I learn from it?
- What would I do differently now as a result of this experience?

Gibbs' model of reflection

Gibbs (1988) described a reflective cycle (see Figure 9.1). This emphasises the need to continue to reflect on actions in order to develop professionally. If you modify a lesson as a result of reflecting, does the change have the desired effect? Would you use the same strategy again? This is the concept of 'double loop learning'; the practice of reflection is a very useful way of developing this skill.

Reflective questions

1 How do you enable your students to reflect on their learning?

2 Could you show an example of the use of a reflective model in your lesson plans?

3 What changes could you make to you teaching to incorporate aspects of the models of reflection described above?

Problem solving – a toolkit

The Old English derivation of the word 'problem' described a riddle or question for academic discussion, not necessarily something that is potentially harmful. Problems relevant to professional practice in education may relate to: teaching methodology; learner management; course administration; working with colleagues; or studying for professional qualifications, for example. Problem-solving skills are not only useful for teachers, but a valuable addition to the development of learners' generic skills.

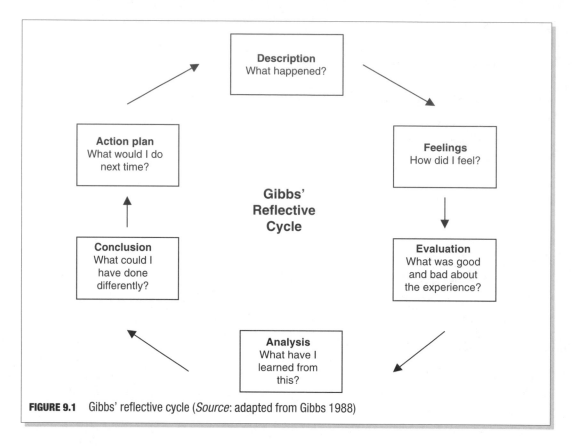

FIGURE 9.1 Gibbs' reflective cycle (*Source*: adapted from Gibbs 1988)

Here is a possible problem-solving strategy:

- Interpret the problem in question. Use all of the senses to do this. Thinking, feeling, the actual facts or truths, assumptions etc.
- Compare this to other experiences you/your learners have had.
- Do you need further information? Where will you get it? Who will you get it from?
- When you have this information you will need to translate this problem into a task with clear goals – visualise what this task looks like.
- Are there other opinions or options you can think of that you could benefit from?
- Have there been similar problems for others that you could refer to? How did they resolve it?
- Have you thought through all of the options? You might brainstorm these options and their possible conclusions.
- Look at the options and select the appropriate course of action.
- Set the action in motion.
- Check your actions as you go along. Reflect on your chosen action and monitor the results – is it working? Do you have an alternative strategy to fall back on?

- Do you need to revise the action?
- Could you use this approach in other situations?
- Can you finally reflect on the outcome and draw conclusions for its use for yourself?

Having arrived at a solution to the problem, would you use the same strategy again, or have you learnt from your solution such that you can improve your problem-solving skills in the future? You may need to seek feedback from others to establish this point.

Summary

- Critical thinking skills have their origins in the works of Socrates, who developed a method of reasoning based on questioning in order to challenge common beliefs and explanations.
- According to Rochelle (2000) thinking skills are ways of assessing and developing how we think and how we argue.
- Thompson (1996) defined critical reasoning as centrally concerned with giving reasons for one's own beliefs and actions, analysing and evaluation of one's own and other people's reasoning, devising and constructing better reasoning. Common to these activities are certain . . . skills . . . and the ability to use language with clarity and discrimination.
- Reflection in an educational context involves recording observations, followed by evaluation, analysis and action planning in order to improve future practice.
- A model for problem solving is provided, which involves analysing the problem, setting manageable goals and producing an action plan.
- The FENTO Teaching and Learning Standards relating to reflection and critical reasoning are shown in Figure 9.2. Full details of these standards are available, at the FENTO website (see 'Useful websites').

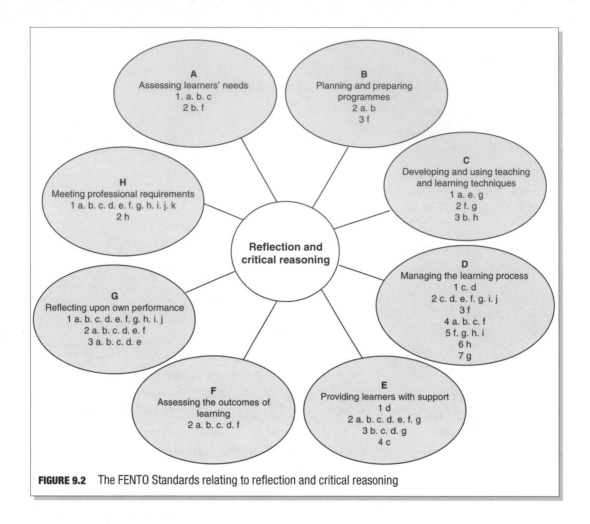

FIGURE 9.2   The FENTO Standards relating to reflection and critical reasoning

Useful websites

www.austhink.org/Default.htm

Resources and links on critical thinking

Last accessed 7 May 2004

www.city.londonmet.ac.uk/deliberations/pbl/urls.html

Links to problem-based learning websites

Last accessed 7 May 2004

www.critical-learning.co.uk/html/approaches.html

Resources on approaches to learning, including problem-based learning

Last accessed 7 May 2004

www.criticalthinking.org

Resources and links on critical thinking

Last accessed 7 May 2004

www.escalate.ac.uk/exchange/Reflection/index.php
A discussion of reflection in educational contexts
Last accessed 7 May 2004

www.fento.ac.uk
The Further Educational National Training Organisation (FENTO) website
Last accessed 7 May 2004

www.itslifejimbutnotasweknowit.org.uk/bib_145.htm
A bibliography on reflective practice, including links
Last accessed 7 May 2004

www.ncteam.ac.uk/projects/fdtl/fdtl4/pbl/index.htm
Problem Based Learning Project Network
Last accessed 7 May 2004

www.uefap.co.uk/reading/readfram.htm
Using English for Academic Purposes website
Last accessed 7 May 2004

References

Blagg, N., Ballinger, M. and Gardner, R. (1988) *Somerset Thinking Skills Course*. Somerset: Somerset County Council and Blackwell.

Bloom, B. S. (ed.) (1956) *Taxonomy of Educational Objectives, the classification of educational goals. Handbook I: Cognitive domain*. New York: McKay.

Boud, D., Keogh, R. and Walker, D. (1985) *Reflection: turning experience into learning*. London: Kogan Page.

Brookfield, S. D. (1987) *Developing Critical Thinkers*. Milton Keynes: Open University Press.

Brookfield, S. D. (1995) *Becoming a Critically Reflective Teacher*. San Francisco, CA: Jossey-Bass.

Cowley, S. (2004) *Getting the Buggers to Think*. London: Continuum.

de Bono, E. (1968) *A Five Day Course in Thinking*. Harmondsworth. Penguin.

Gibbs, G. (1988) *Learning by Doing: a guide to teaching and learning methods*. Oxford: Further Education Unit, Oxford Polytechnic.

Ginnis, P. (2002) *The Teacher's Toolkit*. Glasgow: Crown House.

Johns, C. (1993) 'Professional supervision', *Journal of Nursing Management* **1**, 9–18.

Moon, J. (1999) *Reflection in Learning and Professional Development*. London: Kogan Page.

Rochelle, G. (2000) *An Introduction to Philosophy in Schools Book 1*. Corby: First and Best in Education.

Schon, D. (1992) *The Reflective Practitioner*. San Francisco, CA: Jossey-Bass.

Stiggins, R. J., Rubel, E. and Quellmalz, E. S. (1988) *Measuring Thinking Skills in the Classroom*. Washington, DC: NEA Professional Library.

Thompson, A. (1996) *Critical Reasoning*. London: Routledge.

Research in professional practice

Catherine Matheson and David Matheson

Introduction

FOR SOME YEARS now, teachers in further education, like their counterparts in schools, have been regularly exhorted to become practitioner researchers. The aim of this chapter is to introduce the reader to some basic techniques in practitioner research and to offer guidance on how to put these into practice.

The notion of researching one's own practice goes back, informally at least, to the time when teachers first became aware that their practice need not be fixed. This was the moment when teachers began to realise that they were not obliged to teach as they themselves had been taught (see for example Wells (1918) for a vivid description of the stultifying effect of the teacher who teaches as he was taught and as his own teachers before him were taught) but that they could, at least to a degree, be inventive and imaginative in their pedagogy. Depending on one's perspective and preference, this can take us back at least to the great nineteenth-century headmaster of Uppingham School, Edward Thring, who revised and reformed the pedagogy of his establishment or to such reformers as Thomas Arnold of Rugby School. Arnold improved diet and housing, moral tone and discipline with a new way of using the prefect system. He widened the curriculum to included mathematics and languages along with Greek and Latin; he thought about more efficient teaching methods in order to get the interest of the pupils (Staunton 1877).

These, however, were lone figures and their methods lacked a significant following until progressive education flourished in the twentieth century. However, they showed a willingness to examine their own practice, ascertain where improvement was needed, develop a strategy for improvement and not only put it into practice but also amass evidence to show to others how well it had worked.

Since the Second World War, practitioner research and evidence-based practice has come to signify a set of well-defined processes whereby the practitioner – no longer isolated as were Thring and Arnold, but working in terms of accepted and established practice – identifies a problem or a situation and sets about increasing his/her understanding of it. The problem or situation is very much a personal decision. The overall aim of the process of some varieties of practitioner research is to develop a solution to the problem or an improvement to the situation and to evaluate its effectiveness. It has become a focus of the Teacher Training Agency and as TTA funding was lost from the highly successful Best Practice Scholarships in 2003 (many of which were devoted to teachers researching their own practice; Fryer 2004), the General Teaching Council (GTC) for England's identified practitioner research as a role for the emergent Teacher Learning Academy (see 'Useful websites').

At this point a distinction needs to be made between two senses of practitioner research. One is concerned simply with research carried out by a person who happens to be a practitioner and which is hoped to have a positive influence (again, this is a personal opinion) on his/her practice, although this may be difficult to quantify. For example, a research project investigating the impact of learners' socio-economic or cultural circumstances on learning may enable the teacher to become more sensitive to their needs, but it would be difficult to directly measure the effect on their learners.

A second concerns itself explicitly with researching what goes on in the course of *one's own* practice. It is principally with this and with one variety of it – action research – that we are concerned in this chapter.

Action research

'Action research has been traditionally defined as an approach to research that is based on a collaborative problem-solving relationship between researcher and client, which aims at both solving a problem and generating new knowledge' (Coghlan 2003: 452). Action research demands a degree of involvement with the 'clients' that is not needed in other forms of insider research (research carried out by someone within their own role), such as contextualising policy and organisational analysis. From this alone, it results in ethical issues which require particular attention; these will be discussed later in this chapter.

Action research 'is an increasingly popular approach among small-scale researchers in the social sciences (education, health and social care) in order to improve practice. It offers a systematic approach to the definition, solution and evaluation of problems and concerns' (Blaxter *et al.* 2001: 67). Currently optional, developments in professional practice may result in teachers having to use action research; it is debatable whether this is a valid strategy given the nature of action research.

The idea of action research is attributed to Lewin who in 1946 coined the term 'action research' and used it as a methodology to investigate and improve major social problems and bring about social change based on democratic principles (Kemmis 1993; Hopkins 1995). Lewin had perhaps grander ideas than the average modern practitioner seeking to improve his/her practice in the classroom or workshop but his fundamental idea still pertains. For Lewin and his associates, action research involves 'a cyclical process of diagnosing a change situation or a problem, planning, gathering data, taking

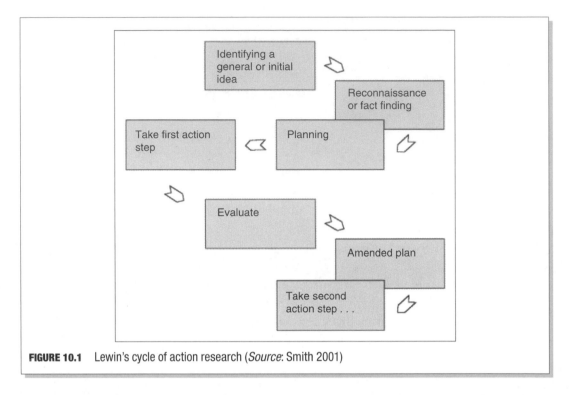

FIGURE 10.1 Lewin's cycle of action research (*Source*: Smith 2001)

action and then fact-finding about the results of that action in order to plan and take further action' (Coghlan 2003: 452).

Nunes and McPherson (2003: 431) suggest the notion of the spiral framework, as shown in Figure 10.1, where one begins by diagnosing a problem or an issue. One then plans action, takes action and finally evaluates the action before conducting a second round of diagnosis and each of the subsequent steps. This iterative process is at the heart of Lewin's vision of action research. The assumption is that time is available to repeat the cycle. There is also an assumption that the plan is not altered during the cycle. In this respect, it is somewhat naïve, if not dangerous. It is naïve in the sense that few practitioners would be content, or able to sit back and watch a process unfold without intervening. It is dangerous in the sense that it implies that even if the project appears to be going completely awry, one should wait until the evaluation phase before doing anything about it. This is hardly a characteristic of professional practice.

In some respects, Lewin's notion of action research resembles Kolb's learning cycle (see Figure 10.2), which is itself derived from Lewin's cycle of adult learning (Atherton 2002).

Discussion point

Comment on the effect of being an 'insider' as in the case of action research, compared with being an 'outsider' when researching another organisation, for example.

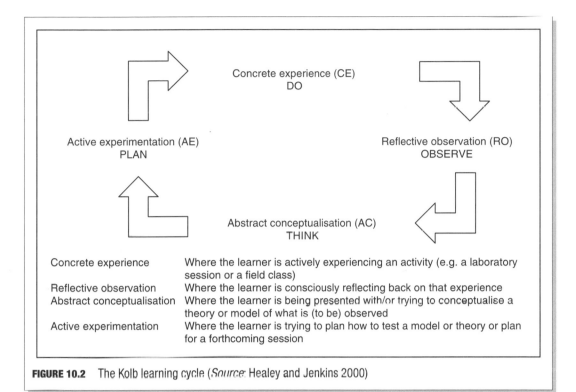

Concrete experience (CE)
DO

Active experimentation (AE)
PLAN

Reflective observation (RO)
OBSERVE

Abstract conceptualisation (AC)
THINK

Concrete experience	Where the learner is actively experiencing an activity (e.g. a laboratory session or a field class)
Reflective observation	Where the learner is consciously reflecting back on that experience
Abstract conceptualisation	Where the learner is being presented with/or trying to conceptualise a theory or model of what is (to be) observed
Active experimentation	Where the learner is trying to plan how to test a model or theory or plan for a forthcoming session

FIGURE 10.2 The Kolb learning cycle (*Source:* Healey and Jenkins 2000)

Planning action research

Coghlan and Casey (2001) stated that 'action research is an approach to research which aims at taking action and creating knowledge or theory about that action' (p. 676). 'It simultaneously involves generating data and analysis together with actions aimed at transforming the situation in democratic directions. It is context-bound producing practical solutions and new knowledge' (Greenwood and Levin 1998: 50). What it does, by definition, is to impinge directly on the lives of those involved in it. It is no exaggeration to say that an action research project can and will change lives, perhaps only to a small degree, perhaps fundamentally; if a teacher's practice changes as a result of research, there will inevitably be an effect on their learners. With this major caveat in mind, how does one begin the planning of such an undertaking?

To engage in the 'type of inquiry that is fluid, emergent and cyclical' (Christenson *et al.* 2002: 260) requires careful preparation. One approach is that advocated by Costello (2003) which consists primarily of signing on at the local Higher Education Institution and taking a module involving action research! While there is an undoubted appeal in this approach, it may be impractical to engage in a formal programme for a variety of reasons. So where should you start?

Every action research project has a similar series of steps:

1 Identify issue

2 Develop aim and objectives/research questions

3 Literature search

4 Develop action plan

5 Implement action plan

6 Evaluate action

7 Revise/repeat steps 1, 2, 3 and 4.

Figure 10.3 shows how these might be arranged. However, nothing prevents steps 1, 2 and 3 being arranged in the order 3, 1, 2. For example, it is not uncommon that reading the literature highlights a relevant issue. Additionally, it is all too easy to assume that how things have always been done is the only way to do them and that there are no alternatives. Reading the literature can be revealing in this respect. This can be an

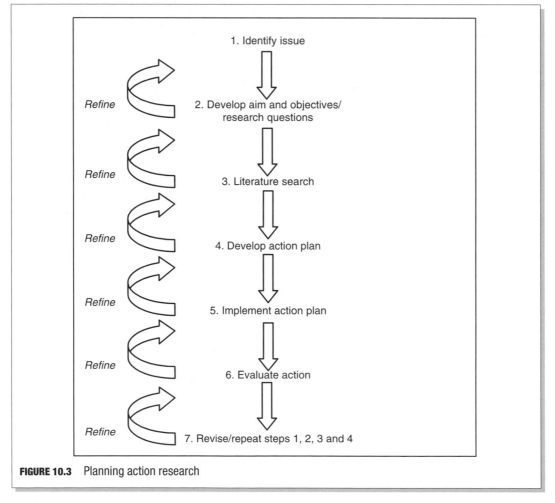

FIGURE 10.3 Planning action research

advantage of a formal programme as library access is usually available, however the Internet is an extremely valuable resource for this purpose.

Discussion points

If you have been the subject of research, what were your feelings about the involvement? Did it change you in any way?

The literature

Education has the wonderful attribute that much, if not most, of its literature is accessible. Macintyre (2000) eulogises over the literature and reminds us that the literature can help us pinpoint a topic 'which would be both relevant and interesting for the researcher and contextually available' (p. 3). This is potentially crucial when undertaking a research project.

Macintyre (2000) also comments that the literature is valuable in order to focus our thinking. It lets us see what others have done and gives us examples to follow, or in some cases to avoid. The literature allows us to build on what has already been done (Brown 1990; Stark 1998) and in doing so it gives our research academic credibility since it allows us to show how our present work is extending knowledge. This term sounds rather grander than it is in reality. Anything which has not been done before extends knowledge. Using someone else's techniques in a new situation – perfectly acceptable provided you don't pretend it's your own invention and you do this by crediting the source – extends knowledge. Extension of knowledge is frequently quite small in both its impact and its scope.

A major issue with the literature concerns just how much of it should be used. Searching the literature can be very time consuming and too much information can be overwhelming, however it is important to do sufficient literature work to avoid missing any crucial information. Enough is needed to demonstrate a reasonable grip on the topic and on related topics. Use not only books (possibly by selecting individual chapters) but also articles in refereed journals. Novice researchers commonly avoid journal articles in the mistaken belief that they are difficult to comprehend. Certainly some are, but most are not. What using journal articles demonstrates is that others' writing is read at first hand, rather than someone else's interpretation. Journal articles are where researchers publish their results; books are a common place for others to discuss them. Anyone can publish in journals and the results of action research projects are certainly appropriate. There are also many serious Internet sources. Many websites present peer-reviewed material, though some do not, so judgement must be exercised when considering the validity of work. The lesser sources will use polemic and assertion, while the better sources will use argument and evidence. Many researchers also present their findings at conferences and a vast number of conference papers are lodged on the Education-line database (see 'Useful websites').

Finally don't assume that *new* literature means *better* literature and that *old* means *worse*. *Old* means historical and nothing more. There are old publications, even from thousands of years ago (such as those of Plato), which might well be relevant to your research. Relevancy is the key, not age. Do remember, however, that every publication is a product of its age and may well refer to events as contemporary, but which from the present perspective are very much historical.

Discussion point

List as many different types of information source as you can. Which ones are most accessible to you?

The aim and the research questions

The aim is simply what one sets out to achieve, or to investigate. It is the direction in which one travels. For example, a teacher using action research to examine issues around numeracy in his or her class might have as the aim *to investigate improving numeracy in a pre-nursing course*. The research questions (see Lewis and Munn 1997) are much more the nuts and bolts of what you are attempting to do. They are the steps on the way towards achieving the aim. One thing to bear in mind though is that the initial research questions (and indeed the aim) may well not be the final ones.

As Sally Brown (1990) reminds us, even the most seasoned researchers can get carried away with ideas of what is possible in a given time period; it is easy to get too ambitious or otherwise unrealistic and have to curb enthusiasm in the light of reality. However, as Brown further states, such modifications have to be done *consciously*.

For the numeracy example above, research questions might be as follows:

1   What is the level of numeracy at the start of the course?

2   What is the attitude of students towards numeracy at the start of the course?

3   What factors during the course affected the students' numeracy and their attitudes towards numeracy?

Notice the use of two base points (questions 1 and 2) while question 3 highlights areas that can be further investigated either with this cohort or with a successor cohort. The action here is the gathering of evidence as to what affects student numeracy. Once this is achieved then teaching materials can be modified and at that point, a further piece of action research can be carried out to determine whether the modifications have been successful.

Data collection

Data can be collected in a range of ways, however, whatever approach is taken, it needs to relate to the research questions. Also of great importance is to only collect data that have some bearing on the research questions. If the age of the respondents to a questionnaire has no bearing on the research questions, then why ask for it? It may be useful as background material on the participants or it may be wholly irrelevant. If you decide to ask for it, make sure you know why you are doing so. Ethnicity is similar but more complex. While there is only one way to label age, there are umpteen ways to label ethnicity and none is really satisfactory. It is safer, if you need to ask for ethnicity, to ask people to say what ethnic group they feel they belong to . . . and to permit 'don't know' as a response. This may lead to a plethora of categories but at least no one will feel offended that their group has been left out.

Interviews can be structured, semi-structured or unstructured. Structured interviews are really just questionnaires that are delivered orally. The order of the questions is fixed for all participants. Semi-structured interviews have a more fluid approach. Opening questions may be the same for all participants. Everyone will cover the same questions or topics but the order can be allowed to vary to suit the participant. Semi-structured interviews resemble a conversation more than do structured interviews. Unstructured interviews are individual conversations around a topic where the conversation goes where it will, within the broad confines of the topic in hand. Questions may be closed, in that there is a limited range of responses possible and the respondent chooses from a list, or open, in that the respondent is free to say whatever she or he feels replies to the question. For more information on research interviews see Drever (1995) and Gillham (2000).

Questionnaires (see Munn and Drever 1995), observations (see Simpson and Tuson 1995) and tests are some of the many alternatives to interviews. Whichever approach is taken, it is essential to pilot the research instrument. An interview is not just a series of questions and neither is a questionnaire. For one thing, the question you think you are asking may not always be the question your respondent hears and the one they hear may not be the one they answer. Piloting with respondents drawn from as close a group as possible to the one you will be examining – and this means trying out the instrument on them and discussing with them what they felt about it – will significantly reduce the chances of problems arising later. Similarly with observations, investigate what you are going to observe and make a conscious decision on how you are going to observe it. Decide whether your observations are going to be structured or not. Decide what you are looking for and from whom; it is well nigh impossible to observe a whole group and indeed observing a couple of individuals can be challenging (Bell 2002).

Data analysis

Data analysis is an essential part of planning the action research. It is important to determine how the data will be analysed before the research begins as additional skills may be needed and the process of considering the analysis method can modify the research plan.

There are entire volumes devoted to research methods which give much space to data analysis. Cohen and Manion (1996) and Bell (2002) are good examples which are useful for the beginning researcher. Data analysis can be complicated or simple, statistical or not. All depends on the data gathered and the information that is required.

Beginning researchers are frequently drawn to questionnaires and interviews and so these will be discussed. Most questionnaires contain some questions demanding simple factual answers. These might ask for the respondents' age, gender, ethnicity, previous educational attainment and so on. Analysis of such responses is done most readily by means of simple statistics to give you, for example, the mean age, the most common ethnicity, the gender balance and so on. Responses to open questions can be categorised and grouped according to how the respondents have replied. In this way, themes can start to emerge and you can see the extent to which they are shared between the participants. This begins the process of analysis and you can then discuss just how significant the themes are. It is at this point that the factual data you have gathered can come into its own. For example, is a particular theme spread equally between genders or is it predominantly restricted to one? What can you surmise from this?

Interviews can be similarly analysed. For detail on the various interview types, see Bell (2002) and Gillham (2000). Interviews may be recorded or videoed, but only with the participant's permission. Recording allows you to listen more closely to what your participant is saying. It also allows you to listen again to what was said and, as importantly, to *how* it was said. Video recording can add another dimension as it enables non-verbal communication to be analysed. There is much more to an interview than just the words that were used. Lastly, recording allows you to make an accurate transcript of the interview. The technical aspects must be sorted out before the interview and it's essential to ensure that microphones can pick up the whole conversation. Multi-directional microphones are essential.

Ethics of action research

Action research has the simultaneous advantage and disadvantage of familiarity with both the respondents and the context within which they operate. A major advantage of this is that the researcher does not have to spend large amounts of time getting to know the situation. A disadvantage is that aspects of the situation may be clear to the researcher, but far from clear to others, so assumptions shouldn't be made in this respect. A greater disadvantage concerns the ethical dimension.

Ethics in this regard can be divided into several categories:

- confidentiality
- consent – real and coerced
- working with the aftermath.

The reader is referred to the British Education Research Association (BERA) Research Guidelines for more detail on some ethical considerations (see 'Useful websites').

Confidentiality

Action research involves dealing with – and frequently experimenting upon – familiar people on a daily basis. This can cause stress in terms of confidentiality. You have to take extreme care to avoid giving information to anyone and especially in circulated material that will identify particular respondents. Of course, if the respondent is the principal of your establishment then non-identification can be difficult, but you must take every precaution to ensure confidentiality in all cases. It is important that respondents are informed and you must obtain agreements in writing. Care has to be taken to limit to the absolute minimum the information that is elicited from respondents as well as limiting the information on them that appears in the final report. Consistently ask yourself whether you need to include a particular piece of information. If the answer is negative then leave it out. It can be worthwhile asking a trusted colleague who knows the respondents if they can identify any individuals. If they can, then others might also be able to, so you need to revise what you are saying about them.

Ideally you should maintain confidentiality about the institution as well. However, this is usually impossible as far as your colleagues are concerned. You need to ensure the institution's confidentiality as far as the wider public is concerned. This may sometimes be straightforward, but other times, the institution's uniqueness is such that it is impossible. For example, if your project was conducted on the Liverpool Institute for Performing Arts, you might have quite a job making it disappear in your reported work as it is a unique institution.

Consent – real and coerced

The current received wisdom is that all participants in a research project should either give their consent or that a person in a role of responsibility for them should act as gate-keeper and give consent on their behalf. This latter applies especially in cases of research with children and young people where parents or teachers can fulfil the gatekeeping role. Nothing of course prevents one from asking children and young people directly for their consent, but this needs to be in addition to asking the gatekeeper, not instead of it.

This blanket injunction can create difficulties for the action researcher in particular and for the reflective practitioner in general. The problem consists of knowing where one's usual practice ends and where the research begins; this may be a difficult question to answer. All practitioners observe their learners whether directly as they undertake tasks or indirectly by looking at assessments or reports, for example; all informally interview their learners; most modify their practice in the light of what they learn from these observations and interviews. So, should you make clear to your learners that at all times they will be subject to a research-type process since this is what reflective pedagogy is all about? And what do you do if someone wants to opt out?

There is no harm in telling learners what the reflective process consists of and how they contribute to your learning, just as you, hopefully, contribute to theirs. Whether they will believe you or not is another matter. As regards opting out, opting out of being part of a reflective pedagogy can only mean opting out of the class altogether. It is our experience that students adopt one of only two attitudes to being told about the symbiotic nature of teaching and learning: they are either happy to be part of it – especially if a publication might arise or they might contribute to the course improving – or they don't care.

More important in terms of explicit consent is when an experiment – for that is what much of action research consists of – is to be introduced with the class members as participants. In this case, the problem can arise of coerced consent as opposed to that which is freely given.

It is impossible to be certain that no class member feels obliged to take part in your action research. What you can do is to be open and honest with them and involve them in the planning and execution of the project. Christenson *et al.* (2002) and Fryer (2004) provide examples of how this might be done. Fryer (2004) mentions the BERA (1992) *Ethical Guidelines for Education Research* (see 'Useful websites') which demand openness and honesty between researcher and participants. These give a reasonable set of rules of thumb to follow, but difficulties can arise in unforeseen circumstances. When people know they are being observed they are liable to alter their behaviour. On the other hand, when people are sufficiently observed then they may well cease to be aware of the observer. The problems arise when time is of the essence.

Consent is not a simple procedure, available as a 'one-size-fits-all'. It is complex and needs to be treated with care and attention. In general though, involving your participants in the project, treating them as responsible persons and taking into account their observations and thoughts – of which there may be many or few – will result in them seeing the project as an occasion to take a hand in determining the shape of their own learning. Often it is necessary for projects to be submitted to an ethical committee; if such committees do not exist, then it is essential to have the agreement of the head of your institution.

Indicative task

1   Obtain a copy of the BERA ethical guidelines (see 'Useful websites'). Review the guidelines and consider how they might affect your conduct of a research project.

2   Are there any controversial issues? Do you disagree with any aspects of the guidelines?

3   Which forms of research are likely to be most difficult in the light of the guidelines?

Working with the aftermath

One of the problems of any form of insider researcher is that, at the end of the project, you cannot simply walk away. Your participants, whether they are students or staff, are liable to be around you for some time to come. You have to decide whether the action research you undertook was a one-off, or whether it might be part of a larger process. It is here that the emancipatory aspect of action research (Kemmis 1993) can come to the fore. If carried out in collaboration with the participants, it can be seen as 'a process of systematic reflection upon circumstances to bring about a desired state of affairs' (Schostak 2002: 192). It can act to get people to think about their situation and to see that the status quo is not the only available option. This can open a 'Pandora's box' or it can simply give a glimmer of hope that can then be extinguished.

Time spent thinking about what happens after the project can be time well spent. Relationships can – and probably will – change during the research process. How you want them to remain needs to be considered.

Developing the action plan

This is where you sit down and decide what exactly you are going to do. The more explicit you are, in general, the better it is. Make sure that you keep the aim and the research questions at the forefront of your mind. Everything that you include in the action plan has to relate to these. It is therefore useful when, for example, you are considering a data collection method, to write down what kind of data you can expect to acquire from the method, what's good about it and what's not and how you plan to overcome the negatives. In any case, if your project is destined for submission for an award or a journal then you will have to include a discussion of methodology which does exactly this. You may, as Price (2004) does, integrate this discussion into the section on data collection. Price (2004) is an excellent example of the use and reporting of action research to improve teaching.

You will need more than one research instrument in order to be able to triangulate your findings. So, if your first main instrument is a questionnaire, then you might want to consider doing some interviews to allow a few respondents the opportunity to provide more detailed responses. In this way, you triangulate by quite literally setting out to measure the same thing from different directions. The literature will also give you some triangulation by allowing you to see the extent to which what you have found matches what others before you have found.

The action plan should also include some kind of intended outcome. Knowing what you hope for at the end of the process will put you in a far better position to evaluate whether it has been achieved.

For the end of the project

A strategy for improvement?

Depending on the extent of the involvement of your participants in the planning and execution of the project then the strategy for improvement may be already incorporated. A question which needs to be asked, both at this juncture and at the stage of developing the action plan, concerns the extent to which the researcher defines improvement by the context within which she or he operates and/or by the participants themselves. If your action research aims at being emancipatory then there is no option but to involve the participants, unless of course you take a paternalistic view of emancipation.

Fundamentally, it all comes down to asking yourself why you are involved in action research and for whose benefit. What is it that you would like to see at the end of the project that was not evident at the beginning?

A strategy for improvement is often expected in what Agyris (1970) terms 'mechanistic-oriented' research. This is where 'the research is framed in terms of managing change or solving a problem' (Coghlan 2003: 453). As Coghlan comments, this is not the only approach and he highlights Agyris' (1970) notion of 'organistic-oriented' research in which 'enquiry into (participants') own assumptions and ways of thinking and acting is central to the research process' (Coghlan 2003: 454). Action research is linked to each of these concerns; it is exploratory in nature and is seeking to better understand the participants, their learning and their context before formulating a judgement as to whether improvement is even desirable or possible.

Evaluation of outcomes?

It is quite feasible to enter an action research project without a clear idea, or indeed any idea, of the outcomes that might result. In this case you would have engaged in action research in which the process itself was the object of enquiry. On the other hand, the opposite is also possible. A frequent, but false, assumption regarding action research is that it must contain a strategy for improvement and that this must be open to evaluation. If we adopt a mechanistic-oriented approach then such is usually possible. If we are organistic-orientated then it may well not be, at least not in any easily defined manner.

The means of evaluation of outcomes can range from simple pre-test and post-test – if the participants did better in the post-test then the strategy has worked – to in-depth interviews in which the researcher tries to ascertain the manner and extent of changes in attitude. Fundamentally, what it comes down to is looking back to the research questions and ascertaining the extent to which you have responded to them. This may be done by further fieldwork or by argument and discussion of your findings or, indeed, by a combination of these. Remember that not all outcomes are measurable and most of these are not measurable in numbers, no matter how tempting this can be. Numbers can serve to give a semblance of objectivity to the proceedings and this may not be merited at all. However tempting it is to rate pain from 0 (= comfort) to 10 (= agony), it is really quite a meaningless exercise since your slight twinge might be someone else's agony or vice versa.

Conclusion

This has been a brief look at researching practice and in particular at action research – 'a form of self-reflective enquiry' undertaken by practitioners 'in order to improve the rationality and justice of their social or educational practices, their understanding of these practices and the situations in which the practices are carried out' (Kemmis 1993: 177). Action research is currently a very popular pursuit, especially among government departments, and organisations such as the TTA and the GTC who see it as a means of creating a reflective workforce, especially in teaching. Quite why they would want to encourage such reflection is open to question but, suffice to say, an inherent danger in action research is that in examining one's practice at a very close distance one loses sight of the bigger picture that surrounds it. With this in mind, it can be very worthwhile considering other approaches to research and using them to expand the picture that one has available.

One might for example take a macro-sociological perspective and consider the wider context within which one's learners and institution are operating. In this way, the larger social forces which stimulate and are stimulated by the context of the learners and the institution are examined. What for example is the role of social expectation in the lives of the learners? What government initiatives are impacting on their lives and hence on their lives as learners?

One could take an historical perspective and consider how an issue was dealt with, if at all, in previous generations. What we perceive as problems nowadays were very often not seen as such in the past. This can impact on the socio-cultural baggage that people bring with them, it can also impact on the expectations made of members of society.

One could take a comparative perspective and consider how other places deal with the same issue, if indeed it is an issue for them at all. We could consider how other places view the way in which we treat the issue and go some way towards seeing ourselves as others see us.

A philosophical approach could be taken and consider the concepts involved. What does, for example, *numeracy* really mean? What are the implications for further education to have what is easily seen as a punitive inspection system?

There are many more perspectives to choose from. However, regardless what you are researching and why you are doing it, taking more than one perspective will almost inevitably serve to enrich your work and let others see it as more than just a cute example that maybe only pertains to your particular situation.

Indicative task

1   Use the information in this chapter to plan an action research project.
2   If time is available, implement and evaluate the project.

Summary

- Action research has been defined as 'an approach to research that is based on a collaborative problem-solving relationship between researcher and client, which aims at both solving a problem and generating new knowledge' (Coghlan 2003: 452).

- Action research can affect people's lives, so it needs to be carefully planned.

- Action research is cyclic in nature with implementation and evaluation followed by further implementation.

- The literature informs action research, but care needs to be exercised when evaluating information.

- Aims and research questions must be formulated before the research process begins.

- Data can be collected in range of ways and consideration must be given to how the data will be analysed before the research begins.

- Ethics are a vital part of research. BERA publishes appropriate guidelines.

- The effect of action research on relationships following the project must be considered.

- An action plan for the research should include a statement of expected outcomes.

- Evaluation of outcomes can be used to inform future research projects.

- The FENTO Teaching and Learning Standards relating to research in professional practice are shown in Figure 10.4. Full details of these standards are available at the FENTO website (see 'Useful websites').

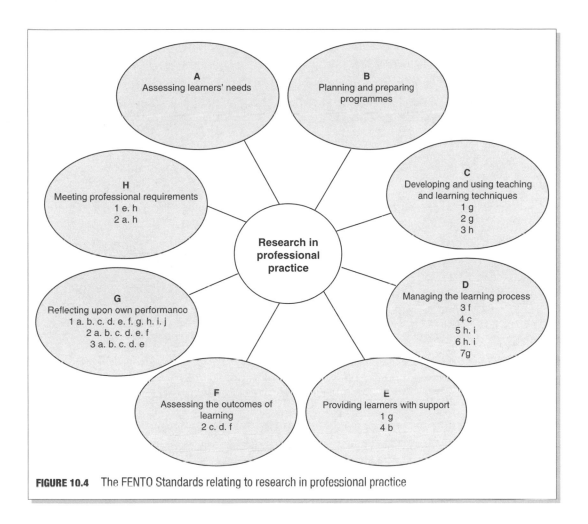

FIGURE 10.4 The FENTO Standards relating to research in professional practice

Useful websites

www.bera.ac.uk/publications/guides.php
British Education Research Association (BERA) guidelines on research, educational writing and ethics
Last accessed 7 May 2004

www.dmu.ac.uk/~jamesa/learning/experien.htm
Experiental learning styles and cycles
Last accessed 7 May 2004

www.fento.ac.uk
The Further Education National Training Organisation (FENTO) website
Last accessed 7 May 2004

www.gtce.org.uk/gtcinfo/tla.asp
The Teacher Learning Academy (TLA) website
Last accessed 7 May 2004

www.infed.org/thinkers/et-lewin.htm
Information on Kurt Lewin
Last accessed 7 May 2004

www.leeds.ac.uk/educol/
The Education-line database: an online database of conference papers and documents supporting educational research and practice.
Last accessed 7 May 2004

www.scre.ac.uk/pdf/spotlight/spotlight67.pdf
Practitioner research material from the Scottish Council for Research in Education (SCRE)
Last accessed 7 May 2004

www.scre.ac.uk/spotlight/spotlight27.html
Planning small-scale research from the Scottish Council for Research in Education (SCRE)
Last accessed 7 May 2004

References

Agyris, C. (1970) *Intervention Theory and Method*. Reading, MA: Addison-Wesley.

Atherton, J. S. (2002) *Learning and Teaching: learning from experience*. See 'Useful websites' (Experiential learning styles and cycles)

Bell, J. (2002) *Doing your Research Project*. Buckingham: Open University.

Blaxter, L., Hughes, C. and Tight, M. (2001) *How to Research*, 2nd edn. Buckingham: Open University.

Brown, S. (1990) *Planning Small-scale Research*. SCRE Spotlights. Edinburgh: SCRE.

Christenson, M., Slutsky, R., Bendau, S. *et al.* (2002) 'The rocky road of teachers becoming action researchers', *Teaching and Teacher Education* **18**, 259–72.

Coghlan, D. (2003) 'Practitioner research for organizational knowledge', *Management Learning* **34**(4), 451–63.

Coghlan, D. and Casey, M. (2001) 'Action research from the inside: issues and challenges in doing action research in your own hospital', *Journal of Advanced Nursing* **35**(5), 674–82.

Cohen, L. and Manion, L. (1996) *Research Methods in Education*, 4th edn. London: Routledge.

Costello, P. (2003) *Action Research*. London: Continuum.

Drever, E. (1995) *Using Semi-structured Interviews in Small-scale Research: a teacher's guide*. SCRE Publication No. 129. Edinburgh: SCRE.

Fryer, E. (2004) 'Researcher–practitioner: an unholy marriage?', *Educational Studies* **30**(2), 175–85.

Gillham, B. (2000) *The Research Interview*. London: Continuum.

Greenwood, D. and Levin, M. (1998) *Introduction to Action Research: social research for social change*. Thousand Oaks, CA: Sage.

Healey, M. and Jenkins, A. (2000) 'Kolb's Experiential Learning Theory and its application in geography in higher education', *Journal of Geography* **99**, 185–95.

Hopkins, D. (1995) *A Teacher's Guide to Classroom Research*. Buckingham: Open University.

Kemmis, S. (1993) 'Action research', in Hammersley, M. (ed.) *Educational Research: current issues*. London and Buckingham: Paul Chapman and Open University.

Lewis, I. and Munn, P. (1997) *So You Want to Do Research! A guide for beginners on how to formulate research questions*. SCRE Publication No. 136. Edinburgh: SCRE.

Macintyre, C. (2000) *The Art of Action Research in the Classroom*. London: David Fulton.

Munn, P. and Drever, E. (1995) *Using Questionnaires in Small-scale Research: a teachers' guide*. SCRE Publication No. 104. Edinburgh: SCRE.

Nunes, M. B. and McPherson, M. (2003) 'Action research in continuing professional development', *Journal of Computer Assisted Learning* **19**, 429–37.

Price, J. (2004) 'A parent in the classroom – a valuable way of fostering deep learning for the children's nursing student', *Nurse Education in Practice* **4**, 5–11.

Schostak, J. (2002) *Understanding, Designing and Conducting Qualitative Research in Education*. Buckingham: Open University.

Simpson, M. and Tuson, J. (1995) *Using Observations in Small-scale Research: a beginners' guide*. SCRE Publication No. 130. Edinburgh: SCRE.

Smith, M. (2001) *Kurt Lewin: groups, experiential learning and action research*. www.infed.org/thinkers/et-lewin.htm – Last accessed 07/05/04.

Stark, R. (1998) *Practitioner Research: the purposes of reviewing the literature within an enquiry*. Edinburgh: SCRE.

Staunton, H. (1877) *The Great Schools of England*. London: Daldy, Ibister and Co.

Wells, H. G. (1918) *Joan and Peter: the story of an education*. London: Macmillan.

Management and leadership in post-compulsory education

Jim McGrath

Introduction

THE FURTHER AND HIGHER EDUCATION ACT (1992) paved the way for the incorporation of colleges of further education. They became separate legal entities, free from the control of local councils and responsible for their own decisions on such matters as finance, personnel and estates management. Along with this new-found freedom came new responsibilities including the need to devise an annual strategic plan, maintain a balanced budget and recruit and retain students to target.

Inevitably, questions concerning the management and leadership of colleges would become increasingly important as managers recognised the new realities of further education. It is not an exaggeration to say that management in FE has been revolutionised in the last 12 years. Senior and middle managers have been constantly required to increase productivity while controlling costs. The model that has been promoted, by successive governments and their agents, the funding agencies, has been one predicated on the private sector.

This chapter examines the phenomenon of managerialism and how managers in FE have integrated the demands for a more businesslike approach to management and leadership with their existing educational values. Types of organisational cultures that staff in FE are likely to encounter and what this means for management and leadership styles are discussed and the nature of educational leadership and how this might differ from that exercised in the private sector is considered. These concepts are developed with a discussion on the differences between management and leadership. Finally, the role of middle managers in FE is addressed.

Managerialism

The term managerialism 'Is generally used to refer to the adoption by public sector organisations of organisational forms, technologies, management practices and values more commonly found in the private sector' (Deem 1998: 47). The managerialist agenda has been promoted under various labels including New Public Management, New Managerialism, Entrepreneurial Governance and Neo-Taylorism (Power 1997) with each giving 'a different level of emphasis to the components of managerialism' (Trowler 1998: 94). In this chapter the single term managerialism has been used to refer to all these initiatives.

Managerialism can be thought of as a set of beliefs or as an ideology that gives rise to a particular approach to management (Wright 2001) that may include:

- elevating the importance of management above that which is to be managed;
- emphasising the manager's right to manage;
- using cost centres and devolved budgets to achieve greater financial control;
- applying value for money (VFM) principles in order to ensure economy, efficiency and effectiveness, where: economy is concerned with obtaining goods and services of the required standard and least cost; efficiency is concerned with maximizing the production of goods or services at the required standard from the least input; and effectiveness is a measure of how successful the organisation has been in achieving its objectives. Of the three concepts effectiveness is the most important as it is pointless being economic and efficient if the organisation does not achieve its objectives or pursues the wrong objectives;
- the extensive use of performance indicators in order to monitor and control staff activities linked with an assertion of the manager's right to manage;
- the creation of a quasi-market environment that promotes competition and transforms students into customers;
- weakening of trade union and professional ties within the workplace as a prelude to the creation of a more flexible workforce and the introduction of appraisal systems and performance-related pay as a means of aligning the individual's aims and objectives more closely with those of the organisation;
- the atomisation of large-scale organisations into sub-units that are viewed as chains of low-trust relationships linked only by contracts.

(List adapted from Dunleavy and Hood 1994; Prichard 1996; Randle and Brady 1997; Deem 1998; Trowler 1998)

The application of the above practices are intended to bring the management, reporting and accounting processes of public sector organisations ever closer to those employed in the private sector. In education, the emphasis has been on financial discipline and performance monitoring (Trowler 1998).

With a change of government in 1997, the emphasis on economy, efficiency and competition was reduced and replaced with an emphasis on effectiveness and partnership working (Fergusson 2000).

Reflective questions

How many of the above practices have been adopted by your organisation? Which practices are emphasised the most? Where does the pressure to apply these practices come from?

Despite widespread opposition to managerialism in education there are a number of indicators that imply that it has become the dominant ideology in educational management. First, there is now a greater emphasis on the need for effective management and leadership in schools, colleges and universities as the means by which governmental and organisational goals maybe achieved (Simkins 1999), an example of which has been the creation of the National College for School Leadership.

Secondly, as workloads have increased, staff have been required to do more with fewer resources. To cope with this the responsibilities of middle managers have become more clearly defined and they have been made accountable for the performance of staff under their control (Simkins 1999; Deem 1998).

Thirdly, in many colleges hierarchical structures have been subject to a process of delayering with responsibility for the achievement of recruitment and retention targets being delegated to course teams. Often this process has been promoted as a means of empowering staff. However, for many staff the reality is that they are required to take on additional responsibilities while the gap between them and the next layer of management increases (Simkins 1999).

Randle and Brady (1997) argue that these changes have distanced managers from their staff and suggest that 'traditionally staff and managers aspired to a common set of educational values', but that this settlement has broken down to be replaced by, 'a new type of manager whose primary concern is resource management' (p. 232). However, Simkins (1999) warned against assuming that managerialism is now universally and uniformly accepted and applied in colleges and universities. He suggests that older bureau-professional identities and allegiances can co-exist alongside the values that underpin managerialism.

Gleeson and Shain (1999) explored the changing managerial cultures in the FE workplace among middle managers who often find themselves acting as the ideological buffer between staff and senior managers and have the unenviable task of translating policy into practice in such a way as to satisfy both senior managers and staff. Their conclusion was that the complex situation in colleges was often oversimplified and that 'managerialism is not as complete or uncontested as is often portrayed' (p. 461). They found that middle managers adopted one of three major strategies in order to cope with the demands of managerialism. These are:

- **Willing compliance**

  This is characterised by the manager's wholehearted identification with institutional aims and objectives and the strategies used to achieve them. With such staff, 'The dominant managerialist discourse is consciously internalised and guides the daily working practice of those involved' (Gleeson and Shain 1999: 474).

- **Unwilling compliance**

  This is characterised by the individual's rejection of the organisation's managerialist agenda. This can take one of two forms. Either the individual finds it impossible to relate to the new management approach and hankers after a bygone age when bureau-professional values ruled (values characterised by concern for students' well-being, academic standards and professional values; see Randle and Brady 1997; Power 1997 and Simkins 1999) or conversely, they believe that the institution has not gone far enough and should embrace even more fully the ethos of the private sector.

- **Strategic compliance**

  This was displayed by the majority of middle managers surveyed by Gleeson and Shain (1999). As an approach it is characterised by the sophisticated way in which managers deal with the managerialist agenda while at the same time accommodating their commitment to older professional values such as collegiality and student support. This requires the individual manager to balance the demands of the organisation with their own professional values. What sets such managers apart from willing compliers is that they do not identify strongly with the image of the organisation as promoted by the senior managers but recognise that their job requires them to 'sell the party line'. This act of distancing enables them to retain credibility with their staff while enacting instructions received from above.

Reflective question

Which, if any, of these three strategies best describes your approach and that of your line manager?

The implication from Gleeson and Shain's work is that middle managers have not wholeheartedly embraced managerialism but that senior managers who determine the image of the organisation have. This view is contested by Lumby and Tomlinson (2000) who reject the notion that there is a 'polarization of associated groups into apparently oppositional cultures' (p. 139). Similarly the claim that managers have adopted a different value system to that held by staff is rejected on the grounds that there is insufficient empirical evidence to support such a contention and that it oversimplifies a highly complex situation.

Managerialism grew out of the 'New Right's neo-liberal modernisation programme' for the public service and since 1979 has supplanted bureau-professionalism to become the dominant ideology in education management. However, the degree to which it has been implemented varies between organisations and even when it appears to be fully utilised there is evidence that managers and staff continue to interpret and apply its concepts by reference to older professional and educational values.

Reflective questions

What do you understand by the phrase 'The New Right's neo-liberal modernisation programme'? Based on your experiences and observations do you think that the senior and middle managers in your organisation share a similar set of values? If not what are the differences?

The trend towards managerialism has undoubtedly impacted on the organisational culture to be found in colleges of further education. The next section considers four common cultures and the form of leadership that they encourage.

Models of organisational culture

Commentators have proposed various models that can be used to explore an organisation's culture. Schein (1992) uses a three-tier model that examines the organisation's culture through its artefacts, espoused values and basic underlying assumptions. Morgan (1997) uses eight different metaphors which look at the organisation as a machine, a living organism, a set of cultures, a brain, a political system, a psychic prison, a vehicle for domination and as a system that is in constant flux and transformation. Handy (1991) suggested that an organisation's culture is formed by the unique combination of four archetypal cultures which he names: club, role, task and person. It is Handy's model of organisational culture that is used here.

Handy (1991) rightly stresses that it is highly unlikely to find only one of the archetypal cultures in an organisation, rather there would be elements of two or more to be found with perhaps one being dominant. The precise mix will depend on the relative importance of a range of factors, including the organisation's size, workflow, environment and history. Handy and Aitken (1986) suggested that one will often 'Find a role culture topped by a spider's web (club) with task-culture project groups round the edges and a few individuals of the person culture studded throughout like raisins in a cake' (p. 92). All four cultural archetypes are discussed here, but as the role and task cultures tend to dominate in educational settings it is these that have been discussed most fully.

Club culture

A club culture exists when there is one central power source and for that reason it is sometimes referred to as a power culture (Handy 1993). The power source can be an individual or a small group of like-minded individuals such as the senior management team. Power and influence radiate from this central source and are communicated to the functional or specialist departments. Handy likens this culture to that of a spider's web, where any movement by the spider at the centre reverberates to all parts of the web. Such organisations rely on precedent or on anticipating the wishes and decisions of the central power source. There are few rules or procedures and very little bureaucracy. Control is exercised by the centre largely through the selection of key individuals who are chosen because they reflect the attitudes and beliefs of the central power source. In effect management places considerable trust in individuals and very little in committees. Such organisations are political in that decisions are taken on the outcome of the balance of influence rather than on procedural grounds. Management, concerned as it is with outcomes, tends to judge performance on the basis of results and is tolerant of the strategies used by staff to achieve those results (Handy 1991).

The full range of management and leadership styles, from autocratic to laissez-faire, can exist in a club culture and the dominant style is likely to reflect the preference of the central power source. For example Virgin's management style, at all levels, reflects the values and attitudes of its founder Richard Branson and while discipline and control is exercised the relationship between management and staff is professional, friendly and informal.

Reflective questions

To what extent does a power culture exist in your college? Which person or group is the source of power? Does a power culture exist in any of the faculties, schools or departments within the college?

Role culture

The 'role organisation' is basically a bureaucracy. Handy (1991) likens such cultures to a Greek temple where the specialist departments form the pillars of the structure and a small executive at the top forms the pediment. In such cultures the work of the departments and the interactions between them are tightly prescribed by rules and regulations and the role that a person plays is more important than the individual who fills it. Individuals are selected on the basis that they can satisfactorily perform the role and it is so prescribed that a range of individuals could fill it. Performance over and above that prescribed is not encouraged, as this can be disruptive. It logically follows from this that positional power dominates, personal power is frowned upon and expert power only tolerated in appropriate circumstances.

Today, the term bureaucracy is commonly used pejoratively as a synonym for inefficiency. Yet originally it was used to describe any 'Formal organisation, which seeks maximum efficiency through rational approaches to management' (Bush 1995: 35). Bureaucratic organisations stress the:

- separation of officials from ownership
- importance of hierarchical authority and the organisation's structure

- achievements of goals that are clearly specified by officers at the apex of the organisation

- division of labour with staff specialising in particular tasks

- primacy of rules and regulations over personal initiative in matters of behaviour and decision making

- impersonal nature of the relationship between staff and clients with decisions based upon pre-written rules and regulations

- use of qualifications and/or previous performance as the basis for appointing or promoting staff.

(Bush 1995; Cole 1993)

Educational establishments share many of these characteristics and colleges in particular appear to have a clear preference for bureaucratic and hierarchical forms of management. This may be because further education colleges have had a long and close working relationship with local government.

Leadership within bureaucratic models 'is ascribed to the person at the apex of the hierarchy' (Bush 1995: 43) and it is assumed that the leader's positional power is sufficient to compel compliance. Such models see the implementation of policy and plans as unproblematic. This implies that the leader may, if he/she wishes, adopt an autocratic approach to management. Such a view has significant limitations. For, while formal authority will reside with the head, he will inevitably require the co-operation of staff to implement his ideas and the support of senior colleagues to manage the volume and complexity of work that arises within even a small educational establishment. The result of this has been an increase in the importance of the organisation's senior management team. Hence, as the leader delegates responsibility to senior colleagues for defined areas of work the hierarchical structure remains but the apex expands to accommodate a team (Bush 1995).

Reflective question

To what extent does a role culture exist in your organisation? Describe some of the practices in your organisation that exemplify a role culture.

Task culture

The 'task culture' is concerned with the successful completion of the job or task. In this culture the organisation attempts to bring together the staff and other resources required to complete a specific task. The culture is represented as a net because of the way the various strands required are woven together to form a team. In such task groups, expert power is highly regarded and individual objectives, status and style are subjugated to the needs of the team. Such a culture is highly adaptable and can act quickly when required as each team contains the expertise, resources and power to make and implement decisions. The management and control of such groups is difficult, as day-to-day management of the project will reside with the team; senior management control is limited to deciding which projects will be resourced, how and to what level (Handy 1991). Within the team it is likely that a participative style of management and leadership will be adopted and the views of all members sought before decisions are made. This approach shares many similarities with the traditional collegial approach to education management. However, not all models of collegiality can be described as inclusive.

Collegiality attempts to draw on expertise from all parts of the organisation in order to maximise the effectiveness of decision making. The notion that a collegial approach is the most appropriate way to run an educational organisation has, according to Bush (1995), entered into folklore. His use of the word 'folklore' is significant as it implies that such an approach has never been the norm in schools and colleges and that education-alists are invoking a golden age that never existed as a response to the managerialist policies of successive governments. But what is this collegiality that so many hanker after? Bush (1995) stated that:

> Collegial models assume that organisations determine policy and make decisions through a process of discussion leading to consensus. Power is shared among some or all the members of the organisation who are thought to have a mutual understanding about the objectives of the institution.
>
> (Bush 1995: 52)

Expanding on this definition it can be seen that collegial models have the following characteristics. According to Bush (1995) they:

- reflect the prescriptive belief that management should be based upon agreement;
- are particularly suited to organisations that contain a high number of professional staff such as colleges;
- assume that the members of the organisation share a common set of values and that therefore agreement on organisational objectives and the means of achieving them is possible;
- require that the decision-making group is kept to a reasonable size. To achieve this, the model advocates that staff have formal representation on decision-making groups. Therefore informal consultation with staff does not constitute collegiality;
- assume that decisions are reached by consensus and that differences of opinion are overcome by argument and persuasion rather than majority voting.

The collegially inspired plea for a democratic approach to management finds reson-ance in the hearts of many lecturers and other professionals. However, the models found in practice seldom match the idealised versions described in theory. Involvement in collegial decision making may be limited to senior staff and therefore many of the models in use could be described as elitist rather than democratic. Even where there is a degree of collegiality there may be a dichotomy between the management of academic policy, which may be arrived at through the collegial model, and the allocation of resources that remains the responsibility of the principal or senior management team. Thus, while the committee system that is evident in many colleges might imply collegiality, the method of allocating resources remains firmly situated within the higher reaches of the bureaucratic model discussed earlier. Indeed, the wish to involve staff in the decision-making process may conflict with the organisation's need to demonstrate accountability to external funding and inspection agencies; these see the managers as the policy and decision makers and are concerned to identify clear lines of accountability (Bush 1995).

Collegial models also assume that staff share a common view as to the purpose of the organisation and that organisational goals have been agreed. To reach agreement it may be necessary to consciously define the purpose of the organisation in a vague and ambiguous manner (Bush 1995).

In large organisations, like colleges, there may develop several distinct cultures leading to a 'Balkanisation' of cultures with different cultures existing in faculties or departments. Such Balkanised cultures share four characteristics. First, each sub-group is a separate entity and there is 'low permeability' between the groups. Secondly, once established it is difficult to remove the barriers that separate sub-groups. Thirdly, people become attached to and identify with their sub-group. Fourthly, the sub-cultures develop a set of self-interests that they actively promote (Hargreaves 1996).

The style of leadership available to managers in a collegial environment is influenced by, and in turn influences, the decision-making process. Because policy is constructed using a participative approach, the leader has to acknowledge that ideas and initiatives may emerge from any part of the institution and should be considered through the participative processes that signify collegiality. Hence, 'heroic models of leadership are inappropriate when influence and power are widely distributed within institutions' (Bush 1995: 64), as effectively the leader in this situation is the first among equals. This means that transformational or charismatic approaches, where one person is perceived as the 'The Leader' are unlikely to be popular with either management or staff.

Leadership in a collegial environment requires the leader to be willing to seek out and be responsive to the views of professional colleagues and to encourage the creation of formal and informal opportunities to discuss, test and elaborate possible policy initiatives with them. The leader must also be sensitive to the dominance of expert authority over positional authority and make it clear that they see their role as leader being one of facilitation and leadership as a shared responsibility. This is achieved by encouraging other senior and middle managers to become co-leaders (Bush 1995).

Person culture

The person culture is comparatively rare but many professionals still cling to aspects of it as a means of negotiating how they should be treated by their employing organisation. In such cultures the organisation exists merely to assist the individual to perform their job. An example of such a culture might be an architects' practice where a group of architects come together, rent premises and hire administrative staff in order to practise their profession. The organisational structure would be minimal and focus on the needs of the architects. In such organisations, management and control mechanisms can only operate with the consent of the individuals and expert power is the accepted currency. Although such cultures rarely exist it is not uncommon in colleges for some individuals to believe that the organisation exists purely to assist them in their work. This can be the source of considerable conflict if the dominant culture is different (Handy 1991).

Educational leadership

Many commentators suggest that the type of management and leadership required in educational settings is fundamentally different from that which exists in the private sector. Organisations that operate in the private sector are, according to Handy and Aitken (1986), relatively easy to run even if they have more than one objective, as all decisions can be reduced to monetary terms and the one that maximises future cash flow selected. This view would be contested by most, if not all, writers on financial management as they point to the difficulties modern companies have in satisfying the often competing demands of stakeholders (Bennett 1999, Samuels and Wilkes 1986). However, it is generally recognised that educational aims are not only contested but 'diffuse, value-based and to some extent self selected' (Fidler 1997: 31). Typically, the aims of educational institutions are to:

- provide appropriate education

- contribute to the spiritual, moral and physical development of the student

- provide certification of learning

- develop the students' social skills

- provide a variety of instruction to meet the needs of students

- meet the Government's economic agenda

(Handy and Aitkin 1986)

Similarly, Fullan (1994) argues that because education is concerned with providing access to knowledge and encouraging enquiry and the inculcation of truth, it has a moral purpose. This reflects the views of Hodgkinson (1991) who asserts that education is special and he refers to its various objectives as 'the constellation of purposes'. He argues that any leader in education must be aware of 'the deep roots of purpose which underlined their organisation ... (and if) education is special then it follows that educational leadership ought likewise to be special' (Hodgkinson 1991: 27).

Although the above education aims relate to schools there is similar uncertainty at the FE level where staff simultaneously act as a critical friend, teacher, judge and guardian of standards.

Despite claims that education is special, the importation of commercial practices and the use of commercial management tools accelerated during the 1980s and continued into the 1990s. How applicable many of these tools are is questionable. Law and Glover (2000) recognise that 'the language of reform has undoubtedly reframed educational management around business related concepts' (p. 6) but warn that:

> While we need to recognize that a number of commercial concepts may be applicable to education scenarios as it becomes more market driven, it is clear that there are no ready made or universally applicable theories we can simply call off the shelf.
>
> (Law and Glover 2000: 4)

Certainly it would seem reasonable to assume that different styles of leadership suit different types of organisations for:

> We erroneously talk of management skills rather than the distinct and specific skills required to manage a school, factory or business. Moreover, a widely accepted corollary is that training programmes in management in one area like education can draw uncritically on ideas in another, especially, nowadays, (from) the domain of industry and business.
>
> (Warren 1998: 51–2)

Against this background of unclear objectives the role of the education leader has become more pivotal as greater emphasis has been placed on the overall performance of the organisation and individual managers have become accountable for that performance (Deem 1998, 2000).

Discussion points

Do you think that education management is different from management in the private sector? If so, how is it different?

The difference between management and leadership

Leadership is a complex process with multiple dimensions. Warren (1998) believes that 'the notion of leadership is not only one of the most difficult in social science to define but is a vacuous and dangerous concept' (p. 65) and that theorising the notion of academic leadership is particularly problematic. Certainly, leadership is a multi-faceted concept and is not paradox free. For it appears that 'No one theory, nor any one approach can subsume the complexities of leadership and, indeed the search for such an all encompassing theory may be illusory' (Fidler 1997: 27).

Stogdill suggests that there are almost as many definitions of leadership as there are commentators (Northouse 2001). Rather than add further to the list of existing definitions Tables 11.1 and 11.2 seek to differentiate management from leadership. Such differentiation may not be necessary or worthwhile because:

- the vast majority of managerial posts contain elements of both leadership and management and holders do not consciously differentiate between the two processes;

- context may determine whether an action is management or leadership;

- what followers recognise as management or leadership may differ depending upon time, place and context.

Thus the tables seek only to summarise how a range of commentators have sought to differentiate between management and leadership, but it would be wrong to assume

TABLE 11.1   The differing perspectives of managers and leaders

Managers are concerned with	Leaders are concerned with
The present	The future
Plans	Vision
Maintenance of systems	The big picture
Maintaining the status quo	Change
Feedback	Inspiration
Objectives	Outcomes

TABLE 11.2 Activities undertaken by managers and leaders

Managers are concerned with	Leaders are concerned with
Monitoring and control	Exercising influence over followers
Providing a sense of order	Providing a sense of purpose and direction for followers
Spreading organisational culture	Building organisational culture
Doing things right	Doing the right things
Acting in accordance with managerial requirements	Acting as the leading professional internally and the chief executive externally
Dealing with complexity within and around the organisation	Change and dealing with the effects of change
Producing order and consistency	Producing change and movement
Planning and budgeting	Vision building and strategising
Organisational structure and staffing	Aligning people behind common objectives
Problem solving	Problem seeking
Economy and efficiency	Effectiveness
Staying on the right path	Making new paths

that there is an impermeable boundary between the two concepts. Table 11.1 seeks to delineate the different perspectives that managers and leaders have while Table 11.2 seeks to differentiate between managers and leaders on the basis of the actions they undertake. (Tables 11.1 and 11.2 are adapted from the work of Fidler 1997; Grace 1995; Handy 1992; Law and Glover 2000; Middlehurst 1993 and Northouse 2001.)

Missing from these tables, because it is neither a perspective nor an action, is the notion that leadership is bestowed on the individual by their followers whereas the title manager often accompanies accession to a particular post.

Discussion points

Do you think that management and leadership are different? If so what do you think are the main differences? If you don't think that the differences between these two concepts are important, suggest why you hold this view.

Reflective questions

Which do you think is more important in running your college, good management or good leadership? Why have you chosen either management or leadership?

The role of middle managers

Paradoxically, while the term 'manager' has fallen into disrepute, and the cult of leadership has grown, there has been a significant growth in the interest accorded to middle managers. *The Economist* (Anonymous 1995) noted that after the delayering of industry in the 1980s, which had seen the culling of many middle management posts, there were clear signs that such positions were enjoying a renaissance.

A middle manager is someone who has management responsibilities but who is not part of the organisation's senior management team (Busher and Harris 1999). Functions often associated with the role include:

- encouraging staff to cohere and develop a group identity and a collaborative culture;
- using expert knowledge to improve the performance of staff and students;
- interpreting organisational strategy and operationalising it;
- acting as a representative for their team or department both internally and externally;
- using their detailed knowledge of the organisation and its systems to get things done;
- acting as a champion of innovation;
- building alliances with middle managers in other organisations – networking;
- developing and implementing strategies at the local level that are aligned with the organisation's aims and objectives.

(List adapted from Anonymous 1995; Busher and Harris 1999;
Briggs 2001; Hancock and Hellawell 2003)

Briggs (2001) found that middle managers were reluctant to call themselves leaders, even though they recognised that it was not possible for senior managers to lead on every issue.

Reflective questions

Given the discussion above, who do you think are the middle managers in your organisation? What are the most important functions undertaken by middle managers in your organisation?

A management strategy for middle managers – situational theory

Situational theory was developed by Hersey and Blanchard in 1969 and has been revised several times since (Northouse 2001). Essentially, 'it examines the interaction between situational variables and the leader's behaviour' (Richmon and Allison 2003: 48). The theory focuses on leadership within given situations with its basic tenet being that different situations require different types of leadership and therefore that the leader has to adapt their style to fit the situation (Northouse 2001).

Situational leadership is composed of two dimensions, supportive and directive, and both must be applied correctly and simultaneously in any given situation if success is to be achieved. To do this the leader has to evaluate each employee's commitment and competence. In this context commitment relates to the employee's level of motivation to the task in hand and competence to complete the task. The four leadership styles that this approach generates are:

- Directive (D1), where a high level of direction and a low level of supportive behaviour is demonstrated by the leader. This is used where the employee lacks or may have lost competency but is enthusiastic and committed.

- Coaching (D2), where the leader demonstrates a high level of direction and a high level of supportive behaviour. This is used where the employee has some competence but lacks or may have lost commitment.

- Supporting (D3), where there is a low level of direction and a high level of supportive behaviour demonstrated by the leader. This is used where the employee is competent to carry out the task but lacks self-confidence or motivation.

- Delegating (D4), where there is a low level of both directive and supportive behaviour displayed by the leader. This is used when the employee is both competent to carry out the task and has the motivation and self-confidence to do it successfully.

(Blanchard *et al*. 1985)

To use Blanchard's approach a leader has to know where on the continuum the employee is at any time and act accordingly, while recognising that this can vary from task to task and over time (Northouse 2001).

Situational theory emphasises flexibility and is practical and easy to understand. It is intuitively sensible and can, in theory, be applied across all sectors and provides actual directions on how to lead. Unfortunately when applied to 300 secondary school teachers and their principals it was found that the theory worked well with newly hired teachers, who preferred principals to have a highly structured leadership style, but that the performance of more experienced teachers was unaffected (Northouse 2001).

Reflective question

What management approach do middle managers in your organisation adopt?

A strategy for survival

In order to survive and prosper in any environment it is necessary for an organism to adapt to its changing environment; failure to adapt leads to extinction, as the dinosaurs found to their cost. In order to be able to adapt people need to understand the changes and pressures that are impacting on them. This chapter has provided a guide to the major factors that a lecturer or middle manager in FE must be aware of if they are to survive and prosper in the sector.

Indicative task

Analyse your own organisation and the role you play in it. Questions that might help you to do this include:

1 To what extent has your organisation and the managers within it adopted the managerialist agenda?

2 To what extent do you support the approach adopted?

3 What strategy have you adopted to cope with the demands of a managerialist environment?

4 How well do you understand your college's organisational culture?

5 Given that organisational culture affects how decisions are made do you understand where the power lies in your organisation and how decisions are made? Only if you understand the process can you influence it.

6 As a middle manager or one who aspires to a middle-management post have you been able to identify the dominant management and leadership style within your organisation? What is your preferred management style and is your style compatible with that used in the organisation? Would the situational-based approach to leadership be useful to you?

Summary

- Indications including the need for effective management in FE, increased accountability of middle managers and the delayering of FE management structures suggest a culture of managerialism in post-compulsory education.

- Models of organisational culture include: **club culture**, in which there is one power source; **role culture**, essentially a bureaucratic culture; **task culture**, with a focus on the successful completion of tasks; and **person culture**, in which the organisation exists to assist in fulfilling job roles.

- One of the challenges of educational leadership is that it is generally recognised that educational aims are not only contested but 'diffuse, value-based and to some extent self selected' (Fidler 1997: 31).

- When considering the differences between management and leadership, it must be considered that the vast majority of managerial posts contain elements of both leadership and management and holders do not consciously differentiate between the two processes. Context may determine whether an action ismanagement or leadership. What is recognised as management or leadership may differ depending upon time, place and context.

- The role of middle managers in FE suggests that they should adopt a broadly situational-based approach to the management and leadership of staff under their control. This involves the manager adopting a supportive and/or directive role according to circumstances.

- The ability to adapt is the key to survival as a manager in FE.

- The FENTO Teaching and Learning Standards relating to management and leadership are shown in Figure 11.1. Full details of these standards are available at the FENTO website (see 'Useful websites').

Useful websites

www.acm.uk.com
The Association for College Management
Last accessed 7 May 2004

www.escalate.ac.uk/
Part of the Learning and Teaching Support Network (LTSN): provides resources and events, including those related to education management.
Last accessed 7 May 2004

www.fento.ac.uk
The Further Education National Training Organisation (FENTO) management standards (The National Occupational Standards for Management in Further Education)
Last accessed 7 May 2004

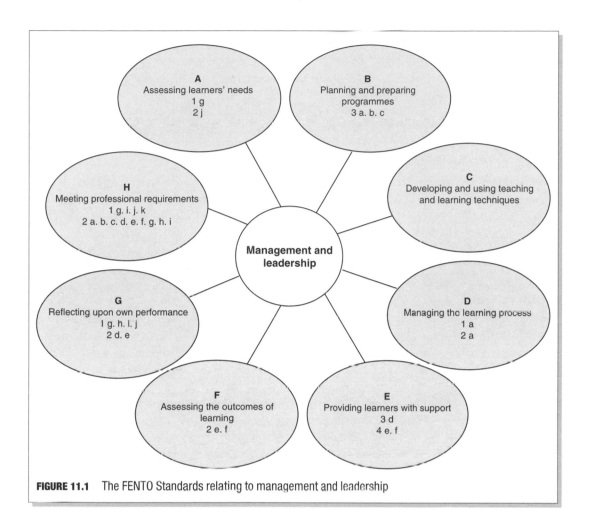

FIGURE 11.1   The FENTO Standards relating to management and leadership

References

Anonymous (1995) 'The salaryman rides again', *The Economist 4/2/95*, p. 82.

Bennett, R. (1999) *Corporate Strategy*, 2nd edn. London: Financial Times/Pitman Publishing.

Blanchard, K., Zigarmi, P. and Zirgami, D. (1985) *Leadership and the One Minute Manager*. London: HarperCollins.

Briggs, A. R. J. (2001) 'Middle managers in further education: exploring the role', *Management in Education* **15**(4), 12–15.

Bush, T. (1995) *Theories of Educational Management*, 2nd edn. London: Paul Chapman Publishers.

Busher, H. and Harris, A. (1999) 'Leadership of school subject areas; tensions and dimensions of managing in the middle', *School Leadership and Management* **19**(3), 305–17.

Cole, G. A. (1993) *Management Theory and Practice*, 4th edn. London: D. P. Publications.

Deem, R. (1998) 'New managerialism and higher education: the management of performances and cultures in universities in the United Kingdom', *Studies in Sociology of Education* **8**(1), 47–70.

Deem, R. (2000) *New Managerialism and the Management of UK Universities*. Report presented to the Department of Educational Research and the Management School, Lancaster University. Lancaster: Lancaster University.

Dunleavy, P. and Hood, C. (1994) 'From old public administration to new public management', *Public Money and Management* July–September, 9–16.

Fergusson, R. (2000) 'Modernizing managerialism in education' in Clarke, J., Gewirtz, S. and McLaughlin, E. (eds) *New Managerialism New Welfare*. London: Open University Press and Sage.

Fidler, B. (1997) 'School leadership: some key issues', *School Leadership and Management* **17**(1), 23–37.

Fullan, M. (1994) *Change Forces*. London: Falmer Press.

Further and Higher Education Act (1992). London: HMSO.

Gleeson, D. and Shain, F. (1999) 'Managing ambiguity: between markets and managerialism – a case study of "middle" managers in further education', *Sociological Review* **47**(3), 461–90.

Grace, G. (1995) *School Leadership*. London: Falmer Press.

Hancock, N. and Hellawell D. (2003) 'Academic middle managers in higher education: a game of hide and seek', *The Journal of Higher Education Policy and Management* **25**(10), 5–12.

Handy, C. (1991) *Gods of Management*. London: Century Business.

Handy, C. (1992) 'The language of leadership', in Syrett, M. S. and Hogg, C. (eds) *Frontiers of Leadership*. Oxford: Blackwell.

Handy, C. (1993) *Understanding Organisations*, 4th edn. London: Penguin Books.

Handy, C. and Aitken, R. (1986) *Understanding Schools as Organisations*. London: Pelican.

Hargreaves, A. (1996) *Changing Teachers, Changing Times: Teachers' work and culture in the post modern age*. London: Cassell.

Hodgkinson, C. (1991) *Education Management: the moral art*. New York: State University of New York Press.

Law, S. and Glover, D. (2000) *Educational Leadership and Learning*. Buckingham: Open University Press.

Lumby, J. and Tomlinson, H. (2000) 'Principals speaking: managerialism and leadership in further education', *Research in Post-compulsory Education* **5**(2), 139–51.

Middlehurst, R. (1993) *Leading Academics*. Buckingham: Open University Press/Society for Research into Higher Education.

Morgan, G. (1997) *Images of Organisation*, 2nd edn. London: Sage.

Northouse, P. (2001) *Leadership: theory and practice*, 2nd edn. London: Sage.

Power, S. (1997) 'Managing the State and the market: new education management in five countries', *British Journal of Education* **45**(4), 342–62.

Prichard, C. (1996) 'Making managers accountable or making managers'?, *Educational Management and Administration* **24**(1), 79–91.

Randle, K. and Brady, N. (1997) 'Further education and new managerialism', *The Journal of Further and Higher Education* **21**(2), 229–39.

Richmon, M. J. and Allison, D. J. (2003) 'Towards a conceptual framework for leadership enquiry', *Educational Management and Administration* **31**(1), 31–50.

Samuels, J. M. and Wilkes, F. M. (1986) *Management of Company Finance*, 4th edn. Berkshire: Van Nostrand Reinhold (UK).

Schein, E. H. (1992) *Organisational Culture and Leadership*, 2nd edn. San Francisco, CA: Jossey-Bass.

Simkins, T. (1999) 'Values, power and instrumentality: theory and research in education management', *Educational Management and Administration* **27**(3), 267–81.

Trowler, P. (1998) 'What managerialists forget: higher education credit framework and managerialist ideology', *International Studies in Sociology of Education* **8**(1), 91–109.

Warren, B. (1998) 'On the curious notion of "academic leadership": Some philosophical considerations', *Higher Education Review* **30**(2), 50–69.

Wright, N. (2001) 'Leadership, "bastard leadership" and managerialism: confronting the twin paradoxes in the Blair Educational Project', *Educational Management and Administration* **29**(3), 275–90.

12

Change, partnerships and collaboration in post-compulsory education

Peter Hipkiss

Introduction

THIS CHAPTER SEEKS to offer some insights into changes that have occurred in the further education (FE) sector during the last three decades in particular, to offer a context for the sector's responses to those changes and to highlight current strategies and responses to the need for collaboration and development. FE colleges have had to adapt to external influences that have at times required them to compete and then to collaborate with each other and with other training providers. The message that has been fully embraced by FE sector colleges is that it is no longer possible to work in isolation as a stand-alone college. Collaboration with employers, higher education institutions (HEIs) and the community is essential, not only to achieve the objectives set for the sector by its funding bodies, but to add value to what colleges seek to achieve for their stakeholders. The changes and the responses from the sector are set within the context of various government and other documents.

Managing change

The management of change in FE has to be seen within the context of its development as a sector and its relationships with local and national government, local businesses and local communities. Many have attempted to define FE. It is unique within the education sector in that it has always been very much a 'home-grown' product, without equivalence elsewhere in the world. There has not been a national plan for FE as a whole, so most developments have been relatively *ad hoc* in response to historical circumstances.

Franklin subscribes to the view that the historic growth of FE 'has run parallel with economic development' (Franklin 1991: 22) reinforcing the views of Tipton (1973). The implication is that during its development FE has adapted to meet the needs of not only its students, but employers, funding bodies, community groups, partners in schools and universities, successive governments and local councils.

Developments during the last three decades have largely been driven by national government. Prior to the 1988 Education Reform Act, the 1944 Education Act was a watershed for FE, defining further education as an entity for the first time (Smithers and Robinson 2000).

In 1976, with increasing threats to jobs and the economy from foreign competition, the then prime minister, James Callaghan, made his famous Ruskin College speech. He was critical of the education sector for its failure to provide the right levels and types of skills required by employers. As an attack on the 'progressive' approaches to teaching in vogue at the time, it highlighted the disparity between what government saw as necessary for industry and what the education system was providing. The teaching profession was identified as complacent and not paying enough attention to the skills and attitudes required to regain Britain's declining prosperity (Esland 1996). An important message for FE from the speech was that it was failing to provide the right skills for industry.

The Government established the Manpower Services Commission in 1976 to commission training and reskilling through specifically funded courses in colleges and with other providers, under initiatives such as Training Opportunities Programmes (TOPs). This was followed by the locally based Training and Enterprise Councils (TECs) in 1983 which directed and provided local industry-orientated training. TECs had to agree colleges' strategic plans in relation to their Work Related Further Education funding – some 25 per cent of college budgets. This reduced the ability of local authorities to influence the scope and type of training provided.

The 1988 Education Reform Act

The 1988 Education Reform Act brought many changes to the education sector as a whole, but specifically required local councils to earmark part of their education budget to FE (the general colleges budget) and further to produce a Scheme of Delegation, to be approved by the Secretary of State. This provided for a formula-driven apportionment of that budget among the colleges in the LEA according to the relative 'costs' of the different curriculum areas and the planned student numbers associated with them at the individual colleges. *Managing Colleges Efficiently* (DES and Welsh Office 1987) highlighted performance measures that could be applied in colleges. This document focused upon the need to improve college efficiency and effectiveness, and stimulated the already growing requirements of the sector for management information systems.

The 1992 Further and Higher Education Act – *incorporation*

The separation of colleges from local authority control was accomplished at incorporation, which created colleges as corporations in their own right and moved the funding of post-16 FE to a new body – the Further Education Funding Council for England (FEFC) – thus creating a defined FE sector. FE was unusual in having funding, audit and inspection controlled by the same organisation. With incorporation came a demand for 25 per cent growth in student numbers over three years, with annual reductions in the budgets available to support them.

The funding methodology spawned a new language that portrayed students in terms of 'units' thus beginning the process of commodification of students. At the same time, it gave enormous power and influence to principals.

Each qualification attracted a number of units and each college received a different fixed rate per unit. A college's funding was based upon its agreed annual plan of provision in unit terms multiplied by the unit rate. This rate reduced (or increased, depending on the starting price per unit by college) each year on a taper under a scheme called 'convergence' with the initial aim to bring all colleges to a single unit price after a period of years. Initial pricing of units was based upon historic data and therefore reflected the historical relative generosity of LEA funding rather than the relative costs of provision.

Only 90 per cent of the previous year's funding was payable so there had to be continuous growth year-on-year with growth paid initially at a lower unit rate, then subsequently rolled into the following year's allocation. An uncapped Demand Led Element fund paid for additional units over and above the agreed growth units, but at a marginal rate of just £6.50 per unit. These units could also be rolled subsequently into the allocation of full-rate units for each college and thus provided an opportunity for uncontrolled growth. The relatively low rate per unit reflected the minimal costs of including extra students in existing classes and was designed to reward efficiency, but to do so at negligible cost. This was a complicated and reductionist system with units having relatively little value (£17.40) against a typical college budget of £12 million.

Incorporation presented a real human resource challenge to colleges as it provoked: managerialist attitudes from college managers; a contracts dispute of over two-years duration with lecturers; significant changes to the curriculum for students and staff and to the information requirements and funding streams; and the need to compete with other colleges for students. In contrast, college principals and senior managers actually co-operated together through the Association of Colleges (AOC) to influence policy developments.

Incorporation was a major step in the Government's agenda for the quasi-privatisation of education, and the reduction of the power of local authorities; at the time, largely in the control of the other political party. Cynics might say that the Poll Tax issue was the reason for taking FE out of LEA control. What is particularly significant is that Conservative policies were not altered by the incoming Labour Government in 1997. Both parties appear to have embraced the centralisation of power in Whitehall and the distancing of responsibility implied by the development of the FEFC as a body with responsibility for funding and performance. Subsequently, it was the FEFC that was blamed for the various financial scandals that shook FE, for example those affecting Bilston and Halton colleges, among others.

The Learning and Skills Council (LSC)

In April 2001, the FEFC was disbanded and TECs were abolished. In their place the Government established the Learning and Skills Council (LSC). This body received the funding previously made available to the FEFC and the TECs. Inspection services moved to the new Adult Learning Inspectorate (ALI) and in some cases to Ofsted.

The LSC had 47 local offices (Local Learning and Skills Councils; LLSCs) with each taking responsibility for a specified geographical area and for the funding of training for the 16+ population. With the new funding body came a new vocabulary, new rules and new Management Information System (MIS) requirements. Colleges were still paid in units, but negotiated targets, scope of provision and performance with their LLSC. FE found itself in competition with private providers on a level playing field for the first time.

Success for All (DfES 2002a) set a challenging agenda for change and development including raising learner numbers, increasing employer engagement, improving success rates and fulfilling the need for all FE college teachers to be qualified to teach. In addition, from April 2003, LLSCs started Strategic Area Reviews with their partners so that colleges can incorporate their outcomes in their three-year plans. Other recent developments have seen the appointment of regional directors to oversee groups of LLSCs in order to provide a viable planning and reporting structure similar to the FEFC regions, and the proposal to initiate a 'plan-led funding' methodology, whereby bureaucracy will be reduced, and colleges 'trusted' to perform (LSC 2004). A significant plus is the proposed removal of retrospective clawback where targets have not been met (see also Chapter 2).

Under the control of the LSC, there has been a change of approach with collaboration as the byword. Colleges are now working with each other and with other providers to meet their targets. Colleges have always been affected by government legislation, but there has been an increasing rate of change during the last three decades.

Discussion points

1 What management changes has your college made during the last year?

2 Consider what has driven those changes.

Flexibility and adaptability in post-compulsory education

The sheer volume of the FE sector is overwhelming. There are some 1,700 qualifications on offer, some £4 billion spent each year, some four million students enrolled each year and over 400 colleges providing courses in England alone. 'Complexity remains a key characteristic of the sector' (Elliott 1996: 1). Nonetheless, FE was always and still is an enigma; ill-defined, multi-faceted, distributed, subject to the vagaries of local politics and funding variations (Hall 1994) and the 'Cinderella service' when considered against schools and universities (Randle and Brady 1997, Wells 2001). Commenting on the technical and vocational education being provided by the FE sector, McGinty and Fish (1993) cited in Randle and Brady (1997) suggest that 'the academic value system has accorded this type of education little attention and low priority'. Wells (2001) uses the term 'Cinderella' to reflect the hidden asset that he considered FE represents within the national economy and also the wrongfulness of its perceived low public status.

The local development base of colleges makes them adaptable to external pressures. This characteristic was evident even 60 years ago as Hall (1990) made the point that, where students needed intensive training at the beginning of their courses, colleges could accommodate them; flexibility being their byword. As he wrote when discussing the wartime training needs situation 'The techs were flexible enough to rise to this challenge' (Hall 1990: 4).

Franklin (1991) identified the late 1970s as the 'servant to industry' phase in the development of FE where colleges had a categorical *raison d'être* due to their relationship with the needs of local industries. It epitomised the *local* aspect of the colleges, supporting local industry to remain competitive. With the fall in numbers seeking technical training and apprenticeships in the 1980s, new markets were sought and gradually a new order came into being with the colleges providing a different type of service to a new set of clients. Franklin (1991) and Green and Lucas (1999) have described this new order as the 'New FE', serving, as it did, a whole range of disadvantaged and socially deprived groups, and increasing numbers of full-time 16–18-year-olds. This period for FE was particularly characterised by its links with the Government and industry through training contracts with the Manpower Services Commission (MSC), and support for unemployed people in the face of a national recession. There was also a relationship with the burgeoning new knowledge industries and with the introduction of computer technology into companies across all sectors on a large scale for data processing and secretarial work. As a result, the use and applications of computing became a major new subject area for colleges.

Significantly, this era proved to be a fruitful development period for FE as colleges once again proved their versatility and ability to metamorphose into a different type of institution as the national environment and their local environments demanded. At that time Training and Enterprise Councils (TECs) awarded many training supply contracts to colleges, principally because of the relatively broad base and extensive range of facilities and skills available in comparison to those from private training providers. Another important factor was the relatively inexpensive cost of the training provided by the colleges; average TEC costs per trainee at the time were almost double those of colleges.

At incorporation Elliott argued that in 1988:

> FE college principals and governors found themselves in a highly competitive market-led busi-
> ness. Colleges were required to bid for funding for work-related FE courses to the Training and
> Enterprise Councils (TECs): quangos with a majority of business representatives appointed to
> their boards of directors.
>
> (Elliot 1996: 2)

He went on to discuss the idea that FE has operated in a market situation since the early 1980s. His contention was that incorporation wasn't the groundbreaking event for FE that was described by many writers. Elliott didn't see that the 1992 Further and Higher Education Act had changed the pre-incorporation model of FE. He quotes an earlier argument by Theodossin (1989) that no single event

> brought about a shift from a democratic to a market model of FE. For practitioners at least, the
> development of a market-led conception of FE is perhaps better characterised as evolutionary.
> Its antecedents can be found in the broad collectivity of reforms across all educational sectors
> brought about by preceding government legislation, associated government sponsored
> reports, and an increasing inclination within the sector itself to provide a responsive service to
> a wide range of customers and clients.
>
> (Elliott 1996: 3–4)

However, the scale of the changes can be judged from comments by David Melville (last Chief Executive at the FEFC) writing in November 2000 prior to the planned demise of the FEFC in 2001, when he praised the sector's achievements:

> Student numbers have grown dramatically since incorporation, despite a small recent decline.
> The increase is from about 2·5 million in 1993–94 to 3·5 million in 1999–2000. This means
> that 860,000 more lives are changed by further education each year. This remarkable expansion
> has been carried out while unit costs have plummeted and retention rates have remained
> constant. . . . what were euphemistically called (at that time) 'efficiency gains' . . . meant, in
> effect, a 5 per cent cut in real terms, every year for several years. . . . Funding per full-time
> student has fallen in cash terms by 5 per cent since incorporation – 35 per cent in real terms . . .
> the sector coped with this . . . with remarkable flexibility.
>
> (Melville 2000: iv)

FE has been through some 30 years of constant development and change and has emerged under the LSC as a vibrant, still-growing sector which more than ever before is meeting the needs of its client groups by adapting and collaborating with other providers and funders.

Discussion point

What do you consider to be the main strengths of FE colleges in coping with change?

Reflective questions

1 Consider your role in relation to current new initiatives in FE.

2 How will the initiatives impact on you, your organisation, your colleagues and your learners?

3 What professional development do you need in order to respond to these changes?

Work-based learning

The continued development and growing acceptance of work-based learning provides a mechanism for the development of skills in the workforce, itself a target for every government since the Second World War. Work-based learning provides the opportunity for skills to be assessed in the workplace and for supported learning to occur.

FE colleges have been providing support to employers and companies through the day release mechanism for decades, but the development of virtual learning environments and the ability to access learning materials over the web have greatly enhanced the options open to employees to learn new skills. National initiatives such as Learndirect and UK Online have provided online courses and the opportunity to access the Internet and e-mail facilities.

The development and adoption of National Vocational Qualifications (NVQs), with their emphasis on competences have made it possible for qualifications to be gained through assessment either at college or in the workplace, with assessment by a work-based assessor. However, employers do not yet trust NVQs in the same way as the (O) Level/GCSE and GCE (A) Levels, being swayed by the relative testing methods; evidence has shown that it can take up to 10 years for new qualifications to be understood and recognised by employers.

Work-based learning for young people is usually associated with Modern Apprenticeships which are available at Foundation (FMA) and Advanced (AMA) levels. An apprenticeship agreement is made between the apprentice and the employer, and ideally the learning provider. The apprenticeship provides: on-the-job training at the workplace, which leads to the award of an NVQ at either Level 2 (FMA) or Level 3 (AMA); technical certificates (such as a City & Guilds Progression Award or a BTEC National Diploma); and, with training from the provider (college), Key Skills qualifications. Depending on their entry qualifications, young people can start on an FMA or AMA. Apprentices are paid a wage by the employer while working. Entry is available for anyone aged 16–24, not in full-time education.

The Cassels Report (DfES 2001), which considered the problems associated with Modern Apprenticeships, produced a number of recommendations. These included an expansion of the scheme to eventually target 35% (230,000) of the 16–21 age group to enter apprenticeships but with a target for 2004 of 28% (175,000) as against the present participation rate of 20% (140,000) each year. His report also proposed an:

> Entry to Employment programme, with distinctive expertise and funding which would specialise in preparing young people identified as needing help either to enter an apprenticeship or, if this is not a realistic aspiration, to settle into other stable employment.

> (DfES 2001: 7)

This became the 'E2E' programme which works on the basis of a collaborative partnership including the LLSC, the local Connexions Service, and training providers including colleges. This programme supports people who, for one reason or another, are not able to access Modern Apprenticeships or cope with normal college courses. Subsequently, in its response to the Cassels Report, the Government made a commitment to place any young person with the necessary aptitude, ability and enthusiasm. Colleges play a major role in supporting Modern Apprenticeships and this commitment will provide further opportunities for involvement in partnerships.

Discussion points

What are your views on NVQs? Do you rate them less highly than 'academic' qualifications? If so explain why.

Partnerships with external groups

This section discusses partnerships with community and other groups. Two main methods were used to provide locally based provision: outreach and franchising.

Outreach

Outreach has been an integral part of many colleges' operations for decades. It met the need to provide access to training for specific groups of students in cases where accommodation at the college site(s) was unavailable or unsuitable, or where it was not viable to teach the students in college due to cultural or religious reasons. These classes have, by necessity, generally been in relatively local locations, and in subjects that can be delivered with minimum resources. Thus humanities and languages are popular while recent developments such as UK Online centres and Learndirect facilities in community locations and libraries have made IT training and Internet access available in local venues. Quality, assessment, staffing and administration were all handled by the college.

Franchising

Fletcher defined franchising as:

> just one mode of delivery of further education. It involves a college contracting with a third party to deliver education away from college premises. The third party, which might be

an employer, a community organisation or a private training provider, operates under the direction of the college, which has full responsibility for the quality of the programme.

(Fletcher 2000: 3)

The principle was that the college paid the franchisee, who then paid their member of staff. In outreach, the college would also have provided a number of other services including accommodation costs, personnel facilities, examinations and assessment. The college would pay a lump sum or rate per student to the franchisee for some, if not all, of these services; that sum would be a proportion of whatever funding was received by the college.

Franchising has been both a blessing and a bane for FE. It has been a blessing in that it enabled colleges to increase participation immediately following incorporation in 1993, while cutting overall operating costs and supporting the convergence of funding rates. However, it has been a bane in that it focused attention on the failure of some colleges to manage their franchises effectively. Part of the problem for the sector was that, initially, the FEFC did not constrain colleges to operate in what might be considered their local area. Some colleges franchised across the country and this caused imbalances in the FEFC funding methodology that affected all colleges. Local colleges found distant colleges undercutting their costs and poaching their students into franchised provision. The rapid growth in franchising destabilised the funding methodology by diluting unit values as Demand Led Element (DLE) rates were absorbed into the franchising colleges' unit allocations as growth units. When faced with an unacceptable claim in 1996, the Government, through the FEFC, moved to reduce franchising by severely limiting DLE payments in 1995/96 and introducing strict rules to curb out-of-area contracts (FEFC 1996). This resulted in several colleges experiencing financial difficulties and at least one college was forced to close.

Franchising provided the Government with a low-cost method of vastly increasing participation rates with hard-to-reach people; many franchisees were community organisations that brought people together for social and other purposes. Education became something else that they could offer and generally it came with money towards their running costs. For colleges, it was anticipated that the costs of provision would be cheaper; a point since recognised in the LSC funding methodology. This should have been a win-win scenario, but the reality was that quality, management and assessment systems were inadequate in some cases and what should have been an opportunity for FE became its downfall.

Possible lessons from franchising?

Not all colleges pursued franchising as a mechanism to achieve their FEFC targets in response to the demands of incorporation. For individual colleges, in some cases, its strategic importance was transitory. However, in some notable cases such as Bilston, its effects were long-lived. Perhaps the greatest legacy from the franchising undertaken by colleges has been that, while it certainly provided a competitive model for development in FE, it also presented a cost-efficient model for the management of training generally. This was providing that appropriate local management structures were in place. It could be argued that the disbanding of the FEFC and the TECs, and the establishment of a national LSC with its 47 local 'branches' has provided that local control structure, which is now maturing and affecting training provision as management systems embed, and that the operation of the LSC is essentially franchising, albeit on a grand scale.

Franchising by colleges still takes place both within and across local LSC borders. It currently attracts a discounted rate of funding, designed to account for the perceived lower costs of provision. In the longer term, it is possible that cross-border franchising will reduce significantly as locally sourced provision, meeting local needs, is developed.

Indicative task

Put yourself in the place of a community organisation leader with some 100 members. Your local college approaches you with a view to providing learning opportunities at your venue. What type of provision arrangement would you wish to consider?

The school/post-compulsory interface

Schools and colleges have worked together over a number of years. However, they differ fundamentally in a number of ways. Attendance at school is compulsory until the age of 16, whereas attendance at college is voluntary. School teaching staff have professional status, recognised by compulsory registration with the General Teaching Council (GTC) and possession of Qualified Teacher Status (QTS), while for college lecturers, the Institute for Learning (IfL) has been established, yet currently, there is no opportunity for them to gain QTS (see also Chapter 3). Funding for schools has generally been on a census day/pupil year numbers basis, rather than on fulfilment of recruitment and achievement targets. Colleges have developed to meet local training needs whereas schools have developed in line with national plans, implemented through LEAs. Plans to 'privatise' schools through opting for Grant Maintained Status were not successful while colleges were all 'privatised' at incorporation. Colleges are essentially providers of vocational training with 80 per cent of qualifications gained being in vocational areas (Ainley and Bailey 1997) whereas schools work towards a limited set of examination outcomes, which are primarily perceived as academic. The desire to include some form of vocational training in schools is not new.

Sharp (2004), in a comprehensive paper summarising the development of the vocational curriculum for 16–19-year-olds in schools and colleges between 1979 and 1995, saw the CPVE (Certificate of Pre-vocational Education) as a response to the Further Education Unit (FEU) publication *A Basis for Choice* (FEU 1979). This publication addressed the question of what should be provided to address the needs of 16- and

17-year-olds with 'average or less than average' abilities so that they received vocational training that would prepare them for employment, but importantly that they should have an assessment methodology that involved the preparation of portfolio evidence as against being solely based upon examinations.

The original intention was for the CPVE to be the full-time counterpart to Youth Training Schemes (YTSs) which were employer-based, and that it should address the needs of some 80,000 young people each year (DES 1982). The CPVE was introduced in 1986 to be run in colleges and schools for students over the age of 16 as a one-year course in preparation for work or further vocational study. Schools that offered it struggled with the resourcing implications in terms of both equipment and appropriately experienced staff. Many used college facilities to provide a reasonable range of options and in that sense, the programme might be seen as successful in that it provided a showcase for colleges and a bridge for schoolchildren to vocational training (see also Chapter 1 for related discussion).

Wolf (2002), in considering the new vocational GCSEs proposed in the Green Paper *14–19: extending opportunities, raising standards* (DfES 2002b), expressed the view that the Government sought to establish some sort of parity between academic and vocational qualifications and this had resulted in a series of initiatives and qualifications following the launch of the CPVE.

> Starting in the mid-1980s, we had, in succession, CPVE (certificate of pre-vocational education); BTEC first diplomas; City and Guilds Foundation; the diploma in vocational education; GNVQ Foundation, intermediate and advanced, GNVQ part one, and running alongside, YOP, YTS, YT, modern apprenticeships, foundation apprenticeships, and NVQs. In every case, the intention has been to create 'parity of esteem' for vocational and academic pathways.
>
> (Wolf 2002)

She argued that parity of esteem is misleading; what young people need are relevant qualifications for the modern workplace. West and Steedman (2004) agree that:

> the quest for parity between academic and vocational subjects is a wild goose chase. Far from raising the reputation of vocational courses it is likely to distort them and make them pale imitations of academic studies with little purpose of their own.

Significantly, school performance tables are to include vocational qualifications; a reinforcement of the parity stance.

Current developments

The Green Paper *14–19: extending opportunities, raising standards* (DfES 2002b) proposes changes to the 14–19 curriculum, the GCSE examinations structure and the development of a Matriculation Diploma qualification (see also Chapter 8). It also proposes that employers, colleges and schools should work together in collaboration, and that a pilot programme of Pathfinder projects should be used to help to map the difficulties and provide a vehicle for testing possible solutions.

Increased collaboration is vital in order to deliver the new opportunities that the 14–19 agenda offers. The aim is for schools, colleges and other providers to respond better to the needs and circumstances of individual young people, and no single school or college can expect to offer the full range of 14–19 options on its own.

(Teachernet – online resource for teachers)

Twenty-five Pathfinder projects started in January 2003 and an interim evaluation report has been produced by a joint team from the Universities of Leeds and Exeter. A brief summary of their findings indicates that: average students are not being engaged; there are issues about partners working together; there is scope to improve the work element; and there were concerns about sustainability.

Increased Flexibility Programme

An important part of the Government's strategy, as outlined in the Green Paper *14–19: extending opportunities, raising standards* (DfES 2002b), was to provide the opportunity to 14–16-year-olds to study vocational GCSEs. The Increased Flexibility Programme (IFP) began in September 2002 with the aim of launching eight new GCSEs in vocational subjects (see Chapter 8 for further discussion). In practice, it provides school-aged pupils with vocational and work-related learning opportunities in a post-16 environment. A second phase commenced in 2003. The initial round included some 270 partnerships, mostly led by colleges, while the second phase is expected to have 290 partnerships, but with a doubling of the current 40,000 participants to some 80,000. Total funding of £38 million is provided through the LSC, with partnerships each receiving £50,000 in support funding. In 2003/4, their local LSCs will receive £100,000 each in discretionary funding.

Discussion point

What are the implications for your college when considering introducing learners aged 14–16?

The post-compulsory/higher education interface

The 1944 Education Act placed the duty for providing education below university level within the remit of local authorities and thus encompassed FE as a sub-set of local education provision. However, in the intervening years, universities and colleges have worked together to ensure that the provision of Higher National level qualifications was available on a local basis. Many colleges have made Access agreements with local universities to enable their mature entry students to receive guaranteed places on degree courses. There have been franchising arrangements between colleges and universities, with courses delivered at colleges and accredited by the host university.

Arrangements whereby the first year of a university degree course has been offered at a college have proved popular with mature students and in some cases, only the final year has been completed at the university. The advent of sophisticated e-learning facilities and a wider acceptance of distance learning at Level 4 and above will accelerate the trend towards degree-equivalent study on a local basis.

Current developments

Many colleges now offer teacher training on franchise from universities. Colleges generally require a franchising agreement from a validating university in order to offer the Post Graduate Certificate of Education (PGCE). As there is a requirement for full-time FE teaching staff to become teacher trained within two years of commencing work as a college lecturer, there is a strong demand for the qualification. This demand can be efficiently met by providing classes at the college, thus minimising disruption to the working day, encouraging participation and retaining students. It is cost effective for the universities which determine the fee payable to the college, while retaining an accreditation, quality and administration charge from the income received.

The Department for Education and Skills (DfES) has recently completed a consultation exercise in relation to *The Future Of Initial Teacher Education For The Learning And Skills Sector – an agenda for reform* (DfES 2003a). This document sets out proposals for a professional training programme with the possible introduction of Qualified Teacher of Further Education (QTFE) or Qualified Teacher of Learning and Skills (QTLS) as equivalents to QTS as the award. It recognises the diversity of the teaching staff in FE, but proposes that higher education institutes be responsible, as now, for quality of delivery. (See also Chapters 1, 3 and 5 for further reading on FE teaching qualifications.)

Foundation Degrees

In April 2000, the Government launched an initial consultation exercise and a subsequent bidding round in July 2000, for the development of Foundation Degrees. The outcome of the initial consultation was the proposal that consortia, comprising Higher Education Institutions (HEIs), FE Colleges and employers be established to develop and deliver these degrees. From the bidding round, 21 consortia were chosen to develop the first Foundation Degrees.

> The ideas of partnership and collaboration are central to the concept of the Foundation Degree. . . . The contribution of a range of partners in foundation degree programmes should keep programmes relevant, valid and responsive to the needs of employers and learners.
>
> (QAA 2002: 6)

Partnerships can also comprise representation from employers, FE colleges, professional bodies, sector skills councils and students on the programme. Where an FE college delivers an HEI-validated Foundation Degree, their relationship will be governed by the requirements of the Quality Assurance Agency for Higher Education (QAA) *Code of Practice on Collaborative Provision* (QAA 1999) and in accordance with the Higher Education Funding Council for England (HEFCE) document *Indirectly Funded Partnerships: Codes of practice for franchise and consortia arrangements* (HEFCE 2000).

Foundation Degrees have been specifically developed to meet the needs of employers, particularly in respect of employability skills and to provide advanced technology to compete on a global level. They have also been developed with the aim of increasing access to higher education and providing a potential progression route to other qualifications. All HEIs offering a Foundation Degree have to guarantee articulation to at least one bachelor's degree with honours. A major part of the structure underlying the development and delivery of Foundation Degrees is the involvement of employers from the outset as part of the design, development and review partnership. Proposals for Foundation Degrees have to ensure that local and regional industry skill needs will be addressed and that any application supports local and regional skills strategies. Foundation Degrees should be designed to be available through flexible delivery and study modes including, full or part time, work-based, distance or web-based, depending upon the needs of learners.

The Government's commitment in the White Paper *The Future of Higher Education* (DfES 2003b) to expanding Foundation Degrees has led to a bidding round by HEFCE for further development funds. Some £5.5 million is available to support the conversion of Higher National Diploma (HND) programmes to Foundation Degrees, and a further 10,000 Full-time Equivalent (FTE) places are to be made available on Foundation Degrees, with prescribed regional place allocations (HEFCE 2003: 7). Significantly for FE, the proposals include a welcome for bids from colleges that have proposals currently supported under the Centre of Vocational Excellence (CoVE) programme, and also the expectation that delivery will be provided through colleges.

In support of these developments, the LSC has announced that the 'Aimhigher' programme (HEFCE 2004) will commence in August 2004 with the aim of widening participation in HE and increasing the number of young people who have the abilities and aspirations to benefit from it. Existing partnerships will be encouraged to work together to achieve the objectives for the programme.

Indicative task

1   Research your organisation's HE provision.

2   Use the organisation's strategic plan to identify future developments.

3   To what extent are Foundation Degrees an essential part of that strategy?

Summary

- FE colleges have a history of successfully managing change and adapting positively to new initiatives; the challenge is to develop new alliances with schools, universities and employers and to continue to collaborate with current partners.

- There is a challenge for FE colleges in supporting the development of Modern Apprenticeships following the Cassels Report and the innovation of Entry to Employment programmes.

- FE colleges need to continue to develop stronger links with, and address the learning needs of their local communities and businesses.

- The 14–19 Green Paper (DfES 2002b) holds many challenges and opportunities for colleges; there is a need to strengthen links with schools, but also to address the training needs of staff working with this age group.

- *Success for All* (DfES 2002a) has set the agenda for development in colleges with challenging headline improvement targets.

- The Foundation Degree offers the opportunity for FE colleges to take a leading role in the development and delivery mechanisms of this new HE qualification.

- The FENTO Teaching and Learning Standards relating to change, partnerships and collaboration are shown in Figure 12.1. Full details of these standards are available at the FENTO website (see 'Useful websites').

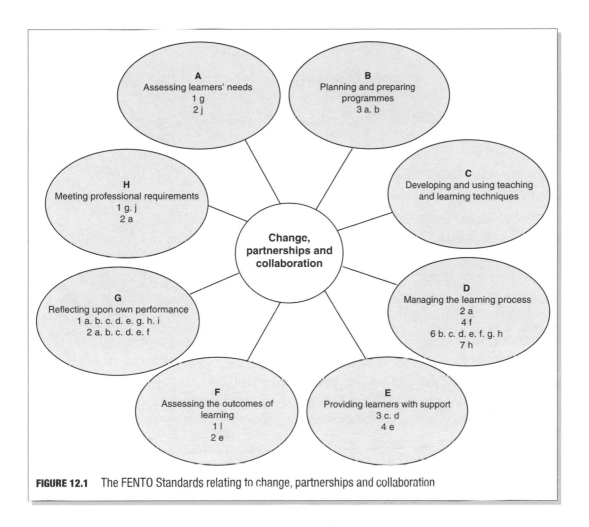

FIGURE 12.1   The FENTO Standards relating to change, partnerships and collaboration

Useful websites

www.dfes.gov.uk/14–19greenpaper/download/raisingstandards.pdf
Consultation document for *14–19: Extending Opportunities, Raising Standards*.
Last accessed 7 May 2004

www.dfes.gov.uk/ma.consultation/docs/MA_The_Way_to_Work.pdf
Report of the Modern Apprenticeship Advisory Committee on *Modern Apprenticeships: the way to work*.
Last accessed 7 May 2004

www.fento.ac.uk
The Further Education National Training Organisation (FENTO) website
Last accessed 7 May 2004

www.lsc.gov.uk/National/Partners/PolicyandDevelopment/YoungPeople/Increased+
Flexibility+Programme.htm
The Increased Flexibility Programme (IFP): information on the eight GCSE
vocational subjects
Last accessed 7 May 2004

http://www.lsc.gov.uk/National/Documents/Series/Circulars/Circ0401.htm
Relates to HEFCE (2004) *Increasing Participation in Higher and Further Education*
Last accessed 7 May 2004

http://www.lsc.gov.uk/National/Documents/Series/Circulars/circular0402.htm
Relates to LSC (2004): *Plan-led Funding for Further Education*
Last accessed 7 May 2004

References

Ainley, P. and Bailey, B. (1997) *The Business of Learning*. London: Cassell.

DES (1982) *17+ a New Qualification*. London: HMSO.

DES and Welsh Office (1987) *Managing Colleges Efficiently*. London: HMSO.

DfES (2001) *Modern Apprenticeships: the way to work*. Report of the Modern Apprenticeship Advisory Group. London: DfES.

DfES (2002a) *Success for All: reforming further education and training*. London: DfES.

DfES (2002b) *14–19: extending opportunities, raising standards*. CMD 5342. London: DfES.

DfES (2003a) *The Future of Initial Teacher Education for the Learning and Skills Sector – an agenda for reform*. Sheffield: DfES.

DfES (2003b) *The Future of Higher Education*. CMD 5932. London: HMSO.

Education Act (1944). London: HMSO.

Education Reform Act (1988). London: HMSO.

Elliott, G. (1996) *Crisis and Change in Vocational Education and Training*. London: Jessica Kingsley.

Esland, G. (1996) 'Education, training and nation-state capitalism: Britain's failing strategy', in Avis, J., Bloomer, M., Esland, G. *et al.* (eds) *Knowledge and Nationhood*. London: Cassell.

FEFC (1996) *Franchising*. Circular 96/06 Coventry: FEFC.

FEU (1979) *A Basis for Choice*. London: Further Education Unit.

Fletcher, M. (2000) 'Franchising – a case study in FE funding', in Fletcher, M. (ed.) *For Better or Worse*. London: FEDA.

Franklin, W. L. (1991) 'Change in further education' (PhD thesis). *Collected Original Resources in Education* **16**(2), 1–85.

Further and Higher Education Act (1992). London: HMSO.

Green, A. and Lucas, N. (eds) (1999) *FE and Lifelong Learning: realigning the sector for the twenty-first century*. Southend-on-Sea: Bedford Way Papers.

Hall, V. (1990) *Maintained Further Education in the United Kingdom*. Blagdon: Further Education Staff College.

Hall, V. (1994) *Further Education in the United Kingdom*, 2nd edn. London: Collins Educational/The Staff College.

HEFCE (2000) *Indirectly Funded Partnerships: codes of practice for franchise and consortia arrangements*. Bristol: HEFCE.

HEFCE (2003) *Foundation Degrees 2003/48*. Invitation to bid for additional places and development funds 2004–05. Bristol: HEFCE.

HEFCE (2004) *Integration Plans for Aimhigher Programme*. London: HEFCE.

LSC (2004) *Plan-led Funding For Further Education*. London: LSC.

Melville, D. (2000) 'Ready to meet the challenge' *Times Higher Educational Supplement*, Further Education Section, 17 November 2000, p. iv.

QAA (1999) *Code of Practice on Collaborative Provision*. Gloucester: QAA.

QAA (2002) *Foundation Degree: qualification benchmark* (final draft). Gloucester: Quality Assurance Agency for Higher Education.

Randle, K. and Brady, N. (1997) 'Managerialism and professionalism in the "Cinderella service" ', *Journal of Vocational Education and Training* **49**(1), 121–39.

Sharp, P. (2004) *The Development of the Curriculum for 16–19 year olds in Colleges and Schools, 1979–95*. Post-14 Research Group Web Page http://www.leeds.ac.uk/educol/documents/00002218.htm – Accessed 24/04/04.

Smithers, A. and Robinson, P. (2000) 'The making of a new sector', in Smithers, A. and Robinson, P. (eds) *Further Education Re-formed*. London: Falmer Press.

Teachernet, *Collaboration*. http://www.teachernet.gov.uk/teachingandlearning/14to19/collaboration/ – Accessed 20/04/04.

Tipton, B. (1973) *Conflict and Change in a Technical College*. London: Hutchinson International.

Wells, A. (2001) 'Alan Wells and Alan Tuckett on twenty-five years of striving for adult literacy and numeracy', *Education Guardian*, Rostrum, 16 October 2001. Available at http://education.guardian.co.uk/print/o%2C3858%2C4277445108283%2C00.html – Accessed 25/06/04.

West, J. and Steedman, H. (2004) *Finding Our Way: vocational education in England*. http://cep.lse.ac.uk/pubs/download/occasional/OP018.pdf – Accessed 21/04/04.

Wolf, A. (2002) 'Same courses, different name', *Education Guardian*, 28 May 2002. http://education.guardian.co.uk/egweekly/story/0,5500,723024,00.html – Accessed 24/04/04

Glossary

ABE	Adult Basic Education
ABS	Adult Basic Skills
ACAC	Qualifications, Curriculum and Assessment Authority for Wales
AiL	Average numbers in Learning
ALI	Adult Learning Inspectorate
AMA	Advanced Modern Apprenticeship
AOC	Association of Colleges
APEL	Accreditation of Prior Experience and Learning
APL	Accreditation of Prior Learning
AQA	Assessment and Qualifications Alliance examination board
AS	Advanced Subsidiary (Level)
ATL	Association of Teachers and Lecturers
AVCE	Advanced Vocational Certificate in Education
BERA	British Education Research Association
BSA	Basic Skills Agency
BOPCRIS	British Official Publications Collaborative Reader Information Service
BTEC	Business and Technician Education Council
CATS	Credit Accumulation and Transfer Scheme
CCEA	Northern Ireland Council for the Curriculum, Examinations and Assessment
CEF	College Employers' Forum
Cert Ed	Certificate of Education
CIF	Common Inspection Framework
CoVE	Centre of Vocational Excellence

CPD	Continuing Professional Development
CPVE	Certificate in Pre-vocational Education
CRB	Criminal Records Bureau
DES	Department of Education and Science
DfE	Department for Education
DfEE	Department for Education and Employment
DfES	Department for Education and Skills
DLE	Demand Led Element
DoH	Department of Health
E2E	Entry to Employment
EDAP	Ford Employee Development and Assistance Programme
Edexcel	Edexcel examination board
EFL	English as a Foreign Language
EMA	Education Maintenance Allowance
ESF	European Social Fund
ESOL	English for Speakers of Other Languages
FE	Further Education
FEDA	Further Education Development Agency
FEFC	Further Education Funding Council (England)
FENTO	Further Education National Training Organisation
FEPDF	Further Education Professional Development Forum
FEU	Further Education Unit
FMA	Foundation Modern Apprenticeship
FTE	Full-time Equivalent
GATS	General Agreement on Trade Services
GCE	General Certificate of Education
GCSE	General Certificate of Secondary Education
GNVQ	General National Vocational Qualification
GTC	General Teaching Council
HE	Higher Education
HEFCE	Higher Education Funding Council for England
HEI	Higher Education Institution

HESDA	Higher Education Staff Development Agency
HMP	Her Majesty's Prison
HNC/HND	Higher National Certificate/Higher National Diploma
ICT	Information and Communication Technology
IfL	Institute for Learning
IFP	Increased Flexibility Programme
ILP	Individual Learning Plan
ILT	Information and Learning Technology
ISR	Individual Student Record
IT	Information Technology
ITB	Industrial Training Board
ITE	Initial Teacher Education
ITT	Initial Teacher Training
LDD	Learning Difficulties and Disabilities
LEA	Local Education Authority
LLLSSC	Lifelong Learning Sector Skills Council
LLSC	Local Learning and Skills Council
LPP	Legitimate Peripheral Participation
LSC	Learning and Skills Council
LSDA	Learning and Skills Development Agency
LSRN	Learning and Skills Research Network
LTSN	Learning and Teaching Support Network
MA	Modern Apprenticeship
MIS	Management Information System
MSC	Manpower Services Commission
NATFHE	National Association for Teachers in Further and Higher Education
NC	National Curriculum
NIACE	National Institute for Adult Continuing Education
NQF	National Qualifications Framework
NTO	National Training Organisation
NVQ	National Vocational Qualification
OCN	Open College Network

OCR	Oxford, Cambridge and RSA examination board
OECD	Organisation for Economic Co-operation and Development
Ofsted	Office for Standards in Education
OU	Open University
PAULO	The National Training Organisation for community-based learning and development
PGCE	Post Graduate Certificate in Education
PLSU	Prisoners' Learning and Skills Unit
QAA	Quality Assurance Agency for Higher Education
QCA	Qualifications and Curriculum Authority
QTFE	Qualified Teacher of Further Education
QTLS	Qualified Teacher of Learning and Skills
QTS	Qualified Teacher Status
RSA	Royal Society of Arts
SAR	Strategic Area Review
SCRE	Scottish Council for Research in Education
SEU	Social Exclusion Unit
SQA	Scottish Qualifications Authority
SSC	Sector Skills Council
SSDA	Sector Skills Development Agency
TDLB	Training and Development Lead Body
TEC	Training and Enterprise Council
TES	Times Educational Supplement
TESOL	Teaching English as a Second or Other Language
THES	Times Higher Educational Supplement
TLA	Teacher Learning Academy
TOPs	Training Opportunity Programmes
TQ(FE)	Teaching Qualification (Further Education)
TTA	Teacher Training Agency
TUC	Trades Union Congress
TVEI	Technical and Vocational Education Initiative
U3A	University of the Third Age

UCET	Universities Council for the Education of Teachers
UfA	University of the First Age
UfI	University for Industry
VCE	Vocational Certificate of Education
VFM	Value for money
WBL	Work-based Learning
WEA	Workers' Educational Association
WRNAFE	Work Related Non-Advanced Further Education
YOP	Youth Opportunities Programme
YT	Youth Training
YTS	Youth Training Scheme
ZPD	Zone of Proximal Development

Index

Note: **Bold** indicates figures or tables